Cover art work by Sully

Also by Chip Walker

The Terrible Battle for Billy Watson

Child of Hern

The Devil Wears Maroon

This book is dedicated first to my late wife Janet, without whom this writing would never have started. Then to my wife Carol who encouraged me to pick things up again.

I am very grateful to the many people who have helped me make this book a reality. The list is long but they include John Sullivan, Tommy Onions, Terry Walker and many more.

Finally I offer this work as a tribute to all the men; past, present and future of the British Airborne Brigade, for it is their proud professionalism and sincere camaraderie that has and continues to inspire me.

If any characters, names, units or establishments named or inferred feel that I have made any remark or criticism unjustly then please accept that it is not nor ever has been my intention to insult or upset anyone.

Remarks made have come from observations as I experienced and understood them at the time. I fully accept that occasionally specific names, dates and quotes may be inaccurate. However I have tried throughout to remain true to my memory.

ISBN-13: 978-1517352783
ISBN-10: 1517352789

Copyright Chip Walker, 2006

A CIP catalogue record for this book is available from the British Library.

***

CHAPTER ONE

IS THIS WAR?

Spiked dry grass pushed hard against my face and the smell of composted soil threatened to overwhelm me. I gagged and though I had been here only minutes, I was already gasping for air. The whole of my upper body felt like it was being crushed under the weight of my equipment. Fatigue meant that my muscles were working at only half speed and with very limited strength. I was completely exhausted.

I tried again to force my head up above the grass; I needed to know what was going on. Lifting my eyes I fought the instinct to compel my body to go ever lower. I was inquisitive and I needed information but the instinctive half of me urged caution, more than that, it wanted me to hide. There was a lot of noise but a distant shout from an unknown officer was the only voice that I could make out clearly. "Has anybody seen the enemy?"

As I peered over the long grass the muscles in the back of my neck stretched tight.

I was carrying a heavy Bergen back pack and earlier when I had stood, it had towered over the top of my head. Now with my belly firmly on the ground I found that my helmet knocked against the top of the Bergen. The back of my neck and shoulders pushed against the restriction but it was as if someone had a foot on the back of my neck. Try as I might, my head was forced back downward. Other than a few inches above the ground, I could not get a decent view.

Arching my over-burdened back I pushed my body upward and onto all fours. I just had to know what was going on. In three different directions, I saw the tops of Bergens and the odd Para' helmet, all sticking up amongst the undergrowth. There were no surprises: everything looked like I had expected.

A drum roll of shots rang out. I recognized the repeated chatter as that of a medium sized machine gun. It came from way over on my left, perhaps a third of a mile away. Remembering my training I dropped as low to the ground as I could and held my breath, listening for the crack of the shots, trying to count the seconds before the 'thump' as rounds passed over head. Maybe I shouldn't have bothered for there was no thump and it was therefore impossible for me to accurately gauge any distance.

My mind wandered for a second. A feeling of total calm took over, everything now seemed so far away. The sun was out; its warmth filtered through the back of my legs. The grass began to take on a wonderfully summery smell; memories of being a kid playing in the fields came rushing back. Such childhood thoughts were only interrupted when an unexpected toot from a distant and old fashioned hunting horn trumpeted the still air. The call was repeated; in my mind's eye. I half expected to hear a shout of, "Talley Ho!" What next, perhaps a squadron of red tunics astride grey horses and bounding over to me in the hunt for a scurrying fox? However, I knew that the sound emanated from B Company's eccentric commander; signalling an all clear and for everyone to start making their way to the RV points.

Just two hours earlier I had been listed as number one port stick. It was my first ever opportunity to be the guy in the door. To a novice airborne soldier it was somewhat of an honour.

Chip Walker

Like ants on a food trail we walked in long lines through the hangar and out to the aircraft. Already the kit was wearing me down. As I stood at the front of the queue I reflected on the weight about me. My Bergen came in at just over ninety pounds, the parachute at thirty and the reserve at twenty. My SLR weighed another twelve.

Not long before and to ensure that our weight did not exceed the limits for the parachute, we had stood upon old fashioned butchers scales to be weighed. I am sure though that the RAF Corporal and the other guys who stood around him were making hideous bets and having a laugh at our expense. As I hauled my massive self and equipment onto the old cast iron platform, I watched the faces of the airmen. The corporal pushed a few steel slides along the top of the scale then giggled. To the delight of his companions, the corporal muttered, "This one will come in fast". Something about the way he had said it had caused my blood to boil. Right there and then, I wasn't sure then whether to laugh or deck him. I wandered off trying bloody hard not to think about what the airman had meant. After all, surely they were just joking, right?

On the tarmac outside and still in the queue, a short squat soldier wearing the DZ flash of 3 Para strolled past and deposited himself in front of me.

"Oi!" I protested, "I'm number one!"

The little man pivoted swiftly on his heels and stared straight at me. He must have been at least eight inches shorter than my six feet yet uncannily, he appeared to match and even exceed my height as his dark eyes bore directly into mine. Erupting into a deep Glaswegian accent, his voice let out a slow growl.

"I'm a mortar man."

I heard his voice but I am sure his lips hadn't actually moved. They were like the rest of him: tight and poised ready to   fight.

3

Nevertheless, I was not about to stand down and surrender the honoured position of number one. I stretched as tall as I could and twisted by body pushing my right arm into the face of the little Jock. I was confident. Slowly and calmly I ventured,

"The manifest says I'm number one."

I paused for just a second before brushing my fingers over the row of three chevrons stitched to my right sleeve,

"But more importantly, these stripes say so!"

The young Scot hardly blinked then pushed forward a heavy looking piece of equipment wrapped and ready to be fitted to his parachute harness. Nudging the toes of my boots, it came to halt with a metallic clunk.

"Fine! You take the fucking base plate then!"

He turned his back on me and stayed at the front. He didn't say another word, he didn't need to. He knew he had won that particular argument.

The base plate of a mortar weighs about sixty five pounds and with that, a mortar man would generally carry three mortar bombs too. Each of those would weigh an additional twelve pounds each. There was no way that I wanted that lot added to my already burgeoning weight.

Thinking about it, it seemed to me that most of the mortar platoon were short guys. Perhaps it was planned that way. After all, if your body weight is less than the average, your parachute can carry above the average. My body weight was already perilously too heavy. Simple arithmetic really.

Not wanting to lose face I discreetly peered through the corners of my eyes hoping desperately that nobody had been watching and even worse, rolling around the ground in hysterics. Fortunately for me, if anybody had seen this minor altercation, nobody was letting on.

Chip Walker

The Hercules aircraft dropped altitude and began its run up to the DZ, hedge hopping along the way as the pilot tried to avoid enemy radar and at the same time, make it as difficult as possible for enemy ground troops to hit us with triple A.

We were stood up, hooked up and ready to go. The overbearing weight of my equipment tried to drag me back down forcing me to arch my back. I had no idea of the temperature outside but it was bloody hot inside this plane. Sweat cascaded down my face, running in rivulets down my back.

Strangely the dampness of my sweat felt cool and almost welcome against the heat of my skin. The heat coupled with a lack of air meant it was difficult to breathe. There was no air-flow inside the aircraft. Instead the stench of hot bodies mixed with the pungent smell of aviation gasoline filled my nostrils and stung at my throat. It was no surprise to see that the floor at my feet ran deep with swirling lumps of vomit.

I looked over the shoulder of the compact mortar man in the door, I could see that already the sun was up and that the sky was clear. This was not good. The drop was supposed to have been in near darkness. The very nature of a Parachute unit is that they are lightly equipped; in quickly, maximising the element of surprise. Paratroopers are at their most vulnerable when in the aircraft and when flying under a parachute. Darkness provides at least some protection.

Suddenly the giant aircraft shuddered and the green light above the door illuminated. A shout of "Green on!" cascaded away from me and behind down the darkened tunnel that was the fuselage.

I was out! A God somewhere must have flicked a switch because just two seconds before, my body had strained under the weight of equipment and the stifling heat. In an instant the weight was snatched from my back and instead, it now hung gently beneath a beautiful canopy of shimmering green nylon. Cool morning air buffeted my face, gently stealing the feelings of nausea. I was relaxed, calm yet fully aware of what I was diving into.

Once I was away from the aircraft I had the chance to go through the drills; check canopy, watch out for other Paras in the sky and for those who might get too close. I tugged at the strap on my waist releasing my Bergen and rifle pack from my leg, which then dropped to dangle just ten feet below.

Suddenly at about two hundred feet, the wind started to blow in fierce gusts flinging the parachutes and their cargo headlong toward a heavily wooded area. I reached up, yanked hard on the lift webs, two of four thick leather straps which in turn spewed out dozens of nylon cord leading to the canopy above. I was desperate to get down and avoid the trees. I pulled as hard as I could on the straps, trying hard to fold the parachute and cause it to steer away and dive. There was no effect. I tried again and using both hands, I selected a single lift web on my front left.

The prospect of landing in trees loomed ever nearer and I was petrified. Mental pictures of being skewered on a huge wooden branch filled my mind. I fought desperately for height or a new direction; I'd settle for either.

For a second or two I contemplated releasing my equipment and dumping it, letting it fall. Glancing down, I could make out men already on the ground. They were busy clearing up their collapsed parachutes, the produce of an earlier wave. I didn't fancy the idea of dumping a hundred pounds onto some poor bugger below so now the decision was made for me. I'd keep my equipment.

I heaved downward bringing the left web to my chest. Fortunately the parachute capitulated and rapidly leaned over before beginning its swift decent. The ground rushed up to meet me, barely providing an opportunity to react. Abandoning the lift webs I tucked my elbows in swiftly. Seconds ago I was trying to force the parachute to change direction, now my priority was simply to protect my face.

With a wallop hard enough to force the air out of my lungs, I struck the ground, landing on my back. Streams of nylon cord wrapped themselves around my upper body and face as I was dragged along the ground. Thankfully my hands remained free. I punched at the giant metal button on my chest, unlocking the harness. Twisting around, I reached up and at the same time, pulled frantically at the parachute cords, collapsing the canopy. The drag came to a sudden halt. In half a moment I was up on my feet. Continuing a fluid motion I threw the harness to one side and pulled my equipment pack to my feet. My SLR rifle came out first. In a fraction of a second I had visibly checked it for damage and had immediately slung a full magazine into it, cocking it at the same time. Shouldering the SLR, I scanned about me. I was in an open field of long golden grass. Three sides of the field were fenced in with thick mature woods and the on the remaining side, the ground gave way to acres of sloping ploughed farmland.

Behind me the wooded area broke away into two parts, separated by a single tree much taller than the rest. In that tree alone there were three parachutes dangling. I considered myself very lucky indeed.

Once at the RV we sped off tabbing through the wooded trails. Our objective was to take the nearby airfield.

For weeks we had all seen the newspaper articles covering the story of how a country had degenerated into a bloody military coup and then in the last week, foreigners including a number of British citizens had been rounded up and taken hostage.

The news articles covered every event. The central African country of Omberia was a mess. Most of us had never heard of Omberia or its murderous dictator, General John Mboke but the news was there for all to see. Thirty six hours ago I had stood outside the cookhouse in the Lines at Aldershot and wondered to myself, "Is this war?" The press releases were quite detailed and the newspapers were full of speculation that British troops might be sent to Omberia to rescue hostages.

For some the answer was obvious but for a good many, it took several days to realise, as elaborate as this was, it was another bloody exercise!

CHAPTER TWO

WILL SOMEBODY PLEASE LISTEN!

For a moment I was a small boy standing next to my Dad, a big man towering at six feet three. An RAF policeman, immaculate in his khaki uniform. He had collected my brother and me from school that day in his blue police Land Rover. Obeying his instructions without question I crouched down in the back until we were clear away, far from prying eyes. Civilians, even as children of airmen were not permitted to travel in service vehicles without express permission. The excitement for me at only five years old was electrifying. My Dad was great and I loved to be with him.

Bumps and holes in the uneven hard baked ground seemed to fight with the Land Rover as it thudded and shuddered forwards. Red volcanic dust spewed out from under its wheels. I had no idea where we were going and I didn't really care. All journeys were a great adventure and at that moment I loved every second of it.

We had been living in the British colony of Kenya, East Africa for about a year. Ever since he had started his post at RAF Eastleigh near Nairobi, Dad had spent much of his time away. The Aden emergency continued and Dad found himself being sent there for months at a time. Now that he was back I simply wanted to be near him. Mark, who at a year older, was for some reason known only to him, content to sit quietly in the back. I though wanted to soak it all in. I couldn't sit still or shut up. I wanted to see everything and I wanted to know everything.

It wasn't a long drive and pretty soon my Dad pulled the whining Land Rover to a halt. I remember that there were large buildings nearby but I didn't know what their function was. This was a large corner of near deserted land situated within the far reaches of this massive airfield.

With shovel like hands smoothly sliding under my armpits Dad picked me up and guided my feet onto the rigid bonnet. High above me, Dad pointed to an almost cloudless sky,

"There!" He said excitedly.

I followed his finger direction up and beyond. Far off but clearly visible I could see aeroplanes. Large, lumbering hulks of grey, each with twin tail booms.

"Beverlys", explained Dad.

He knew a lot about planes and his enthusiasm unwittingly fuelled my growing excitement.

I watched transfixed as the giant bulbous aircraft began to disgorge their loads. Seemingly hundreds of tiny black dots spilled from their booms and fell into space. As the tiny dots fell toward the ground, each would explode into billowing mushrooms of silk khaki.

Extending an arm affectionately around my shoulders Dad brought me close to him in a hug. Filled with patriotic pride he emotionally whispered,

"They're the Red Devils. Paratroopers,"

I don't know if I completely understood what exactly a paratrooper was but those words were enough. They pictured in my mind images of tough fighting men. My Dad was proud of them so I was too.

Nearly twelve years later I sat in a cold and boring classroom full of excitable teenagers, yet I felt very alone. Something was missing from my life. There was no purpose, no direction. I of course had mates and we often got into all sorts of mischief and had some laughs too but still I felt incomplete. I had just had a disastrous two years at this school and three others. I had changed schools several times and that at least wasn't my fault. I was at an age when most kids were trying to settle down to do exams; circumstances clearly prevented my chances of settling.

My Dad had just been told that he was to be sent back to London after his posting in Cyprus had been unexpectedly curtailed by the Turkish invasion of that island. The return of my Dad wasn't simply a much wished for reunion with my absent father, it also meant yet another change of school.

The problem didn't even end there. In school I had foolishly and stupidly created a reputation of rebellious behaviour and downright mischief. Now teachers were warning me that I could soon be expelled.

The school gates were wide open and the signs were glaringly obvious, it was time for me to leave.

Suddenly, leaving school without a single academic qualification was not as big and clever as it had earlier seemed and my classroom boasts now felt very foolish indeed. It dawned on me that the prospects of me getting any half-decent job in this depressed area of Nottingham were at best, slim and at worstimpossible.

Mixed ambitions and confused teenage values prevented me from making any decision as to exactly what it was that I wanted to do or what I should do, though I did feel a certain influence from a couple of lads in the class who had recently been accepted into the army.

For years as a young boy I had wanted to be a Royal Marine Commando, but since about the age of thirteen I hadn't given it any serious thought. Instead the later years saw me convinced that any form of service life was the exact opposite of what it was that I wanted. However, interest in military life was once again stirring within me.

My best mate at the time, a lad called Alan "Scrappy" Dean was firmly fixed on the idea of enlisting into the Royal Anglican regiment. I toyed with that idea myself for a while but then like a light being flicked on inside my head I found myself thinking about joining the Parachute Regiment.

Unfortunately for me, I had an extreme dislike of all activities that even remotely involved physical exercise and if that wasn't enough I was also acutely scared of heights. I guess that the idea of being a soldier and especially of jumping out of aeroplanes didn't last long. I didn't know what to do. I was lost.

One night whilst lying awake in bed, I made a decision. I reckoned that there was no other choice; I was going to join the Army. I really had no idea which Corps or Regiment that I should try for, nevertheless my mind was made up, in the army I must go.

In the last few weeks of his time in Cyprus my Dad wrote to me telling me that he was happy for me to enlist into the army but he had great misgivings about me joining the infantry. Too many friends and relatives, he said had served good and full careers in the front line of our army only to find that later on, Civvy Street didn't want them. His letter concluded, "Join the army if you wish but get a trade".

On the face of it, it sounded like good advice; my problem was that I couldn't think of a single trade that appealed to me.

Just days after making my first enquiry, a tall uniformed Recruiting Sergeant from Nottingham's Army Recruiting Office delivered a glossy brochure to my door. The brochure was titled with a slogan something like;

"Two hundred trades in the army".

So many to choose from? There were jobs covering almost everything, train drivers, clerks, mechanics, chefs and many more. Sadly though, few caught my eye and even fewer caught my attention.

Ever since I'd had inkling to enlist I had fancied working on motor bikes. Actually I knew very little about bikes but it was pretty macho to pretend that you did. Not only that, but imagining myself as a wartime dispatch rider as I wrestled my machine through enemy territory was very appealing. It seemed a glamorous and adventurous pastime. One which any sixteen year old could fancy and eventually aspire to.

Hopes were soon dashed though when I next saw the Recruiting Sergeant for he informed me of the long waiting lists and queues to join the two trades which dealt with motorcycles, the RCT Junior Leaders Battalion and the REME apprentices. I could, he advised, either wait another year and then enlist into adult service or alternatively I could simply select another trade, one with vacancies.

After the Sergeant had gone I sat alone in front of the glowing coal fire, just staring at the dancing flames. In silent thought I searched for guidance and inspiration. The idea of waiting another year definitely didn't appeal. I needed something now and anyway; I'd just spent the previous two years doing nothing and I definitely didn't feel like I waiting for another year.

I snatched up the pamphlet from the floor and began to flick through its glossy pages. Any thoughts were interrupted abruptly when my Mum entered the room. Mum was spoiling me and had placed onto the coffee table behind me a large

13

wooden tray neatly displaying a supper of cakes and sandwiches. Pausing to close the pages of the army pamphlet I found myself staring at an open page.

There looking straight up at me was a full colour photograph of a young soldier chef immaculately turned out in his crisp white hat and tunic. Out in front he proudly offered a tray of delicious looking cakes and buns. In less time than it took to blink, my mind flashed back to all the times that I had tinkered with food here at home. In an instant I had found a choice and a decision was made.

The Army Catering Corps (ACC) trained at St Omer barracks in the heart of the Aldershot garrison. It was inevitable that here, in the home of the Parachute Brigade that I would occasionally come across Paratroopers.

Throughout my training in Aldershot I was taught to look at our neighbours from other Corps and Regiments with a certain disdain. This was particularly so of the Paras.

Perhaps this started as simple and healthy rivalry, friendly and certainly encouraged, but over the years it had somehow got out of hand and some feelings on both sides had evolved into near hatred. I suspect that at least some of this dislike stemmed from envy.

As an impressionable sixteen-year-old I absorbed this exaggerated snobbery with fervour. Like thousands of others I was brainwashed by a few silly narrow-minded attitudes.

Outwardly I exhibited a profound dislike for anyone who wore a maroon coloured beret. Secretly though, many of us knew that those lads who we had seen about town strutting their stuff were undoubtedly very good soldiers, some of the best in the world. These were real fighting men with a very well-deserved reputation for toughness. The resident 16

Independent Parachute Brigade held in me, a hidden but a deep respect.

It wasn't until two years later on completion of my army apprenticeship training that I was to be thrown in amongst the man eating monsters of local legend. I had expected to join the Blues and Royals in Chelsea, London but for some reason, which was never explained to me, the posting order was quickly cancelled. In its place a new order arrived, I was to join the 7th Parachute Regiment of the Royal Horse Artillery, known simply as 7 RHA or 7 Para.

I tried hard to look forward to joining the regiment but at the same time I couldn't help but feel deep apprehension of what might lay ahead.

The fateful day came on a warm but overcast morning. I cautiously approached the guardroom at Lille barracks in Northcamp, a Victorian town straddling the boundary between Aldershot and Farnborough. This was the home of the Regiment and had been for the last seventeen years.

On the far side of Lynchford road I stood paused, alone for a moment, savouring the last few seconds of boy service.

On the other side of the road I would have to stand up and be accepted as an adult and a trained soldier. Somewhat timidly I inched across the road and entered a place which I expected could easily have passed for the gates of hell!

The red brick 1950's built guardroom surrounded by polished red oxide cement looked quite impressive with its huge gleaming wombat shells stood proudly either side of the door.

Outside a uniformed young soldier lifted the red and white wooden barrier that blocked the road. He said nothing, just scrutinised my MOD90, the army issue plastic identification card, and then waved me over to a small blue framed kiosk style window adjacent to the guardroom door.

A little man with black hair and squat features, and who I later learned was known (at least behind his back) as Jimmy the Pig, leaned forward into the window space stopping just inches from my very worried face. Speaking abruptly he introduced himself as the Regimental Provost Sergeant, a type of localised military policeman. He looked down, ticked a list and directed a NCO to escort me to the RHQ building.

The burly bombardier wearing an already out of issue but much loved old style Dennison parachutist's smock beneath his cherished red beret, marched along with me   towards   the various HQ buildings.

As we went, and without once turning to face me, the NCO asked several questions but it didn't take long before the Bombardier became red faced and   agitated.   He   snapped angered comments at my answers and me. At first I couldn't figure out what I'd done wrong but just as we reached our destination it suddenly became glaringly obvious. Without realising I had repeatedly addressed the big man as Corporal instead of Bombardier as his artillery heritage dictated. He by now definitely didn't like what I had said and it was even more obvious that he didn't like me.

Inside and upstairs I was told to sit down at the highly polished dark red mahogany table centred in the Regiment's conference room. The room adjacent to the RSM's office was filled with other men already sitting down; some were talking but most sat still and stared into oblivion. They all looked as nervous as I and it was easy to see that all of us here were new.

Most of the blokes were young Gunners but one was a cook (or a chef as they more often like to be called). Little Scouse Wright sported close-cropped fair hair and deep rosy cheeks. Like me he was just eighteen years old and wearing the cap badge of the ACC, but unlike me he could have easily passed for a kid of fifteen. He had just passed out from the training battalion of the ACC, the establishment responsible for the training of adult recruits.

To the army an adult recruit is anyone who enlists after their seventeenth and a half birthday. Adult recruits were rushed through about a third of the training that I had received but still it was high by civilian   standards.

Pleasantries and handshakes were exchanged and the atmosphere relaxed becoming immediately friendly.

A loud crash shocked everyone back to their senses and the burly Bombardier burst back into the room shattering the idle chitchat into momentary silence. His mouth barely opened but from it came the scream,

"STAND UP!"

Jolted by the high voltage vocal electric shock all of us newcomers shot to our feet knocking chairs and each other aside, instantaneously adopting the stiff position of attention.

A wide shouldered man wearing the crown of Battery Sergeant Major upon his sleeve marched over to the top of the table at the end of the room. He wore a large bushy moustache and what looked like half shaved sideburns not quite reaching his hairline yet not extending as far down as his moustache either. Unused to the sight, I found myself for a moment staring.

"Hairy cheeks". I thought, allowing myself a silent chuckle having found the spectacle somewhat comical.

A powerful voice erupted from the BSM. His words boomed across the room, intense and piercing. I don't know what it was that he shouted but it sure as hell frightened me! Pushing the chair behind him he leaned over the table towards us till his shoulders cast horrible ghoulish shadows over me.

At the same time he banged his heavy fists onto the table and barked some unrecognised noise which I am sure was in a language that he just made up as he went along. Nobody, including me or perhaps especially me had the nerve to ask for a translation. His by now captured audience of novice soldiers bounced further and further backward in startled fear with each and every collision of his white knuckles and the shuddering table.

I gathered that we were being told that we must all reach the standards expected in this Brigade and now that we were part of this Regiment and standards had to be higher still.

As suddenly as he had started he stopped. In the pause I dared to glance about the room at my fellows. Unmoving and completely mesmerised, stunned by the ferocity of his speech, they each stared at the Sergeant Major without even blinking.

The CO entered the room and the atmosphere immediately calmed with the welcome change of pace. The Lieutenant Colonel, a greying sedentary man in his forties, thanked the stiff upright BSM. The CO paused, then brushed his fingers comb like through the long thin strands of hair above his ear and then flicked the hair over his balding scalp.

Turning to the new members he uttered a well-practised welcoming speech, all the while looking down at the table as if reading from some invisible script.

I remember that actually he said very little apart from a promise to see every one of us personally at some time during the next few weeks. I couldn't help but get the impression that this welcome was someone else's idea and that he had simply but reluctantly agreed to it. Surely it was a chore dictated by etiquette rather than military efficiency.

Chip Walker
I don't remember ever seeing him again.

Scouser Wright and I were pointed off to the Regimental Cookhouse and away we went dragging our kitbags and suitcases with us.

Once there we met the Master-chef, known affectionately within the Regiment as The Duffman or occasionally shortened simply to Duff.

Staff Sergeant Nobby Clark was well liked by many in the unit despite being thought of as an eccentric. A short man, bespectacled and showing some grey in what used to be a head of shocking yellow hair, he introduced himself and detailed our immediate duties then appointed a LCPL Johnny Wilkes to ensure that we signed our various documents and drew extra kit, then bedding from the stores.

The Duffman went on, informing us that the Regiment was soon to lose its parachute status and with it, its right to wear the coveted red beret of the Parachute Regiment and the Airborne Forces. 7 PARA were being posted to Osnabruck in West Germany to take up a new role as a field regiment.

James Callaghan's Labour Government was hard at it implementing their much-publicised savage cuts in the country's armed forces. Politicians and Generals said that the airborne soldier was obsolete in modern warfare. War, if it came, they added would be with the USSR and fought on the plains of central Germany by a motorised push button army, defending its ground.

The government didn't want a lightly equipped attacking group such as 16 Parachute Brigade. The conclusion for many was worrying but still inevitable.

The Parachute Brigade was an independent brigade. It had never been restricted to a purely NATO role. Instead it served as a quick response unit ready to deploy or operate anywhere in the world at short notice to protect the interests of Great Britain and her citizens. British interests overseas though with the collapse of the empire were fast shrinking and with it, the political will to defend it.

The famed 16 Brigade was to be disbanded. The Government at the time, like so many since, was playing a distasteful and dangerous game of chopping huge chunks from the armed services and with it some of our country's proudest and finest units.

Both Scouse Wright and I had volunteered to undergo parachute selection, the course known as P-company, but the answer to our very simple request was an equally simple "NO". In fact it was no longer possible.

The course running at this time and nearing its end was the last for this Regiment. Open to all soldiers other than those of the Parachute Regiment, it was known as the 'All Arms Parachute Selection Course'. It was shutting down, its future   uncertain.

A few months later and we were on parade really early. Germany was waiting. Ordered to remove their cherished maroon berets and replace them with the dark blue, almost black beret of ordinary ground troops, disgruntled Gunners climbed into unfamiliar left hand drive Land Rovers ready to commence their long drive to Osnabruck.

Barely distinguishable from their British based counterparts, the convoy of brand new Land Rovers left the barracks turning left into Lynchford road and passing the guardroom for the last time.

Standing to attention, a lone gunner stood on the roadside and solemnly saluted his departing colleagues. Behind those men lay the memories and pride of a great airborne   Regiment.

Ahead of them was the beginning of a newly formed field artillery Regiment.

Before the lead vehicle had even passed the now demolished Queens quarters along Lynchford Road a young Lance Bombardier climbed through the open window of his Land Rover. With his feet firmly pushed into the seat he anchored his shins against the door and stretched outwards. He gripped the flapping tarpaulin which was hooded over the Land Rover and with his free hand, made exaggerated pointing movements to the top of his head and bringing everybody's attention immediately to the fact that he had once more donned his prized maroon beret!

Soldiers in the following vehicles let out raucous cheers and yelps of approval then every one of them to a man followed suit. Seeing the laughing faces on the soldiers behind him, the leading soldier reached inside, grabbed his newly issued black hat and ceremoniously chucked it straight across the road. I sat still, watching their antics and laughed with them.

Nonchalantly I removed my black beret. I felt that I didn't deserve to act as my comrades had but, out of respect, I pushed the hated black hat away and out of   sight.

The driver of my Land Rover was a tough Scot from the Blackhill area of Glasgow. Turning to face me he scowled,

"Until we get to Osnabruck this is a Parachute Regiment. If you want to stay in this wagon then you'll keep that fucking thing off your head!"

I promised myself there and then that I would remain bare headed until it was safe to do otherwise.

Maroon berets, pride of the   airborne   soldier   gained   a temporary reprieve. For at least the duration of this journey it would be worn with utmost and sincere reverence. The soldiers of 7 Para gained a respect from me that day that would stay for the remainder of my life.

It was nearly eight years later after serving with several other units that I came to the solid opinion that the manner of soldiering, its skills and professionalism found in the Airborne Forces were exactly how I thought the army should be but disappointedly, often was not.

Of course, I did meet some men who were not airborne and were excellent soldiers but my argument is one of collective attitude. No other unit or Brigade shares that level of skill which is accepted as normal practice for Airborne Forces. With few exceptions, ordinary soldiers often don't possess that same pride that get up and go way of life.

Whilst serving with Headquarters, Episkopi Garrison in Cyprus I twice had occasion to work with different airborne units. These units had come to Cyprus to exercise in its near Middle Eastern terrain and weather conditions. Always with them, I felt a sense of belonging.

Here was a bunch of blokes who were like me. Naturally, I began to believe that I was in the wrong job and also in the wrong place. Cook, chef, cabbage mechanic or even slop jockey, whatever title I carried, I knew that I had joined the army to be a soldier and yet few commanders had allowed me to be one.

Over the next few weeks scattered thoughts raced about inside my head, then one blazing hot day in August of 1983 after completing a small part in a waterborne exercise with the Special Air Service (SAS), I came to the conclusion that there must be more from life for me. I felt especially that I wanted more from the army.

With my mind made up, there was no going back. I would immediately volunteer for service with the Paras.

I told everyone who would likely listen or even pay even passing attention. They all heard my voice, friends, NCOs, and officers alike. They all knew how I felt and what it was that I was searching for. Now all I had to do was to express my wishes on paper.

Volunteering for service with Special Forces had to be on an official application letter addressed to ACC manning and records. These were the people who with a large computer and an awful lot of paper piled up somewhere in Taunton, Somerset, controlled the postings and promotions of the three thousand men of the Corps.

From Dave Shott, my WO1, I sought advice about which would be the best way to make my application. I was riding on a steep high but my legs were well and truly kicked away from under me when abruptly he countered,

"Wait son, because you're not due to be posted for another year".

He had thought that I must have been mad or at least foolish to want to give up a warm sunshine posting to go jumping out of aeroplanes. His disagreeable logic cut like a knife. He went on to say that unless I had a damned good reason, Manning and Records would not even consider an application.

Two long months later I again approached Dave Shott once more. I stood in front of the big man as he stared somewhere past me. His appearance was somewhat deceptive because his obvious bulk betrayed his true fitness and prowess on the cross-country field. Indeed this man had more than once beaten me in a race.

As he read from a paper on his desk I watched as his cheeks darkened with a permanent five o'clock shadow, form boyish dimples as he broke into a smile. As if suddenly realising that I was there he said,

"Yeah, um, come in and sit down".

I parked myself on the faded blue chair and without giving him the chance to say anything further I abruptly voiced my doubts about the future of my army career and how I again wished to volunteer for parachute selection but once again I received the same answer,

"This was not the right time".

I waited.

Some three months later and still waiting for the promised, "Right time", the bad news suddenly arrived. It came in the shape of an early posting order.

The order, typed, stamped and addressed to me detailed how and when I should leave Cyprus for a Royal Engineer regiment stationed at Perham Down in the south of England.

A fine unit I was sure but not where I had aimed for and certainly not a unit coloured by the famous maroon beret.

Frustrated and shaking with anger I screwed the paper into a tight ball and squeezed my fist until the knuckles turned white. Without hesitation I went immediately to see that same warrant officer who had twice previously told me to wait.

The urge to leap over his desk and beat him to a pulp swelled inside me, a temper threatening to unleash unless there was something, anything to satiate my anger.

With my bottom lip quivering I fought to remain calm. Concentrating instead, trying hard not to be insubordinate, I forced myself into a position of attention just a few feet from his chair. Through gritted teeth I tried to explain my feelings of extreme annoyance and disappointment in how things had eventually worked out. After all, I reasoned, I had taken his advice and the end result was exactly the opposite of what it was that I had wanted. Of course much of my frustration was for me but also for my Corps because this Corps in particular was struggling to find enough suitable volunteers to serve as an airborne soldier.

Dave Shott pushed his hands forward holding them out as if weighing some invisible commodity. He shrugged his shoulders before going on to speak but strangely no words came out. His head tilted to one side making his eyebrows crunch up in the middle. Then, "What's all this fuss about?" he asked.

I felt that his attitude was one of not really caring or perhaps he could not comprehend why it was that I was bothered. To me my feelings had been trampled and it seemed obvious that nobody at that time gave a toss about which direction my career should go.

I tried to take the discussion further but the he was by now obviously tired of my protestations and he cut me off with a cold, "You should have submitted your letter earlier!"

Before I could even take a breath he blurted, "It doesn't matter; it's probably a good posting anyway!"

A good posting! I thought, incredulously. *What does he know?*

Thoughts whirled around inside my head and I could physically feel the red mist of temper begin to boil inside me once again, rising ever higher. If ever I had wanted Scotty to beam me up, it was now.

Storming away from his office I punched an imaginary foe and let out a short but very relieving scream. Looking back I think I can honestly say that I've had better debates with fish.

Now I was dejected, not wanted and not particularly needed. Sudden realisation dawned; I was just a tiny cog in a very large machine. Despite this so called system it seemed that nobody gave a damn.

Days later after chewing the ears of anyone who would listen I eventually calmed down. A friend and colleague of mine, John Hatfield-Sieman, a man engaged with his own battles for SAS selection, advised that I should ignore the posting order. I noted too that the order had been in the unit for nearly three weeks though I had only received it a few days previously.

Acting as if nothing had gone on before, I applied by formal military letter to serve with Airborne Forces. During a quick break at work I drafted the letter in its regulated format. It read,

Sir,

APPLICATION TO SERVE WITH SPECIAL FORCES.

1. I have the honour to submit this my application to serve with Special Forces (i.e. The Parachute Brigade).

2. My reasons being that I feel that I have the correct physical and mental aptitude and that the experience gained would benefit me greatly.

3.I hope this application meets with your kind consideration and

approval. I have the honour to be

Sir,

Your obedient

servant Corporal

24340155.

No time was wasted. With letter in hand I went immediately to my immediate boss, SSGT Geordie Lowerson.

Geordie an ever cheerful chap, greeted me wearing his prized Green beret. He had earned it whilst serving with 59 Commando of the Royal Engineers and after passing the Royal Marine Commando course.

Now that he was no longer serving with a commando unit, the strict army dress code dictated that he should revert to sporting the ordinary navy blue beret or black hat as it is known. Ironically he was trying hard to keep his beret whilst at the same time I was trying hard to get rid of mine.

Geordie had always refused to replace his Green beret and nobody had dared order him remove it. This muscular man with his Mexican moustache was sometimes questioned about his choice of headdress by officers, those who were uninitiated into his likely response often left wishing that they had never asked. It was the fastest way to learn that Geordie was the master of belittling and a maestro of the curt reply.

Geordie was different to most, a good boss and a good soldier. Such a combination isn't exactly rare in the British army but at times and especially in the ACC at the time, he appeared to be in the minority. He was a leader. Everyone respected him though not everybody liked him and I was optimistic that he would accept and understand just exactly what all this had meant to me.

Patiently he sat back threatening to topple his old and battered chair then, pushed his hands behind his head and let out a long sigh.

The letter was snatched from my outstretched hand as he allowed the chair to crash forward. His eyes darted through the hastily written application. Between clenched teeth neatly hidden behind a bulbous moustache he whispered insulting expletives aimed at the immediate hierarchy.

"Leave it with me, I'll sort it out". He snorted a loud nasal groan, which said nothing, but I took it to be a sign of pure disgust.

Gesturing for me to sit, he pointed to a chair opposite the desk then promised that he would send the application through the system without delay. He paused for a second, waited in silent thought then smiling, he asked,

"Why don't you do the commando course?"

I broke into a near uncontrollable chuckle. Said nothing, only noting the cheeky glint in his eyes, I laughed and walked out.

A week followed before anything further happened, then one afternoon John Hatfield-Sieman (HS to his mates) on his way home from working an afternoon shift, called at my married quarter. In his hand he held a written message from Geordie Lowerson.

The letter informed me that I was to parade before the OC at ten hundred hours of the following morning. No reason was given but HS suggested that it might be about my posting application. When the time came I stood under the shade of the long veranda outside the Major's office.

Flicking my wrist I examined my watch to check the time. As planned I had arrived at around ten minutes early. In the army whenever anyone orders that you should arrive somewhere at a certain time then you would be expected to arrive at least ten minutes earlier. I believe that this practice is normal in all three armed services.

Dressed in best working uniform, I stood checking my kit for any irregularities. There were a few small and tiny pieces of foliage wedged into the welts of my bulled boots, which had collected during the short journey to the OC's office. It took just a few seconds to pick away the crap. Appearance was important to me and I was desperate to make a good impression.

Called in by an unseen voice I marched forward, threw a rigid salute and spurted a monotone but regulation,

"Good morning Sir".

The OC motioned for me to sit down and without looking up he told me to relax. I pulled myself forward and waited for the OC to finish scribbling something on a note pad.

Thoughts rushed around inside my head. The voice of my inner self whispered a warning; *Here it comes.*

Nervously I tried to blot the pessimistic demons from my mind but still they murmured. *He's going to say that you've left it too late.*

I couldn't help but agree with the unwanted thoughts; after all I probably had left it too late. The more that I thought about it the more I convinced myself that I was right. I began to think that I should accept the way that things had turned out; perhaps I would be happy then.

My train of thought was sharply interrupted as the Major peeled his eyes upwards and towards me. His mouth began to move as if speaking yet no words were heard. I watched mesmerised. Suddenly the OC seemed to gather his thoughts and said,

"Corporal, I think you're just the sort of man that the Paras are looking for."

With unexpected glee I fought to suppress the already spreading smile which threatened to split my face in two.

The OC, a Major of the Royal Artillery was nearing the end of his career. Looking tired and aged in this young man's army, he reflected for a moment on his own experiences.   His career had started with the famous 33 Regiment of the RA. These were the airborne gunners of the 1940's and 1950's.

Pride of thought caused him to stand, shoulders pulled back. For a few seconds his mind reminisced of younger and perhaps happier days. Turning obliquely away from me he dropped his right shoulder. I couldn't help but detect the faded wings of a parachutist adorning his upper sleeve.

"I was a paratrooper once you know"

"Yes, I know Sir." Trying to sound as if I'd known all along.

The old soldier eased himself back into his chair and leaned forward. He went on to say that he would of course give my application his complete support, but he too doubted very much whether his opinion could possibly persuade ACC Records to change the posting order at this late stage.

He squinted, gazed out into the sunshine and stuttered,

"They're funny things you know, Record offices."

A wiry grin broke out revealing him to have a humorous contempt for officialdom and the system.

Feeling elated I was not going to let the OC's slightly pessimistic view of things dampen my new born spirits. As far as I was concerned the score stood at two-one. A battle won as they say but the war was still a long way from being over.

Later that day Geordie gave me the official form to fill out. In it I had to specify which of the units considered being Special Forces that I wished to volunteer for. The list was understandably short; Commando, S.A.S., Paras, and perhaps oddly, the RCT Maritime division.

Four days later I was summoned to see another of my superior officers. Once more I was to see a Major but this time one of my own Corps. I had known Major Saunders for some time and generally found him to be a very capable man. He was an exceptionally tall man with a kindly nature. I thought him to be a gentleman officer who held the appointment as the garrisons SO2 Catering.

The Major had very little to do with my ordinary every day duties or indeed any work restricted to the confines of my parent unit. In fact an SO2 is more akin to a district manager responsible for ACC interests within a given region.

Part of those interests included career development.

Before I had even got into his office I had decided on my plan of action. Attack was the best form of defence they say, so my plan was simple. I would put him straight on the spot. I will give him the whole story, I thought, come what may, he will listen. I was sure he would and I will tell him why I wanted so much to join the Airborne Brigade and why my application had arrived on his desk so late.

I wondered what he would have to say but I reckoned that he would most probably accuse me of submitting this application only so that I could get out of a less than glamorous posting with the engineers. Over and over again I rehearsed my speech inside my head. I was ready.

As soon as I opened my mouth the SO2 closed it by speaking before I could utter a sound.

"I've already actioned your application."

I was stunned, almost winded by his opener. Speaking in his soft educated accent he went on to explain that he had agreed fully with my OC and that he written an urgent letter to ACC Manning and Records asking them to alter my posting order.

Major Saunders too, was doubtful of any great success. He speculated that Manning and Records would possibly just keep it on file until another posting was due or at least until I had served a year or so at Perham Down with the engineers.

I was surfing a wave of good fortune, now I could do no more than wait.

Every now and then our printed Routine orders carried a warning not to try and contact Manning and Records direct. There was little truth I am sure but rumours suggested that direct contact would severely piss them off and would then likely ruin any chances of getting whatever it was that you contacted them for.

Days of silence followed with nagging doubts beginning to bite away at my waning euphoria. Slowly I began to resign myself to the fact that despite all of my efforts and all of the support that I had recently enjoyed, I was still likely to end up with that very ordinary unit back in England.

On the ninth day of waiting I received a telephone message from Geordie Lowerson. The line was bad and the receiver crackled with static.

The mild voice on the other end was faint but it sounded happy as it broke into speech,

"I've got a priority signal for you"

Two and two had not yet come together to make four in my head and I wondered what in hell he was talking about. I had just begun to query his statement when he interrupted with a stuttered exclamation;

"If you'll just shut up I'll read it out!"

Assuming my silence as acknowledgement he went on,

"Previous posting order cancelled. Attend Para course 23 April 1984. Posting order to follow."

This little war with bureaucracy had come to an end.

CHAPTER THREE

THE SLOW SLOG

I now knew that I had a place on the course and I was more than satisfied with my soldiering skills, in fact, having spent three years of my previous posting as a Drill and Weapons Instructor to new recruits in Aldershot, I reckoned that I was pretty good. There was a real worry though, and that one bit hard into me. Was I fit enough?

I had been running regularly in the local road and cross-country competitions and had recently been awarded Garrison colours for running. Quite obviously I was fit by most standards. However, I had a nagging doubt about how I would perform wearing heavy boots and army denim trousers, and then on top of that I would have to carry a loaded Bergen pack. It had been a couple of years since I had attempted anything like an assault course. How would I fare now?

I debated the problems in my head trying hard to convince myself that actually I knew all the answers but I was unable to produce a single viable conclusion. My mood was sinking and I found it hard to remain positive.

I needed a Bergen but there were none in Cyprus. At that time Bergen packs were only issued to Special Forces, Airborne Forces and the Commando Brigade. That meant that the rest of us had to cope with the old, uncomfortable and atrociously designed 58-pattern backpack. Luckily, a colleague from the ROAC based at Akrotiri offered me his old 'A' Frame Bergen.

'A' Frames had been obsolete for years and this one showed why. It was twenty-six years old and threadbare around the edges, the pockets were full of holes. Even so it was better than the issued back-packs and it was as close a cousin to the modern Bergen as I was going to get.

The SQMS of his unit was kind enough to arrange for a Sail maker to make urgent repairs on what was fast becoming my pride and joy.

Training started in earnest. Out came my newly repaired but poorly looking Bergen. I had to fill it, both to pad it out and to help me get use to carrying weight. It didn't take long and soon it was filled to the brim, padded out with a real assortment of items; newspapers, tinned food, clothing and very nearly the kitchen sink. Standing over my Bergen I felt a sense of pride and quietly admired my handy work.

Next out came my DMS boots, puttees and a pair of old olive green trousers, known as OGs and the predecessor to the more modern green Denims.

With a complete disregard to elegance, I squatted before pulling the webbed straps toward me and swinging the pear shaped sack onto my back.

Bloody Hell! It felt like I was lifting a grown man over my shoulders. Not only did I find it far too heavy to be comfortable but also the triangle shaped metal frame, the A that gave it its name, dug sharply and painfully into my back. When I tried to move my arms backwards as I might when running or marching I found my shoulder blades protruded outward. They in turn quickly located the tubular frame and at its best it was uncomfortable, at worst it was bloody horrible. It didn't take long before I discovered that my height and build was not best suited to this design of backpack. "At least now" I said to myself, "I can see why they made it obsolete".

Undaunted, I kissed my wife Janet goodbye and set off for the garrison cookhouse. I knew that hidden there somewhere was an old set of butcher's scales. These if set correctly, were accurate and perhaps just as important to me, they were large enough to weigh both my bulging Bergen and me.

I placed the overgrown bag on to the ample scale pan and watched as the needle of the dial shot around to come to a shuddering halt at just over forty-eight pounds.

Is that all? I questioned the reading, surely it must be wrong!

It had felt like a hundred and forty eight pounds but there was no choice but to believe the dial on the scale and put my surprise down to simply being unused to carrying weight on my back and in particular, the way that this weight was carried in the odd shaped and old fashioned Bergen. Still keen to get on with it and start running, I left the cookhouse at a good pace. My simple plan was to run five miles as fast as I could, but after only a quarter of a mile I was already reduced to a trot.

Forty paces later and I was only able to manage a short skip. I didn't plan it that way but it was an action where under the sheer strain, my knees were barely able to bend though I was still able to move my legs forward fairly fast. I was stiff, awkward, but I was moving.

With my enthusiasm hardly daunted and my spirits still high I continued. A mile and a half later I felt as though I was crawling on my chinstraps. I was very fast running out of energy. It wasn't just the weight but the continuous and awful pain from that horrible steel 'A'. The pack refused to stop bouncing onto my back, jabbing persistently and finding bony flesh with every pace. Enough is enough, I convinced myself
and turned around for home.

When I finally arrived back at the married quarter, the skin was completely off the small of my back and again over my shoulder blades. With the Bergen away from my body I felt like gravity itself had been removed and with it, the pain.

I needed a shower. I was really sweaty and still sore. As soon as I stood in the bathtub and allowed myself to relax, my body enjoyed the rain of warm water. The water gently washed the dried sweat down off my back and I enjoyed the relaxing warm tingle through my skin as it forced an involuntary shoulder shake.

Aching muscles slowly began to return to normal when without warning the cascading water became suddenly and sharply violent. Stinging pains shot through the very fibre of my body. Salty sweat had found the open red sores on my flesh!

Something had to be done about that 'A' frame! It didn't take a lot of brains to figure out what to use as padding to put around the offending bits. I suppose that I could have simply wrapped something like a soft towel around the cross of the 'A', but I decided to go for something a little more permanent.

Armed with only an idea I visited the local hardware store.

In the heart of the Episkopi Garrison was a small shopping centre made up of temporary buildings of corrugated tin. A three-sided square with a car park in the middle, the whole lot was no larger than a football pitch.

That shopping area was known as Dodge City, probably so named because of its visual similarity with an old frontier town. Dodge housed on its southern edge a rambling shop named, "Wee Woollies".

Inside the darkened interior I crept through the dusty alleyways, long since created by overstocked and unwanted goods. There I began a systematic search amongst the shops hidden treasures. I knew exactly what it was that I wanted and I was sure that it was here somewhere.

Wee Woollies was not best known for being well organised. A bicycle tyre might be found near the men's socks which might be adjacent to the birthday cards. Whereas, a bicycle pump might be found amongst the children's toys along with household paints so it was never as straightforward as heading for the relevant aisle.

At last, buried under the paint-by-numbers kits, I found that what I had been looking for; sheets of versatile foam rubber. Pulling a square yard sized sheet from a pile caused a huge cloud of dirty grey dust to billow outwards and ascend into the cramped space between shelves. The sun's rays filtered through the shadows causing the dust to sparkle as it fountained around me. That dust went on to rain down over me, and then inevitably, it went up my nose, which immediately erupting into a storm of sneezes.

Quickly I gathered my senses, brushed myself down, wiped my nose and headed back towards the sunlight and the cash till where I could pay for the cache of cushioning.

At home I began to cut the foam rubber into thin strips, each big enough to cover one of the bars on the back of my Bergen. Every piece was fully wrapped around the metalled tubes and then carefully secured, fastened with black gaffer tape.

I had decided not to run the next day, mostly because my back was still really sore and painful, but also I reckoned (perhaps foolishly, but at that time anyway) that running three times a week would undoubtedly be enough.

Of the thrice-weekly runs each was planned to achieve something slightly different. The first run of the week was to be completed whilst wearing DMS boots and denim trousers. This was the standard dress for the BFT. Only I had already decided that I would carry my Bergen. The second run was to be speed training, a run of between five and eight miles and ran as fast as I could. Third and last would be stamina training. The week's final run was going to be my favourite, a long distance jaunt of between fifteen and twenty miles. For both the speed run and the long distance I had planned to dispense with the military stuff and just run in my regular cross-country kit.

I figured that if I stuck rigidly to those three runs for each and every week, I would easily build up enough strength to carry weight and enough speed to keep me happy. With continuing to compete in the cross-country league as well as the planned long distance runs, I expected to build up plenty of stamina.

Two uneventful weeks passed and though my working shifts did cause some problems, forcing training times to alter, I had so far managed to keep to the regime, at least roughly. Leg strength and stamina were, I believed, coming along exactly to plan.

I had given very little thought to improving my upper body. It really was a silly mistake because it was obvious that to an airborne soldier, a strong arm was equally important as the ability to cover long distances on foot, even if it were over some of the world's toughest terrain.

The simplest of solutions are often the best and in this case it was to be found less than half a mile from my quarters. The Garrison Gymnasium had very recently acquired a brand new multi-gym machine. It didn't take much to make my mind up to make use of the gym in between my chosen running days.

As I left the comfort of my home, long shadows stretched out in front of me, the morning sun still low in the sky glared at my entry to the outside in what was to be the first run of the week.

Despite the slowly healing sores on my skin I was back to carrying the old Bergen. Still it felt very heavy and even though

I had spent so much effort padding out the bars they did continue to rub quite a bit on those tender parts.

That previous back-ripping journey of mine had taught me not to set off so fast but instead to try and adopt a type of skipping. I might have looked pretty stupid but it did seem the most natural mode to use when carrying weight. With this in mind I set my sights on completing the same route and distance as before. That way, I thought, I could accurately measure and compare.

As I started, I straight away found the going to be a little more comfortable. Physically it was perhaps just as taxing but because I knew what was coming next I found it easier to cope with. The Bergen was definitely less bothersome but some parts of the frame continued to rub away at me.

Strangely though, this time the offending bits were not my carefully cushioned bars and tubes but the canvas straps which were worn across my shoulders. I tried pushing my shoulders back, closing the gap between the bony blades, then I pushed them forward, arching my back, but nothing seemed to help.

I was annoyed; these straps hadn't presented any great problem before. They were going to have to get the same treatment as the bars.

CHAPTER FOUR

ONE STEP FORWARD

It was February of 1984 and just over three months since I had begun my training regime in earnest. The unit HQ received an unclassified signal from England. It was in two parts. The first confirmed that a place had been reserved for me on a Pre-Para selection course. This was good news indeed, I knew already by then that I was going but it was still great to see it in black and white. The second part of the signal carried an ominous tone. Its words were simple and to the point, they read;

"The ACC failure rate on last Para course was abysmal. This we are informed was due to lack of fitness and determination. Units are to ensure that ACC attending course are especially fit and have undergone specific training. Merely having ability to pass BFT is insufficient."

Once that copy of the signal had reached the next day me it had gained an additional and separate note stapled over the front. My CO had signed the note. It ordered me to report with the attached signal to the Sergeant Major Instructor (SMI) of the Army Physical Training Corps.

The instant that I finished my morning shift in the Officers mess I went off to find the SMI. I told him everything that appeared relevant at the time and though he was quite receptive, it was unfortunate that he didn't know a great deal about the specific training required for the Paras selection. Luckily for me though, sharing the office with the SMI was Quarter Master Sergeant Instructor (QMSI) Bell.

He was a tall dark haired Warrant Officer of the APTC and was at the time attached to the Scots Guards. QMSI Bell had transferred to the APTC from the Parachute Regiment and he knew exactly what sort of training I should be undertaking. For the next six weeks, he and his two Corporals would take me under their wing, Their "Pet project" he called it.

He set about assessing my standard of fitness and then he enquired what had I actually done up to that point. Proudly and eagerly I launched into the story of my training so far, how I had got myself organised into three runs a week and about the weight training sessions on the multi-gym. To me at least, the QMSI seemed more than impressed. Throughout my speech he sat silently and motionless, all the time expressing a slight smile.

At the end of my ramble he sat bolt upright. Talking through a friendly grin he laughingly made it clear that he actually wasn't that impressed at all but he had enjoyed the way that I had made it sound impressive.

He said that he would give it some thought and then he sent me away with instructions to return early for the following morning.

As ordered I reported to the gymnasium wearing PT kit. I was to undergo an annual personal fitness assessment (APFA). The test consisted of a number of short exercises, which would measure aerobic recovery, strength and suppleness.

The test was then to be followed by a circuit in the weights room. During this time I would be monitored closely by both of the Corporals.

The test started with five minutes of reasonably fast step-ups. This initial test required me to repeatedly step up and down onto a wooden bench. The pace regulated by the clicking accompaniment of a metronome. Immediately after the five minutes one of the instructors noted my recovery rate by measuring my pulse and then twice again at one minute intervals.

I felt pretty fit and I was convinced that I would easily achieve a really good score from this and the remaining tests. One hundred and sixteen points were the minimum score required to get into my target zone and achieve an A-grade.

The instructors though felt differently. They thought that a score of one hundred and forty or beyond was what they considered to be a decent score and actually worthy of the sought after A-grade.

With all that now out of the way I was guided straight into the remaining tests. From the step-ups I went over to the hanging beam where I did my best with chin-ups, then onto sit-ups and then triceps dips on the parallel bars. All of those tests rated their score by the number of good repetitions that I could manage. Inevitably it meant that some of my efforts were immediately disqualified for not being just perfect. A standing jump completed the test.

Standing side onto a large wall mounted chart and with my arm stretched upwards, I readied myself. With knees bent I crouched slightly ready to jump. At the whistle blast I launched myself upwards. One of the Corporal instructors named Kev' Vest watched whereabouts my hand would slap the chart.

On completion I had only to wait for a few minutes while the other Cpl did some arithmetic to calculate the total score. When he emerged from the office I noticed that he didn't look up from his clipboard. I gathered that this was either because he was still counting or more likely because he wanted to avoid eye contact, as he was undoubtedly the bearer of bad news.

Eventually he stood in front of me and loudly tapped his biro on the metal bulldog clip of the clipboard then looked straight at me.

"One hundred and twenty seven".

He just blurted it out, turned around and walked off.

I felt awful. For many soldiers that score would have been alright, but for me and my trainers, it was disappointing.

Kev' stood up, hooked his finger and beckoned me to follow him. Earlier he had said that we would do some weights after the APFA. I guessed that was now.

Hanging my head low I kicked my heels like a sulking school boy and followed him into the weights room.

Kev' set the apparatus and went on to demonstrate each exercise that I was to do. Three quick circuits of ten repetitions on each of the work stations around the multi-gym machine, all completed as fast and as correctly as I could.

Both Corporals watched closely, barely speaking but occasionally scribbling frantic yet secretive notes. Quite obviously I was still being assessed.

With three very quick circuits completed I was barely able to stand. The wind had been sucked right out of me. Struggling to remain on my feet and bent over I tried to support my aching weight upon my knees. My face was burning from excess body heat and I felt bloody awful. I was panting and wheezing like an old smoker, I was wrecked.

Before I could even contemplate failure the QMSI came in. At first he ignored me but turned to his two staff and queried,

"How did he do?"

"Not too bad." Came Kev's quick reply.

His tone though was suspicious; I couldn't help but notice that he had over emphasised the "Too".

Kev' continued,

"He'll probably be alright in a month or so"

My ego sank suddenly and without trace. I put on one of those obviously false smiles to pretend that I wasn't that bothered and uttered something like.

"I'll do better next time".

I didn't really believe myself and I was not expecting anyone else to either. I felt quite feeble and I kinda hoped that nobody had heard me.

Back in his office, QMSI Bell got down to writing a six-day training programme for me. It was a programme that was to be monitored but repeated on each and every week. He didn't hesitate to tell me that it was now that the serious training must begin.

He told me that I was already pretty fit and certainly much fitter than the vast majority of his own men of the Second Battalion of the Scots Guards. They had recently completed a five-year stint on ceremonial duties in London and many of them he said, had become fatslobs.

For me, he dictated two hours a day for six days of the week adding that that was the minimum requirement.

Each day of the training would be different, not just so that I could exercise all muscle groups but also so that I wouldn't become bored with it.

Every morning would start with a one and a half-mile speed run on the running track followed immediately with a session of fast circuit training in the gym. After a break of four to six hours I would have to start the next task. This would vary depending on the day, it could be an eight mile run whilst carrying my Bergen and webbing or it might be something like a faster but shorter five mile run followed by a couple of trips over the garrisons unusually long assault course.

Though every day's training was different the format stayed basically the same, only the distances and terrain providing any variation.

For the first five weeks of that training, Wednesdays were spared the continuous slog of wearing boots and denims whilst running. This was because Wednesday was race day for the local cross-country league and I was still competing and representing the Garrison. The league season was just coming to an end but the road-racing season was about to start.

The training programme devised for me was all very well and good but being an army chef meant working awkward shifts and longer hours than other soldiers did, so my plans didn't always succeed.

Perhaps if I hadn't worked in a trade that was seen as vital to the everyday running of the army then maybe I would have been excused some duties and been allowed to train during work, indeed my training probably would have been scheduled as a duty.

Of course within the ACC this is nearly impossible. Obviously, men have to be fed. If I didn't work my shift for any reason than some other poor bugger would have to it. The demand doesn't go away just because I'm not there.

To escape this predicament I went to see my Sergeant, Alan Bowker. I explained my need to train and where I needed to be and hopefully at a time when the PT staff were on duty. Fine for them but to my great disadvantage they worked much fewer hours and at a much more sociable time.

I didn't give Alan a chance to comment; instead I volunteered an immediate solution, hoping against hope that he would at least consider my idea. Secretly I was confident, Alan was a decent bloke and he'd always been alright with me.

My proposed solution suggested that I be allowed to work permanent afternoon shifts excepting Wednesdays where I hoped to swap for a morning shift which would allow me to run in the weekly road race.

As expected Alan was sympathetic to my cause and after flicking through the duty rosters and his diary he readily agreed that the solution might work without serious hitches. He went on to say that he was happy as long as the remainder of the staff raised no objections. He was adamant though, perhaps quite rightly that he would not order other blokes to alter their duties just so that I could train for something, which I had volunteered for.

It was easy convincing the other chefs that things would work out fine if I were allowed to follow my proposals and work mainly a late shift. Probably everywhere but certainly in Cyprus the men often prefer to work the morning shifts so that they can spend some time with their families enjoying the afternoon sun.

Three weeks into my training I was ordered to undergo the Infantry Combat Fitness Test (ICFT). This particular test meant a soldier covering a distance of eight miles over road and cross-country whilst wearing full webbing weighed down with thirty pounds of ballast and at the same time carrying his personal weapon, in my case an SLR. The QMSI however, ordered that I take forty pounds of ballast and then issued a time limit for completion at less than two hours.

Of course I had run this distance and further many times before and sometimes with an equal amount of weighted kit and I had always finished in a time well under two hours. I should have been supremely confident but two factors bothered me.

The terrain was the first worry. I knew this route well and it was renowned for its extremely formidable going. Just over five miles of this route were uphill, some of it was very steep and much of its surface followed an ancient cobbled and dilapidated road. Many of the cobbles were raised or missing altogether. Every step presented some danger. Twisted ankles were common and bruised or stubbed toes were to be expected.

The route was so arduous that it had recently taken a heavy toll in minor casualties amongst the resident battalion of Scots Guards. The QMSI had confided to me that the Battalion was running at about an eighty per-cent failure rate on this very test.

The second concern for me was the initial time limit of two hours. The QMSI had said that I should easily complete it in an hour and a half. So my new target was exactly that, one hour and thirty minutes.

Kev' Vest stood in the road outside the gym. He waited, stopwatch in hand, seeming relaxed and looking fit. Here I was, I thought, dressed up like action man and the bloke who was to push me around this test was in shorts and T-shirt. I voiced my concern over what appeared to be an unfair choice of clothing but the Cpl simply retorted that the test was for me and not him. A little resentment pocketed itself inside my brain but the QMSI's voice halted any ponderings.

"Don't disappoint me!" He warned.

The Cpl set off at an immediately fast pace, already shouting at me as he went. The first part, thankfully, was downhill. Kev' shouted that we should take full advantage of the easy terrain.

Within seconds of starting off though, I realised that I was going to have problems with my webbing. I had previously visited the unit stores and had exchanged a torn right-hand pouch for a brand new one. Now I was finding that this new pouch had a very hard corner.

Whenever anybody runs whilst wearing webbing they will find instantly that the pouches mimic the runners bouncing motion and naturally, will bounce as well. No matter how hard the runner tries to tie down his 58-pattern webbing there would always be some movement; all you could do was try and restrict it.

My own pouches were filled with heavy and very hard rocks. I had chosen rocks as a weighty substitute for rifle magazines. The result was that every time my right foot struck the ground, that hard corner on my pouch gave me a painful poke in the upper thigh.

At first, the poking pouch was obviously annoying but nevertheless it seemed do-able. As the yards trailed behind me, the pain of being repeatedly jabbed began to piss me off. The helplessness of the situation was extremely frustrating and that frustration was beginning to boil away inside me, so much so that it threatened to erupt into a loss of temper.

After a mile or so the pain had become excruciating. I tried to concentrate on tabbing but my mind kept returning to the pain. Desperately I fought to push the pain out of my head and instead tried hard to focus my thoughts on other things. I admired the scenery, wondered what training I had yet to do, I wondered about all sorts of things, anything as long as it wasn't that bloody pouch!

Cpl Vest continued running slightly ahead of me and turned only occasionally, either to shout encouragement or more often insults. The switch from one to the other demonstrated an ease at remaining forever a typical army instructor. It may sound odd perhaps but the system worked with me.

Still we went on. I was in pain and he was happily enjoying the run, completely oblivious to my plight.

Another mile further and I had wedged my rifle horizontally through the straps of my webbing and had pushed my hand under the offending pouch.

I was trying very hard to keep it from banging into my now very tender and very sore thigh. The pain was somewhat temporarily relieved but before I could enjoy it and allow myself to recover, the terrain would suddenly become more difficult making my running more strenuous. It now seemed worse. I was forcing my webbing out with my rifle; this caused me to run lop-sided.

Downhill running is often problematic and this piece of hill was proving to be just that. The cobbled road meant that every now and then I managed to stub my toe. Once is bad enough but when I kept doing it I got really got angry with myself. Every time I touched the ground my feet shunted around inside my boots. Downward momentum was forcing my toes forward. Inside my boots my feet just kept on moving, inevitably slamming into the toe cap with all my weight. It was alright at first but continuous pounding is something else. It felt like being barefoot and then having to kick a brick wall a few times.

Under battle conditions or even a test the body's natural painkiller, adrenaline is released allowing a man to push pain to the back of his mind. Sometimes injuries are not even realised until afterwards. Right now I wondered where my adrenaline had got to.

Eventually the hills disappeared. Now I thought it was time to get serious and get my act together. Concentrating on the rapidly diminishing time limit, I fought desperately to speed up. I only needed to be fast enough to complete that last but almost flat half-mile return trip to the garrison gym.

Up to now the PTI, Cpl Vest had never altered his position of just a few yards in front; leading the way and yelling virtually non-stop at me. Suddenly he was here with me, right by me side. Arching his neck to blare in my ear, warning me that we were about to run out of time.

Each time that he made a noise his voice would rise in volume, he was getting angry. None of this particularly worried me but it did help because watching his odd and at times wild behaviour took my mind well away from any discomfort that my poor body desperately wanted to remind me about. And anyway, I carried a sense of loyalty, QMSI Bell had asked me not to let him down and I really didn't want to.

After only two or three breathless minutes both of us stood, chests heaving and hands on hips. I was panting and gasping like a grounded fish. Sweat soaked and feeling utterly robbed of all my energy I turned my head to watch Kev'. At least he too appeared knackered. I took comfort from this because I felt utterly wrecked!

The big PTI, now leaning forward, hands on his knees, nodded to attract my attention. Gasping to catch his breath and in between spurts of expelled air he asked,

"What time did we do?"

I examined my cheap but remarkably reliable Casio wristwatch. The final time read one hour and thirty-three minutes. Clearly outside the one and a half hours set by QMSI Bell but still fast enough to please Cpl Vest who had at last decided to stop shouting at me.

Chip Walker

Later Kev' told me that secretly even the boss was fairly pleased with the finish time.

The jubilation quickly expired and the re-emergence of pain was quick to remind me that not all was well. Adrenaline was fast fading and the sting of a dozen sore spots came through. As I walked I couldn't help but be reduced to a limp. My toes were hurting like Hell. They felt like I had just dropped a ton weight down onto them.

At home I threw my boots dispassionately into the corner of the room. Then ever so gently I peeled my socks sticky with blood, from my feet. Prising my toes apart, I inspected the red stained digits on both feet. As I did so my wife made strange sounds which suggested to me that it was she and not I who was feeling the pain. Actually, now that the pressure of stiff leather boots had been removed, the pain wasn't that bad.

The action of repeatedly stubbing my toes had caused nasty looking blood filled blisters to rise where the pressure was greatest. I had managed to kick those rocks with an uncanny skill of striking the very same toes over and over again. Each time that I had done that, the blisters burst splattering blood about my foot. New blisters had then formed underneath and then these too were hammered until they also eventually burst creating a gooey mess around my toes.

Ready for the shower I removed my sweat soaked denim trousers. I stood examining my sore and naked body. A patch, dark blue and about four inches across on my thigh immediately stole my attention. My first thoughts were that a biro pen had exploded inside my pocket but, as I stared at the fist sized stain, realisation told me that this was in fact bruised flesh. Just looking at it made me wince. Anticipating the cascade of cool water I carefully rubbed soothing soap around

51

the wound. A fear of more pain made sure that I was pretty careful.

Continuing the shower my thoughts were diverted to the injurious culprit, that hard cornered bloody pouch! In an attempt to convince myself I thought, Shouldn't be difficult to sort you out.

In the bedroom my attention once more returned to those relatively minor but painful injuries. My toes were the worst. For many years I had suffered lumps of hard skin on the knuckles of my little toes and especially on my left foot. Previously they had been only been uncomfortable but now they had grown into a real major worry.

Today whilst running they had swollen and the skin had been rubbed away onto the top of my boots. I could see now that those lumps had split and the one on my left little toe just would not stop bleeding.

Determination within me to win my wings remained undiminished but it was bloody obvious that nobody should or could attempt Para selection with their feet in this state. It would be simply asking for trouble and would invite failure. I wasn't about to accept that. My feet had to be sorted out.

I have learned many things in life and one of those things is that little is ever straightforward, and the problem of my feet was no exception. I had no doubt that I needed to fix my feet but reporting sick to see a doctor worried me. It seemed likely that the MO would very probably issue a chit excusing the wearing of boots.

In the army if a M.O. excuses a soldier from a duty or of wearing some item of clothing, it isn't simple advice, it's an order.

It was really difficult to choose between these two evils. Wanting support, I turned to my wife Janet. Naturally perhaps, she worried about me but with probably a little more common sense than I could be usually credited with. She told me quite firmly that I must see the doctor. I took in her words but I still wasn't convinced at that time that her advice was as wise as she plainly made it out to be.

Later that afternoon I was back in the garrison gym for a session on the multi-gym.

Despite my foolish attempts to hide my limp, I still attracted the attention of QMSI Bell. He quickly approached me and sought an urgent explanation. I candidly told him about the lumps and cuts on my toes which were still very painful.

Pointing to the door, the QMSI ordered me out, telling me to instantly visit the M.I. room and see the M.O. I protested, saying that I didn't want to miss any training but he, frustrated and slightly angered with my stubbornness, assured me that it was very much an imperative that I get this problem sorted out before commencing P-Company selection.

He continued, telling me that if I worked hard enough I would be able to catch up on any lost time but if I tried to carry on with such an injury, then it could only worsen. I would eventually be forced on to sick parade. When that happens I would lose even more valuable training. I knew deep inside that he was right.

Ten minutes later the Nursing Sister at the garrison's Medical Inspection room examined my feet. She was quick to reassure me that there was nothing seriously wrong, though I already knew that. However she did say that I should see the doctor as soon as possible and an appointment was made for the next day.

The following morning I walked into one of the two doctor's surgeries and sat down while the doctor looked at my feet. Once again I was told that there was nothing serious to worry about.

He gave me some ointment and a block of smelly black stuff. It looked like a piece of old breezeblock but it was for rubbing over the affected areas on my toes. Lastly I was given some padded straps to go over my toes.

I explained to him what I was doing and to my great surprise and relief he didn't order me to avoid wearing boots.

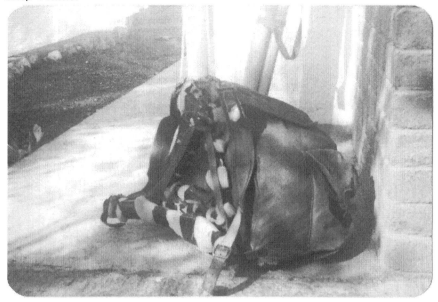

The famed A-Frame Bergen, complete with improvised padding.

The Episkopi Garrison x-country team 1983. Unusual in that it was 100% ACC.
Standing: Derham Gittings. Dave Shott. Jon Hatfield-Seiman.
Kneeling: Chip Walker and Mick Petreu.

CHAPTER FIVE

RUN, RUN MY BOY!

Six weeks of progressively hard training and still I kept up with it. Going well, I allowed myself a little congratulation. Each week the training became somewhat routine with every Monday starting with yet another ten mile run. The route, always the same, took in all the now very familiar hills.

It was impossible to run any distance in Episkopi without encountering hills, and big ones at that! Every day I woke up hoping against hope that I had somehow developed the stamina of a mountain goat but that never did happen.

These runs were always in light order, boots denims and a PT vest. I ran them hard and fast but at least now, because of my vastly improving fitness they had become comfortable.

At the end of the run I darted straight up to the top of the hill and into the Garrison gym for a weight training session. I had always enjoyed this type of physical training. Certainly it left me drained and exhausted. Sometimes, at the end, it was even difficult to simply pick my towel up off the floor, but there was always this great buzz. Some may describe it as an adrenaline high. Whatever it was it was a wonderful feeling. I was exhilarated, refreshed, renewed; there was an all over feeling of health and fitness. I loved it!

Twenty minutes later, showered and feeling pretty good, it was back to the real world of mundane duties. On went my Bergen, (everywhere I went it went too). It hadn't got any lighter, the opposite in fact, and it certainly felt   it.

I must have looked a strange sight as I ran or marched around the camp. Tabbing along in my gleaming white uniform of an army chef but carrying this old patched up Bergen. Silly comments were fast becoming commonplace, some were funny, and most were rude and insulting. I didn't care; I guessed that it just went with the territory.

The alarm bell shrieked at 0430, time to start again. My eyes were clogged and sticky. I forced them apart to once again look upon another fine day. My conscience was way ahead of me and it was shouting at me, but my body could only answer with dreadful aches. In any other walk of life perhaps I would have talked myself into staying in bed but I wasn't in any other walk of life. I was a soldier and I wanted to get through Para-Selection. I forced myself to get up.

Dressed in DPM combats and with Bergen in both hands I completed my now familiar swinging manoeuvre to throw the Bergen onto my back. I left a lovely warm bed behind me and started a slow jog over the short distance to the gym.

Standing just inside the doorway was CPL Vest waiting as usual with his arms crossed and looking every part a man who had impatiently waited for a never arriving bus. He cut a formidable picture, impressive with arms like my thighs but his looks hid his true nature. He was a hard task master but behind those Cpl stripes he was a gentle giant.

The plan, he said, was to complete an eight-mile march and run in as fast a time as possible. The route as always was hilly but Cpl Vest in devising this route had done his evil best. This was bloody steep and very bloody hard.

We stepped off straight away into a good fast pace. Immediately fatigue hit me yet we had only just started. My muscles though were fresh and even skilfully allowing for my weight to help push me along the downhill slopes, I still found myself puffing like an old steam engine. I sucked in as much of that air that I could possibly gulp down and all that my worn lungs craved.

Experience has taught me that the first five or ten minutes of any hard run are always the worst and the most difficult. Heart and lungs startled by the sudden demand to graft are cruelly jump-started into action and then we ask them to work ever harder while at the same time coping with the shock of having to feed starving muscles of oxygen.

Sometimes it took three or four miles of running before I could really settle into a rhythm. Experienced runners and athletes call this their second breath. We are all different I suppose and I know that lots of people achieve second breath within a few minutes, but not me. I have to suffer first. Eventually of course I did settle.

A mile and a half later and well along into the run, we were running on satisfyingly yet rare flat ground. The weight of the Bergen continued to punish my back and upper thighs but all I could do was grit my teeth.

I never did like the design of the 'A' frame Bergen, and I was fast becoming number one militant in a hate campaign against it. This pack, being somewhat pear shaped, allowed the weight to push into the small of the wearer's back. If the straps are tight the weight pulls downward heavily. If however, the straps are loosened, as they dearly beg to be, then the weight pokes and punches in time with the pace. For me, the harder I ran, the harder the thing hit me.

No matter how tightly I tried to pack the heavy kit into the top of the Bergen, it never seemed to work out well either. During any run the stuff inside developed a nasty knack of moving around and eventually ending up exactly where I didn't want it.

It did bother me but I wasn't about to let it finish me. Shit! We weren't even half way round yet. Once again I found myself trying to force the pain from my mind. A long time ago I learned how on any uncomfortable exercise or run, to concentrate my thoughts on some other subject. It could be virtually anything, jobs to do, at work or at home, or more usually, just the scenery.

The beautiful Cyprus countryside kept my mind away from any pain. As we ran the muddy path through the shoulder high evergreen hedgerows of the garrison's Happy Valley sports fields I was able to take in the deep green of the soccer pitches. In a country starved of the colour green this was a most pretty sight.

Concentrating on keeping my mind off running and the pain, I studied the tall sandy cliffs and allowed my eyes to scan the rock formations which boxed in the valley on three sides. But sticky sweat stung my eyes, forcing them to close and flutter. For metres at a time I ran completely blinded.

Majestic griffin vultures cast giant shadows over me as these birds with their six-foot wingspans soared above the cliff tops. I don't know if these giant creatures live elsewhere on the island, I only ever saw them around the Episkopi Garrison area. They were my saviours as for a while at least, all thoughts of pain were forgotten.

I was mesmerised. I watched these incredible birds float apparently effortlessly in mid-air, slowly circling, spreading their feathers to catch any thermal up draft. Absolutely brilliant!

Away from the cliffs we ran into sandy dunes stretched along the side of the beach. The pace slowed suddenly. The sand was loose and extremely fine. Shortening every step, each foot found it difficult to spring back with any sort of power.

Each boot filled with the salt like sand adding even more weight to my already tired legs and making sore feet even more painful.

As we went by, small birds darted from clumps of dried bush, all the while shrieking their loud alarm calls. I wanted to find the firmest parts of the sand dunes, those with some leafy plant protruding upward but most of it gave away under my feet.

The grassy shrubs and dehydrated bushes began to disappear behind me as we pushed ever further on and up the golden slopes. Ahead the beach continued for only three-quarters of a mile, yet it was taking us ages to complete it.

Eight minutes of sweat blinding hard slog followed; my Bergen, a constant reminder of the bruising weight.

Webbing pouches on my belt once again prodded sharply into my thighs. I now wished I had earlier tied the damn things down. Each step that I made became progressively harder, with all the energy sapped from my veins.

My legs seemed to weigh more than a thousand pounds, each only barely clearing the ground in front of them but I remained determined to force them forward. There was no more speed, no more reserves to call upon yet I needed to find that little bit of extra energy. The pace was too slow.

A voice penetrated my struggling mind, jarring my eardrums into paying attention, "Run, run my boy!" Big Corporal Vest was not at all impressed with me. Now screaming.

"C'mon, Move!"

I really, really wanted him to just shut up and then depart from here and go home to make love to his wife, though as I remember, my thoughts were not nearly as polite as that. Tiny voices of conscience argued inside my head. One side offered,

'Tell him to piss off and let's get some rest!' The other countered, 'No! I must keep going.' I kept going.

Off the beach and now back on a tarmac road I found firm ground beneath my feet. Even though we were running uphill it still felt blissfully easy in comparison to the dunes.

At last I managed to find a comfortable pace alongside Kevin. I was now able to run with him instead of endlessly chasing him. Contented, I relaxed and allowed myself to be carried along at a steady pace for the relatively short distance back to the gym.

As the hill road twisted snake like around and up the hill towards the army's housing estate for Warrant Officers and their families I began to find some tiny amount of hidden reserve energy.

In anticipation, like the approaching end to a race, my body geared up for the final few hundred yards and at last the two of us reached the closing patch of road, but one of the steepest so far, Head down, arse up and arms swinging wildly back and forth like pistons, I pushed hard into the hill.

Searing pain burned into my left knee. It was sharp and powerful, enough to stop me dead in my tracks. This was new. I had never experienced this type of hurt before. Many times I have strained and sprained muscles and I have bruised most parts of my body, but this was different. I had stopped running.

I just stood bewildered and hurt. Kev' apparently concerned, immediately ran over to me and asked what the problem was. As he bent to examine my knee the pain vanished from me, departing as fast as it had arrived.

Both Kev' and I were baffled, we looked at each other and at the same time shrugged shoulders. I shook my leg, stomped the ground, looked at Kev' in pleaded innocence and started running again.

As I went forward the pain began to return. Slowly at first but it grew ever more severe with each step. I tried hard to ignore it but it really was fast becoming unbearable. Then suddenly excruciating pain pierced the bony flesh around my knee. It was like a hot knife, slicing deep into the very centre of my knee.

I felt helpless. A scream erupted from my throat. The pain was now so bad that it verged on agony. It was the same kind of pain as the first time but even worse, again I stopped.

Kev' now frustrated at having to stop once more and so near to the end, tried to show his   concern.

"What's up Chip?" He gasped.

Through gritted teeth I squeezed   some   words,   trying   to describe the terrible feelings inside my knee. Kev' took my Bergen and following slightly   behind   him   I   limped   the remaining distance to the   gym.   Patience   gave   way   to frustration and along the way, I shouted and swore at   Kev'.

Kev' had given up much of his own free time to help coach me. Now he allowed me to vent my anger and let off steam, but it still wasn't fair on him. I should have apologised but all I could think of was the pain.

I couldn't believe it, another worry, and another bloody injury! I was so angry with   myself.

In the office my injury was discussed at length. As the staff talked about me but not to me, I felt invisible. Listening to the theories from the conversing PTIs, I too hoped for a nice simple explanation. In the end their collective opinion was that the injury was the result of running miles and miles but putting additional strain on my already overworked joints by carrying heavy weight for too much of the time.

The QMSI explained that when a person runs on a hard surface such as road or concrete, the heel impacts with the ground striking it at a greater force than that of your whole body weight. Add to that any extra pounds that you are carrying, and then it is not surprising that knee joints in particular, protest.

The knee's way of protesting was to become inflamed and very painful.

On that day I had been carrying about fifty-eight pounds with my Bergen. My own weight tended to fluctuate at around twelve and a half stone (175 lbs.). Looking back I am in no doubt that the fact that army issued DMS boots carried a solid heel must have also contributed.

QMSI Bell advised that I rest my weary legs for as much as was possible. He said that I should carry on with the weight training, concentrating on my arms and torso, but under no circumstances was I to carry extra weight especially whilst running.

No more running over the next few days allowed my knee to show good improvement. Luckily for me in one way at least, was that the enforced rest coincided with a period of leave, most of which I happily spent at home in my married quarter.

I needed this valuable time to get the married quarter sorted out and ready for a formal hand-over and March-Out. This included an inspection of the building and all its contents. It was scheduled for some time during the following week. Janet had difficulty doing some of the cleaning work, especially as now she was quite heavily pregnant carrying my son, so I tried hard to do that little bit extra.

On a lazy afternoon having just finished another round of domestic chores I rested my leg, still a little sore from the injury caused during that run a couple of weeks previously. Hearing a rasping sound at the kitchen window I pulled myself from my deck chair to see the toothy smile of a work mate; John Hatfield-Seiman.

On answering the door I could see that John was not alone. Stood next to him was another colleague, Dave Shott. Both were running mates of mine from our very successful Garrison running team.

Once inside and sipping my cool lemonade the two of them interrupted my greetings and each other to explain that they wanted me to enter into the Joint Forces Cyprus marathon scheduled for the coming Sunday. Laughing into near hysterics I collapsed back into my deck chair.

"Don't be daft." I chuckled, and continued,

"I can't! How could I? I've done no training".

I tried to explain how over the last few weeks I had done only a little running on account of the fact that I had hurt my knee. The only run I had done of any substance recently was a fifteen miler. A long run right enough but not as far as the twenty-six miles of a marathon, and anyway, that run was weeks ago.

"No, I'm not up to it", I pleaded but these two were not having any of it. They just would not accept the word, 'No' as an answer. John argued that they were short of a runner to make up their team. All they wanted from me, they said, was for me to simply finish the race so that they could claim the team point.

Flattered at their choice but certainly not convinced, I continued to argue. A rapid but still friendly battle of wills and opinions followed. Outnumbered and outflanked at every turn I eventually and reluctantly gave in and agreed to race.

As I watched them walk away I wondered what on earth I had done.

Janet sat silently but her face said it all, she glared at me angrily. In an attempt to placate her I returned her gaze but with doe like eyes, silently begging for her understanding and approval. She didn't even blink as she growled,

"Look at you! You're bloody stupid! Your leg, oh why can't you say no and just stick to it?"

Janet wasn't simply upset, she was bloody fuming! I know though that she was genuinely worried that I might seriously injure my already weak knee.

Holding her in my arms I gently kissed her neck and around to her tear soaked cheeks. With a promise I said that I would only jog a little on the build up to the marathon and though I would give the race a damned good try, I wouldn't push myself so hard that I could do any damage.

"If my knee starts bothering me, I'll just stop. Trust me" I tried to sound reassuring. I am sure that my wife was not completely satisfied with this little speech but she did perk up.

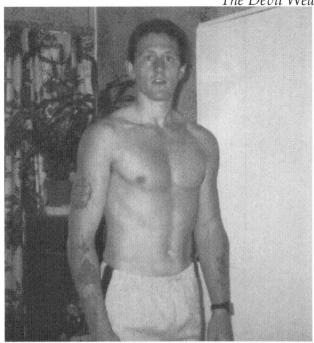

Chip Walker training at home 1984 and just prior to starting Pre-Para.

Regimental boxing with 7RHA. Chip Walker in white, his opponent and eventual winner of the bout, L/BDR Andy Symes.

CHAPTER SIX

MARATHON

The marathon was an annual inter service race staged as the last race of the road running season and prior to the start of the new Cross-Country season. Its venue was the huge peninsular base of RAF Akrotiri. This suited me fine because whilst my own base of Episkopi was incredibly hilly, Akrotiri was completely flat.

The morning of the eighteenth of March 1984 broke into a fine and sunny day. An army bus did the rounds and collected all the runners from Episkopi and took us over to the RAF base.

On the bus spirits were high. Some like me were novices to the marathon race and without exception we tried to take in words of wisdom from the old hands; those who were   more experienced in long distance   races.

As we neared the huge base we started to get ourselves prepared. Some stood in the aisle of our bus stretching their legs. I was not one of those. It was not fashionable for us macho types to be seen prancing about like ballet dancers or pretentious athletes. We were there just to have a good run.

My team-mates and I were all sat close to each other. I looked at Dave and with a cheeky grin he telepathically agreed that it was time for the Vaseline to come out. It was blobbed about thickly over and on top of our eyebrows. It was intended to prevent sweat from dripping into eyes and causing that annoying sweat blindness.

More Vaseline was strategically placed around my groin and over my nipples. I had hoped to stop friction burns.

Then out came my secret weapon, Algipan heat lotion, the cheater's way of warming up. Formulated for people suffering from sprains and rheumatism, it was ideal. It warmed muscles by allowing veins and arteries to expand thereby increasing blood flow. I rubbed the lotion generously into my legs and shoulders.

You have to be careful when applying this stuff and must make sure that the Vaseline is administered first. I've seen runners get the system round the wrong way. They're easy to spot; they're the ones diving about like a cockroach on a hot plate. Even when mixed with Vaseline it stings like hell around your groin.

We stepped off the bus and were greeted with smiles and waves from friends and colleagues. Some were seen only at previous races but we were always pleased to see a familiar face.

For a small island with only a small service establishment, there were quite a few runners. I estimated that for this event there must have been over a hundred people, a good turnout. There was a decent crowd of supporters and spectators too.

Janet, still annoyed that I had actually gone through with my promise to the boys remained stubborn and flatly refused to come to the race and watch.

Nerves had never bothered me much. Occasionally I had that strange feeling of butterflies deep in my stomach but not this time. I'd had a good night's sleep followed by a huge breakfast loaded in complex carbohydrates.

I felt little pressure, after all, all I had to do was finish, and surely I could even walk if I wanted to. Thinking a little more seriously though, I was supremely confident that I would easily finish well under the four hours generally accepted as the time limit for any half decent runner. Relaxed I ambled over to the start.

Standing on the start line, finger poised over the stop watch button of my Casio, I waited. Any second now a gun would blast and the eager crowd would knee jerk into a short sprint until we were able to find our own space and speed.

I had earlier promised to hold back and to run with a guy called Derhem Gittings. He was nice bloke and one of my Sergeants who at that time was employed in the Garrisons Sergeants' Mess.

He had asked me to accompany him during the marathon for at least the first ten miles. Derhem was about ten years older than me and considerably slower. He preferred to jog along at his own leisurely pace rather than compete with the pack. That's fine for him, but it would not normally have suited me. With my recent leg injury though, it seemed to make sense and I decided that I ought to stick to my promise to Janet.

Dehrem had never run a full marathon before, though back in the UK he had run quite a number of half marathons. He was the most laid back bloke I had ever met. We often joked that if he were any more laid back, he'd be horizontal.

For this race I think that all he wanted was someone to chat to for the coming few lonely hours, and it could be lonely out there. Normally that didn't worry me at all and I reckoned that this arrangement with Derhem should work out to be perfect.

The pace as we started was easy, almost carefree, more like a Sunday afternoon jog in the countryside. My running partner and I chatted freely about all sorts of things and all the time Dehrem kept smiling. In his world, words like 'rush and stress' had absolutely no meaning to him.

As we cornered the road onto a mile long stretch known locally as the M1, I could see a water point being operated by wives and children.

 Close to the approaching water point was a hand written sign, clearly made out with large letters in black marker pen. The sign was loosely stuck into the ground at the feet of a race marshal. The sign read, "10 MILES".

The first ten miles had already passed and the time had disappeared relatively fast but unlike Dehrem, who was still grinning like a Cheshire cat, I was far from happy.

I looked around and behind me. There were just nine visible runners to my rear. These were the so-called 'Fun runners'. Most would not last the course. The other hundred or so runners were way off ahead somewhere. The leaders were probably miles in front of me. Feeling frustrated I began to get frustrated.

Running along with Derhem I had been deliberately slow in my pace but this was ridiculous. Even taking it easy I never imagined that I would find myself so far behind my team mates and the rest of the pack.

I looked over toward Dehrem who appeared quite soulful as he took in the obvious hint that I was about to leave him. I could see in his eyes that he wanted me to stay with him but he wouldn't ask.

I tried hard but in vain to encourage his efforts. I didn't want to leave him, I wanted him to speed up and come with me. I guess that I too preferred his company. The argument cut no ice.

His face stretched now taut with effort threatened to split wide open into one of his familiar grins, "Go on Chip. Don't worry about me."

I patted his shoulder and nodded acknowledgement. As I opened my pace forcing my legs apart, I turned and shouted to my already distancing partner,

"I'll have the tea on!"

Derhem pushed his right arm limply into the air, threw his hand upward gesturing for me to go on.

Chest thrust forward and legs stretching, the power of my thighs carried me away. I raced onward. My breathing grew deeper, more laboured but oddly more satisfied. I felt good. Already, runners who were once far ahead of me were now glancing around. They could hear the thump of my fast approaching feet.

Gaps were shrinking and some of those runners who had been way out in front were now just about to be overtaken.

One by one they fell behind me. I was trying to keep tally of those I passed but I soon lost count. I was flying and so was the time.

Still running strong I went right through the next water point without even slowing down. I didn't feel a need for a drink just yet. The next water point came at the fifteen-mile mark. As I passed I grabbed eagerly at an outstretched hand loosely holding a water soaked sponge.

With a practised skill I smashed the soft sponge into my forehead, releasing the cool torrent of refreshing water over my face. I then squeezing the sponge once more to release the remaining fluid, allowing it to rain over my shoulders and down my back forcing my back to throw itself into a shiver and a shoulder shake. God it felt good!

Later I learned that the two hot-favourite runners and supposedly the best on the island had both dropped out at around the fifteen-mile point. Both apparently burned out in their personal duel against each other. Their fierce rivalry destroyed any race hopes that either of them had had.

As I approached the marker for eighteen miles my pace had begun to get a little more laborious. My legs felt heavy but I didn't have any major problems. I was still managing a comfortable speed. I was tired and I truly felt that I could continue and even complete an additional ten miles easily.

The eighteenth mile mark was situated at a small crossroads near to some of the married quarters and here some families gathered to shout support to their passing loved ones. Two young airmen were running alongside of each other a few yards in front of me.

They were obviously tired but tried hard to appear cool and confident to their watching wives. As I closed the distance behind them I raised both arms outward like a kid pretending to be an aeroplane. Simultaneously I started to loudly hum the Dambusters theme.

Shouts of "Fuck off!" immediately filled my slipstream. I know now that it was a little immature of me to behave in such a way, but there has long been a tradition in the services to take the mickey out of each other and this incident was just that. I found it funny anyway.

Just two short miles further on and I hit a wall, not a literal wall but a physiological or perhaps a psychological one.

Over the years many people had told me that sooner or later I would find my wall. I knew that after exerting extreme physical effort over a sustained period of time my body would find itself starved of all energy and with no more calories left to burn. It would quite suddenly want to stop.

I could not even sweat; all my remaining body fluids were being diverted to my organs. I could feel my eyes beginning to bulge and the muscles around my joints, particularly my legs, started to collapse.

I slowed to a jog but strangely I was not too affected with pain. I felt almost normal. I decided to allow myself a little rest. There was less than six miles to go and I reckoned that even if I walked the remaining distance I would still finish in well under three hours forty-five minutes.

Less than a mile later pain surged through my left knee. This was the same type of pain that I had experienced before whilst running up Episkopi Hill with Kevin Vest. It was a bit like cramp but much more painful and it also seemed to be more localised. It was deep inside my knee. Convincing myself that it most probably is cramp I went on, believing that it would soon pass.

Years later I would discover that I had done a fair bit of damage to the cartilage in my knee.

Still jogging, albeit slowly but not quite limping, I tried hard to take it easier and rest my embattled knee. I carried on, determined to finish. I didn't want to give in. The pain mysteriously slid away, not completely gone but certainly bearable. I made a decision in my head that I should continue as I had been; it was only a jog but what the Hell?

Another mile fell behind me and then another. Then, just as I started to feel reasonably comfortable, a new but identical pain shot through my other knee forcing me to momentarily stop. Time for a walk, I told myself.

Fifteen slow and agonising minutes passed. I was demoralised and began to question my own sanity. My thoughts dragged me back to a few days before at my house. I pictured Janet lecturing me over my incredibly stubborn and stupid decision to enter this silly race. I found myself seriously asking whether I should ditch the whole race.

The pain struck at the very centre of both knees. Searing and hot it refused to relent. Every movement now, no matter how slight was agony.

I'd come this far but I wondered if I should give in now? I couldn't. A big part of me, maybe even the intelligent part begged to stop and go home, but there was another part of me. The stubborn half that refused to give in. Somehow I convinced myself that the pain would subside. Painfully I once again I pushed myself into a jog, but each time either heel impacted with the road I groaned. Still I told myself to force my pace to open up. My speed did increase but it was no more than a shuffle.

My left knee began to seize up and I could hardly straighten it. I forced my body to keep going but I was limping terribly.

Equally demoralising for me was that this stretch of the road and at this point on the route, runners completed a U-turn at the end. The stronger runners passed me on the other side of the road going in the opposite direction. They were pushing for the finish. Some shouted words of encouragement as they went.

I struggled to maintain any momentum and eventually found myself approaching the finishing line nearly an hour later.

On the approach to the line, I somehow found hidden reserves of adrenaline. Spurred on by the cheering crowd I picked myself up and forced myself to improve the pace.

As I moved forward I attempted a weird kicking motion. I tried to shoot my right leg forward, skipping to the line, eventually crossing with tears streaming down my face.

Immediately my left leg gave up and I wobbled like a Saturday night drunk. A race official ran up to me and threw an old army blanket around my shoulders congratulating me before disappearing again into the crowd.

A colleague approached and described my finish as brave and emotional but all I remember is that it hurt like hell and that I must have looked like Quasimodo down at the disco.

Despite the heat of the Cyprus sun I was shivering with cold. All of my calorie reserves had been burnt during the long effort to run. Now I had nothing left to even warm my body.

The official results said that I was sixty first in position and that I achieved the disappointing time of four hours and eleven seconds. Still, the team did get its point.

CHAPTER SEVEN

ON THE LINE!

The married quarter had been sorted out and handed over to the MQ Warden and at last Janet and I boarded a bus which would take us to the Pavema Hotel on the eastern side of Limassol ready for the trip home in the morning

Janet was now seven months pregnant and struggling to keep control of my over enthusiastic three year old daughter. They had both found the hand-over and flight preparation exhausting.

In the spartan hotel room, Janet and my daughter Bobbie went for a well-deserved nap. I couldn't as easily relax so decided to go for a run, my last on the sunshine isle. I was still taking it fairly easy after my marathon experience and just jogged for a few miles along the rocky seawall. Once more and finally, I allowed myself to enjoy the wonderful scenery that I hadn't always noticed in the previous two years.

The alarm sounded early inside our room. Breakfast was served at half past and then the rush began. Everything had to be packed and ready by six o'clock. Bobbie fought to wake up but once she was on the bus, excitement took over and from then on the whole day became one huge adventure for her.

After a quick tour around the hotels to collect all those other service families who were flying home that morning, we started on the road to RAF Akrotiri. Time disappeared and before long we were climbing the stairs to a new Tri-Star aircraft of the RAF.

The Tri-Star aircraft, though aged in civilian life, was new to the RAF and represented a significant move forward in the service attitude towards the movement of its passengers. Their excellent and trusted VC-10s were now twenty years old and years of Government defence cuts had reduced the support function of the RAF to a pitiful size.

The turn-around came in just after the Falklands conflict. There weren't enough aircraft in service to fly the thousands of troops now suddenly required for Fortress Falklands. Luckily British Airways announced to the world that they had just placed a huge order for more aircraft from Boeing in order to replace their fleet of old and noisy Trident and Tri-Star aircraft. The Tridents went to China and the scrap yard.

Our Tri-Star had arrived sporting its newly painted grey and white livery of the RAF. The cabin crew however were British Airways staff. They had been seconded to the RAF whilst the RAF's own crews carried out training for these aeroplanes.

During the flight, the crew freely complained of their boredom. They told me that normally on a four-hour flight, they would show films and serve hot meals followed of course by drinks from the bar. However, the RAF didn't do things like that. There was no film or hot meals, instead after about an hour of flight, a cold packed meal was passed to us weary passengers.

With Janet sat on the seat beside the aisle, she began to attract concerned looks from the wandering cabin crew. One of them, a man in his early thirties announced himself as the Chief Steward. He pointed to the very obvious lump around my wife's middle and asked,

"When's the baby due?"

I leaped in with an answer and said,

"That whilst I admit my wife does indeed look like she is about to sprout triplets, she still has two months to go."

The Chief Steward paused then Janet's voice interrupted the momentary silence by groaning,

"I don't feel well."

The colour visibly drained from the man's face and he hurried away. Shortly after, the steward returned bringing with him a large grey book, it was the First-Aid book carried on all British Airways aircraft and it was already opened at the page for Emergency Improvised Childbirth. He thrust the thing under my nose.

Appearing a little flustered he pleaded with me to study the chapter as quickly as I could and then went on to reassure me that he had placed all of his staff on stand-by and that the captain had been informed. I'm sure that he meant well but it was just too much and I ended up laughing out loud. However, real concern was by now showing on Janet's already worried face. Janet had always been a reluctant flyer and now with all this fuss and attention, she felt even more stressed. Fortunately and despite all the concerns, apart from some turbulence, the remainder of the flight passed uneventfully.

Once on the ground we were met at RAF Brize Norton by Janet's Mum and Dad, and then whisked off to their house in Oxford. Our intention was to stay there for about a week and then travel down to London to stay with my Mum. We were hoping that we might visit a few friends and other relatives as well.

The river Thames flows past the huge 1950s council estate where my in-laws lived. During the first week back in England the river banks became my own private treadmill. Each day I ran for miles along the muddy tow paths. With nothing more than an occasionally uncomfortable twinge in my knees, I felt really good. I reckoned that I was easily back on course for full fitness and ready in time for P-Company.

Being on leave, my hair grew long and I looked less and less like a soldier but I remained disciplined to my aims. Runs were kept to about five or six miles with just the odd one taking a distance of ten or more miles. Coupled with this I kept a healthy regime of press-ups, sit-ups and other exercises.

It wasn't until we got to my Mum's flat in west London that that I collected some items that had been shipped back from Cyprus. Now I was able to give my somewhat restricted exercise routine a most welcome and encouraging boost.

Out came my trusty but uncomfortable Bergen. It was repacked and weighted with about forty-five pounds of assorted items. Once more dressed in boots, denims and combat jacket, I lifted the now familiar weight onto my shoulders and set off. This was the first time for a while that I had had a chance to get out and carry some weight so I tried to take it easy.

Happily I just plodded about, blissfully unsure of where to go or how far. I simply felt fit and it really was lovely to get back into things.

The next afternoon I visited the nearby RAF station at Uxbridge. It was only a few miles from my Mum's place and I knew that I could run to and from it easily.

Once there it was relatively easy to find the gym and the guy in charge. Speaking with the PTI there I explained that I was in the army and on leave but that I needed to train as I was shortly to start Parachute Selection. He kindly offered to allow me free use of the gym. He seemed genuinely pleased to help.

I think that maybe all these wonderful shiny apparatus that filled a corner of this huge gym were little more than very expensive ornaments. I certainly did not gain the impression that these machines were used very often. Only once during any of my visits did I see anyone else use the gym.

It was the fourth day of staying with my Mum when one morning I awoke with a nasty cough. As I sat up I could hear myself wheezing like an asthmatic and each time that I even moved my head, I felt the dull pain of a severe headache. It was a bad one, so much so that I'm sure it would have killed ten Royal Marines. I was burning too. Suffice to say that I felt bloody awful.

I dug out my Mum's old medical thermometer and placed it under my tongue. I checked the reading. Surely not? Holding the tiny instrument up against the light I read the figures once more. According to this, I had a temperature of a hundred and two.

Obeying the very sensible rule (not to mention the rule of my wife) of never over exerting oneself when carrying a temperature I rested for the whole day. I was confident that a single day of rest would sort me out. When morning came I found myself feeling a bit better though tired. It was Friday morning, I was still full of cold but I was relieved to see that at least my temperature was back down to near normal. It didn't take much persuading but I decided that I should rest further, at least until the coming Monday morning.

It was the Monday that I was expected to report for duty at the ACC Depot and Training Battalion based at St Omer barracks in the heart of Aldershot's military town. I was confident that by that time I would be over this nasty little cold and be ready to get stuck into some serious training.

Having to start work on the Monday morning meant that I had to arrive at St Omer barracks sometime during the Sunday evening. As soon as I got there I signed for my regulation bedding pack of one pillow, one slip, two blankets, two sheets and a foam mattress, and then someone told me where my bed space was.

Negotiating through the darkened barrack block and unable to flick the light switch because of over laden arms, I finally arrived at my bed space furnished with a single wire-sprung bed and a wooden locker. I sat down on the   bed underwhelmed and depressed.

This was as dingy a barrack block that I had ever stayed in. Everything about it was drab, gloomy and boring.

I was still suffering the effects of a nasty cold and so decided that once I had telephoned my wife I would get to bed. Sleeping was difficult. With my nose running and throat as coarse as sandpaper I started to feel a little sorry for myself. As I lay there I could feel my skin begin to tingle and then to change temperature, climbing rapidly.

Before long, my body went into extremes. First burning wildly then, cooling to a shiver, only to be really hot again.

The morning brought a little relief. With a clearer head and feeling not too bad I completed the booking-in procedure and administration. Somehow, even though I had barely even spoken to the PTIs, I had managed to volunteer myself for a march and run over an eight mile distance and carrying skeleton order (Light webbing belt and shoulder yoke fitted with ammunition pouches but holding only a little weight or maybe perhaps, empty). The run was one of a series of tests for the resident recruits.

We hadn't been out of the camp gates for very long but already some of the recruits were leaving me behind when I should have been finding it quite easy. I just didn't seem to have the energy. The whole thing was very difficult. Nevertheless, I was determined to complete every last yard.

This wretched cold was to blame, I couldn't think of any other explanation for my poor performance. On my return to barracks I showered and just swanned about. I didn't do a thing for the rest of the day.

As day wore into evening I came to feel more and more ill. In bed that night I felt that the devil himself had got inside me. I could feel my skin burning yet inside I was frozen to the core. Breathing was difficult too. Each rasping inhalation stung deeply inside my chest. This was worse than any cold that I could remember.

As another fine morning arrived the sun's rays penetrated the drab thin cotton curtains. I crawled out of bed and trudged down the corridor to the wash rooms. Supporting myself on the cold ceramic sink I gazed into the small mirror weakly and thought, "you are bad". Though unwilling, I knew that I must report on Sick Parade and make some effort to get this infection sorted out.

Of all the army's eccentricities, the procedure for holding a Sick Parade was probably the worst.

For a soldier of junior rank to see a doctor, an array of obstacles were placed in his way. I'm not sure whether this was to make his life awkward or to dissuade a soldier from reporting sick in the first place.

After I had battled to convince the Orderly Sergeant that I really did need to report sick, I was told to come back in half an hour when those on Sick Parade would be seen by the CSM. The CSM had been at the Depot and Training Battalion for many years. Lacking experience of the army in the real world and equally well equipped with tunnel vision, he hated just about everyone. Most of all though, he hated anyone who wanted parachute wings on their arm.

He scoffed at my explanation as to why I felt that I should see a doctor and moaned,

"So you want to be a super duper paratrooper? I thought you were supposed to be fit! My   God!"

His voice rose to near a shout, continuing,

"Going sick with a bloody cold!"

His ridicule bit deep.

My opinion of this guy was fast diminishing. I didn't like him and he quite obviously didn't like me and nothing that I could say or do was likely to change   that.

Nevertheless an hour later I found myself waiting inside the MI room. There was at least another hour to go before the Doctor would turn up, but in any case before the Doctor could see anyone, an army medic must first assess the patient. If he thought it necessary, then the nursing sister will examine the sick soldier. Only after all that could a soldier actually get near the Doctor.

I was lucky. During my short time at the Battalion I had got to know one or two of the medics, at least by face. Fortunately for me, one of them, a Corporal in his early twenties recognised me. He ignored the others in the queue and called out to me,

"Hey Chip! What're you doing here?"

Pushing my way forward I quickly told him of my horrendous previous night. Recording brief details on a pad he scribbled away before sympathetically telling me that he would get me in to see the nurse as soon as she arrived.

The nursing sister finished taking my   temperature   then promptly told me to strip to the waist then wait with the others in the corridor outside the Doctors' surgery. Outside his door and sitting on a wooden slatted bench were four other men. All were stripped to the waist and some were also without socks and boots.

Hardly able to contain myself I began a short giggle. This insane ritual had been the subject of some humour even when I was a recruit here at this barracks some years before. No matter what the ailment, soldiers always had to strip to the waist. A patient could have been suffering from an in-growing toenail or a pulled muscle but still, strip to the waist he must.

Stories and rumours abounded. Many thought that this particular quack was either sadistic or queer maybe both.

Above the doctor's door was a set of little traffic lights. Red meant wait and green meant enter.

After a wait of what seemed an age I became the only person waiting, everyone else having been seen. This included men who had arrived on the bench long after me. There didn't seem to be anything wrong in that. I just figured that as these other men were recruits they had some sort of priority over me. I thought back to my own time as a Recruit Instructor and the pressures we had to keep our recruits on their feet and on our timetable.

When the little green light eventually lit up, I took my turn and entered the doctor's room. Knocking as I opened the door I walked in and approached the empty chair in front of the desk.

"On the line! On the line!" The old man behind the desk shouted loudly.

I wasn't expecting to be screamed at and it took me back a bit. I froze to the spot, a little bewildered. I looked for an explanation from the Doctor. He remained sitting at his desk. His eyes widened and looking genuinely worried he pointed a trembling finger to a strip of white sticky tape on the carpet   a few inches behind me. I took the hint, stepped backwards and stood on the line.

"Beg your pardon Sir" I said pleadingly, but still baffled.

There was a small pause where the doctor did nothing but perhaps choose his next words.

"Do not cross the line unless I say so!" Remonstrated the elderly Doctor. He was a funny old bloke, a retired Brigadier and aged in his seventies.

The note in front of him that had earlier been prepared for him by the Nursing Sister stated that I was suffering from a temperature of a hundred and four degrees. The old doctor leaned over me and with a very cold stethoscope, listened to my whistling chest. According to his diagnosis, I wasn't at all afflicted with the common cold or even influenza but a rather nasty viral infection on my lungs.

He returned to his desk and began to scribble immediately some notes, and then tapping his pen across the knuckles of his left hand he turned to face me. "What are your duties young man?" My reply was hesitant,

"Er.. I, I'm training for P-Company Sir."

"Not now you're not ". The Doctor was decisive and to the point,

"Rest, that's all you're getting."

Armed with a bottle of antibiotics, a foil strip of some other pills and a bottle of medicine, I grabbed the sick note from the doctor. The note ordered me off all duties and to be bedded down for the next week. I left the MI room. I was alone, despondent and very, very worried. Time was fast running out for my training yet I seemed to face one delay after another.

I spent the first two days in bed in my barrack block. The bed space allocated to me was in the Battalion Transit block. Fine, except that it was generally empty or occupied with just a few occasional course personnel. This meant that I was hardly ever seen. I had no-one to talk to and, with my meals forgotten, I was left to fend for myself. I was severely pissed off.

At the end of the second day I asked the Duty Sergeant if I could go home to my Mum's flat. He was at first reluctant to allow me any sort of leave whilst I was sick but I think that eventually I wore him down and he allowed me to go but only until I was due to report fit for duty.

The week flew by and with the arrival of a brand new Monday morning I was raring to go. I felt good and I wanted to get back to do some training. My ambition of passing P-company continued to grow inside me. I didn't just want it. I was hungry for it. Over the next few days I did everything that I could. I trained hard, ran hard and worked hard.

One of the young APTIs with whom I had been sent to train had recently passed P-Company and was now proudly showing off his wings on his sleeve. Several times over the next few days we went running together and it was after one of these runs that he expressed his confidence in me. He commented that because of my fitness and positive attitude I shouldn't have too much trouble getting through the coming course. He warned though, that more soldiers fail because of injury than any other reason. I thought back to all the silly little injuries and ailments that I had already experienced. Would I make it any further? Could I get to the beginning of the course unscathed? Only time would tell.

CHAPTER EIGHT

PRE-PARA

Ordinarily the Pre-Para course started on Monday morning. This time however, Monday fell on a Bank Holiday.

I awoke early on possibly the most important Tuesday of my life. A little nervous, I could feel anxiety twisting the muscles in my stomach. I didn't simply have the butterflies; I had a whole menagerie of wild beasties fluttering about in there. Only now was I beginning to doubt my commitment. Niggling doubts penetrated everywhere. Now, I wondered, what on earth had I let myself in for?

Depending on which Corps or Regiment is running it, Pre-Para is a course of two to four weeks of almost solid physical preparation for P-Company. It was organised by parent units with the aim of bringing their soldiers up to the exacting standards demanded by the Airborne Brigade. It was every unit's intention to build up and assess the physical fitness of each of their volunteers before allowing their men to join the Para selection course with the Parachute Regiment and Airborne Forces at Browning Barracks in Aldershot. Generally speaking, units were unhappy with those who were RTU'd.

Individuals often believed that they would have been made to feel as though they are failures who have let their side down. Some units seemed to give the impression that they resented their soldier's inability to bring back the prized maroon beret.

Up to now the ACC had experienced a high failure rate amongst its few volunteers. This was undoubtedly due to a lack of physical and mental preparation. I knew from experience that sometimes young soldiers were pushed into volunteering when in reality they were far from ready.

In an effort to combat these failures, Officers from ACC Manning and Records tried whereever possible to ensure that its soldiers attended a Pre-Para course. In my case the obliging hosts were to be the 9th Parachute Squadron of the Royal Engineers. They were based at Arnhem barracks which was nestled in the huge concrete sprawl of Montgomery Lines in Aldershot.

There hadn't been any sort of joining instruction for me, only a date and a time to report to the barracks. I didn't know exactly where to report or to whom. Instead I arrived early and went into the cookhouse. There was I thought a fair chance that I might know someone in there, and anyway, whilst I was there I might be able to scrounge a cup of tea.

Down by the wash-up and enjoying a fresh brew were two other chefs who would also be joining the course. One of them, a lad called Jock Elliot was attached to the Squadron and knew where we were supposed to go. The other lad had a name, which at first I was reluctant to accept as true. It must be remembered that this bloke was a member of the Army Catering Corps, his name was Tom Onions.

A little while later all three of us walked the short distance from the cookhouse to the square outside the Squadron HQ where we joined a group of twenty-two other men. Outside in the spring sunshine the men automatically formed themselves into three ranks.

As yet we hadn't seen any sign of an instructor and no one wanted to take charge. Inevitably we turned to face each other and introduce ourselves. Anxiety prevented easy conversation and we got by with just names and occasionally a glance at a cap badge to determine where someone had come from.

Immediately noticeable though were the public school accents of the young and newly commissioned officers of the Parachute Regiment.

In front of us was a long raised outdoor veranda, rather like a concrete loading bay for large vehicles and over to my left leading away from it was a worn and partly crumbling staircase. A wiry man, not very tall and with shocking red hair, dressed in regulation boots, denims and a maroon sweatshirt appeared at the top of the stairs. Striding great steps as he approached, he shouted orders and brought the course to attention. With only a tiny pause he then stood us back at ease.

The red haired man viewed his candidates from his position in front. Slowly and silently he looked each one of us full in the face. To us it was intimidating but to him it was just useful summing up of each man's worth.

I knew from my own days as a Recruit Instructor that even after the briefest of meetings an experienced instructor could tell who the failures would be. I was confident yet nevertheless was feeling very uncomfortable because his stare lingered on me for far longer than I would have wished it to. For what seemed an eternity he stood perfectly still, alone and in silence. I didn't know what was happening, except for the order to stand at ease, nobody had spoken. The silence felt cruel.

As if reacting to some secret signal he pulled a clipboard from behind his back. Then leaning it on his waist and holding it to his front with clasped hands, he began to call the roll. Listening to the names and ranks being called I noted that there were three Officers, two Corporals, a Lance Corporal and the remainder were a mixed bunch made up of Sappers and Privates, including a Driver from the RCT.

According to the roll call there should have been five ACC on this course. I later learned that for reasons unknown to me, two had simply failed to turn up. When it became obvious to everybody that the only missing men were from the ACC it brought sniggers and ridicule followed with the usual bout of old jokes regarding army cooks. These missing men did no favours for me or their Corps on this day.

The instructor eventually introduced himself as Corporal Ford. Regardless of rank, he explained, he and all other instructors were to be addressed as 'Staff'. So as to avoid confusion, Physical Training Instructors throughout the army were usually called, 'Staff'. I suppose that this was because they are often out of uniform or wearing their T- shirts and the like without showing any badge of rank.

Earlier while I was waiting in the cookhouse I had been warned to ensure that my water bottle was filled to the brim. As suspected it was one of the first things that Corporal Ford checked, I of course with the other two from the ACC made sure that the bottles were really full. Most though hadn't done so. Subsequently the Corporal had his first opportunity to scream at people.

Corporal Ford barked out his instructions for everyone to get their bottles filled. All around me men scurried away towards the cookhouse only to return shortly after still fumbling at the fastenings on the canvas pouches which housed their bottles. No sooner had we reformed three ranks than our instructor marched amongst us ordering that we should now present our bottles, opened and held out so that they might be checked. Two of the blokes standing close to me had not heeded the advice and had failed to fill their bottles to the very brim.

Most people of course would have readily accepted that the bottles were indeed full but Corporal Ford was specific in his instruction and when he said 'Full' he meant 'Full'. There should not have been even the tiniest of gaps at the brim.

Quite obviously very unimpressed with this failure to comply with what he saw as a simple command the Corporal snatched the bottles from their hands and one by one he emptied the contents over the heads of the guilty.

"Lesson one!" He shouted, and then jumped back onto the raised platform in front.

More commands were shouted and the course was turned to its left as a squad and was stepped off into a fast double march. Before we had reached about three hundred yards and the bridge over the Farnborough Road, the squad had begun to break up. The pace was much faster than a regulated double march. Even though I had been forewarned that the first run of the first day would be a beasting, it had still taken most of us by surprise, including me. This was hard.

Already shouting insulting names the Corporal halted the group, reformed us back into three ranks and shouted his disapproval. Before we once more stepped away, we were joined by another instructor, similarly dressed as the first. He remained quiet but watched us closely. He too made me feel quite uncomfortable. Then away we went again, as before it was fast.

Taking short steps up the slope of the bridge I tried to conserve energy. I didn't know how far we were going or for how long? Over the crescent shaped bridge we went and onto the Garrison playing fields opposite. To be expected, my lungs struggled to regulate themselves as I fought for oxygen. At the start, Corporal Ford had told us that the first thing that we would do on this course was the BFT. Not understanding just what was actually happening here and feeling a little angry and frustrated, I tried instead to concentrate solely on what I was doing, right here and right now and that was trying like bloody hell to keep up with these two instructors.

Eventually we stopped at a large iron bridge, which spanned the murky waters of the Basingstoke canal. Still in three ranks we stood, chests heaving. Taking the well-earned opportunity to make some attempt at recovery, I slowed my breathing. Looking about me I took consolation that the others in my squad were at least, in a similar condition and some apparently much worse.

Shouting their anger, both instructors seemed very annoyed with our apparent lacklustre performance. Corporal Ford quickly reminded us of our lowly status of crap-hat and then launched into a tirade of obscenities. Only then and when he had run out of swear words to shout, was it pointed out that we had now reached the start of the BFT. The instructors said that because most of the squad was new to the area we must familiarise ourselves by having to run the whole route first.

This time when we set off we doubled at a more comfortable pace. We kept our dressing and stayed together for the relatively quick mile and a half jog which took us across another but near identical bridge and then back again to the first. As soon as we arrived back at the start we were ordered to remove our webbing and place it in a neat pile beside the road. I couldn't help but laugh to myself, for to ask to build 'Pile of neatly placed webbing' was certainly impossible.

Stepping off into the start of the BFT was, in contrast to our earlier fast paced run, quite easy. The initial stage of the BFT is always a march and run of just one mile and a half and it must be completed in or under fifteen minutes. It is usually seen as not much more than a warm up to get yourself ready for the important second half. I took advantage of every step in an effort to claw back some spent energy and of course to appease my already tired legs.

Chip Walker

Occasionally the squad slowed to a regular march only to break into a double shortly after, but as always it was comfortably manageable. Just under fifteen minutes later we were returned to the bridge where we had earlier dropped our webbing. We were brought to a stop and lined up across an imaginary line being drawn by one of the Cpl's pointing hand. Momentarily we waited and listened. The Cpl warned us that the time limit for the second part of the test, a repeat of the first mile and a half along the exact same route but completed in the runners best time, would be only nine minutes and thirty seconds, but he added, "The Squadron doesn't accept a time above   nine minutes!" Again this did not unduly worry me.

For male soldiers under the age of thirty in the rest of the army, the time limit is actually eleven and a half minutes. Eleven and a half minutes over just one and a half miles is an awful long time.

"Anyone not back inside that time", the Cpl threatened, "Will be going for a swim in Nine Squadron's very own swimming pool".

I followed his eyes and watched as he pointed downward. It became immediately obvious that in fact he had meant the Basingstoke canal.

The instructor set us off, quick and stretching, all of us aiming for a fast time. As I approached the half mile point I began to labour. Cursing, I asked myself, What in Hell could be the problem? Anger and frustration at my disappointing start began to swell up into my throat, threatening to push itself out in tears. It was painful. I fought my way around the test route and eventually reached the bridge.

I knew that I hadn't done as well as I had planned. My only consolation being that there were still some blokes behind me. I was told that my time was nine minutes and eighteen seconds.

I had just recorded my slowest time for a BFT for at least three years.

Instructors ticked away at names on a clipboard with loud comments following each entry on the sheet. I didn't catch the remark given with my time but I knew it wasn't praise and probably rhymed with banker. I was pleased though to see Tom Onions was there already and comfortable with a good time. Jock Elliot though was the last to get in.

After refitting our webbing we were split into two groups, each with an instructor. After my embarrassing start I had hoped to be placed in the squad lead by the as yet unnamed instructor but I was quickly disheartened to find that I was to remain with Corporal Ford. We doubled away over the canal toward the tall iron bridge. On the bridge was a sign proudly showing that it was built by the Royal Engineers.

Once positioned at the base of the bridge we were halted once more. I stood listening carefully to the instructions shouted out. We were, he explained, to carry out sprint exercises up the steep slopes right to the top and back again. On the given word I raced a few of the other men to the tiny summit of this rough but man made structure. At the top before I was allowed to return, we had to complete various exercises; press-ups, sit-ups and burpees. I have always hated burpees with their combination of a vertical jump and squat thrusts and this time was no different, of course I did them with maximum effort but I hated every second of it.

There was no slowing down. It was relentless. At the end of each set of exercises there was the briefest of stops. As I stood struggling to breathe, I could feel my heart pounding fiercely within my chest. It felt like my diaphragm was stretching up and down into the cavities of my straining chest, threatening to snap and send my heart and lungs shooting off into orbit.

After what seemed an age, this part of the exercise was brought to an end and as the last man finished; we were reformed into two ranks and lined up on the far side of the bridge. At last! I thought. A chance of a short rest, whilst we waited for the other half of our course to re-join us.

Drowsiness foggily drifted in to my head and I started to see bright lights, everything suddenly started to go green. Like when descending from a flight my ears popped and then my hearing started to disappear. It was a horrible and strange sensation of being unable to hear the outside world but at the same time the sound of my own heartbeat and respiration was amplified tenfold. I hadn't the slightest idea of what was happening to me or why.

I felt faint and thought that my legs were about to buckle under me before my swaying body came crashing to the ground. I had never previously suffered dizzy spells or had fainting attacks but I was suffering both now. Just when I thought my body was about to collapse, the squad received the order to move off.

Men were suddenly all around me and I was moving along with them. In an instant the fogginess went and my head cleared. The experience was totally weird but inexplicably it was no longer with me. Now when I look back I can speculate that it was oxygen starvation caused by the extremes of exercise. It was horrible and I have never forgotten it.

We continued the run through the training areas around Aldershot with the Corporals pointing out landmarks that we would need to know. I felt tired but glad that those dizzy feelings had at least, completely gone.

Finally the run returned us to barracks. There we were stood at ease on the same spot that we all first met and paraded earlier that morning. As soon as we had a chance to speak, we each turned and asked others for their times on the BFT and what they had thought of it so far. I asked around to see if anyone had ever felt what I had when I thought I was about to faint. Most hadn't but one bloke had. However, he hadn't known why he had experienced that either.

This Pre-Para course had only just begun but already I felt that I had let myself down by not being able to demonstrate my best. Doubts began to creep in and I was beginning to wonder if I really was up to this. When we started I thought that I was ready for anything, now I was not so sure.

I had found the previous two hours bloody hard. I had been knocked down off my high horse and had landed with a bump. Over confidence had affected me, even with my recent illness, I thought that I would be one of the fittest men there. Instead I felt one of the weakest.

Showered and changed, I dressed in normal working uniform. The squad paraded again, this time though, ready for a lesson in radio usage and signals procedure. As an assessment exercise to find the right calibre of candidate the Pre-Para course had to cover diverse subjects such as; Signals, Weapon training, Map reading and Section Battle Drills as well of course as working on the more obvious fitness and agility.

The lesson was really good and I enjoyed it immensely. The object was to revise us in the handling of the large man-packed clansman radios and coupled with that, an update on the latest signals equipment to be brought into recent army use. In the ACC we didn't get to use radios much so instead of this lesson being revision as it was meant to be, it was in fact all new. I found it both interesting and valuable.

After lunch I was in the squad and back outside of the HQ building dressed in the already very familiar boots and denims and of course carrying light webbing and an extremely   full water bottle. According to the programme now published and displayed on the notice board inside the OR accommodation, this next activity was to be, 'Run 1'. Few, I suppose could accurately guess what could be in store for us, after all, this morning was shown on the programme simply as a BFT, and that had been so arduous that it nearly finished me off.

He called the roll and then the red haired Cpl stepped us off once more into a fast double march. No time or pace was shouted. With an absence of rhythm I just ran along with all the other men who were also fighting to stay as close to the leading instructor as possible. He by now though was surging ahead.

Almost immediately and just as it was earlier this morning, the squad began to break apart. I struggled through in a determined effort to stay with the small pack now enjoying relative success in keeping up with Corporal Ford.

Through the barracks and back over the high pedestrian bridge, the huddle of men only slightly in front of me would appear to slow down, just enough for me to catch them. Just as I began to think that at last I had secured my position with the leaders the pace appeared to open and I would find myself chasing yet another gap. I had to find more speed.

Across the Garrison playing fields off the main Farnborough Road we continued onto the training areas of Caesars Camp. The speed remained seemingly constant. Running fast and feeling every ounce of the clumsy DMS boots and restricting puttees, I tried to find a rhythm so that I could somehow relax into this demanding journey. Eventually I managed to find my pace and settled into a long hard and fast run.

Two miles on and the squad slowed to allow the disgraced stragglers to catch up. The staff were apparently equally disgusted with our poor fitness. Each screamed obscenities at us and warned that we, 'Hadn't even started yet!' The angry tones ripped into me as simultaneously, I fought to calm my frantic breathing.

The skin on my face was withdrawing tightly into the bone and my temperature soared. I looked and felt like a glowing ember. Sweat was cascading down my face finding the cavities where my eyes had deeply sunk. It was like having soap in my eyes, it stung. Both eyes involuntarily squeezed shut. I tried to wipe the flood from my brow but succeeded only in attracting the unwanted attention, then wrath of an instructor who was most perturbed to find that I was moving when I shouldn't have been. Not for the first time that day, I was loudly reminded of my doubtful parentage and undoubted lowly status.

The squad, now reunited, stood together for only a few moments before the instructors split us again into two separate groups. In file along each side of the hardened track we were made to play leapfrog. Each side raced against themselves. When it came to my turn, I ran five paces then bent down, legs straight but slightly apart and with my hands firmly on the ground. Everyone on the same side of the road as me then proceeded to vault over me. As soon as the last man leaped over it became my turn to leap across all the others, they now being bent and waiting patiently.

At first we saw this game as a very welcome break from the fast running that we had just been doing and with everyone else I giggled out loud at the seemingly childishness of it all. The giggles came to a quick stop though when as one lad pole-axed another, a shattering voice called out, 'Crap hat wanker!

At last, I thought something light hearted perhaps even fun. The boyish antics of us grown men and aspiring airborne brought smiles even to our instructors who up to now had remained in a very serious mood. We were all laughing, but not for long.

About three hundred yards later and the laughing abruptly turned to loud and verbal moans. This was bloody hard work. Inside my head I begged to be allowed to simply run again. I wanted to demand it out loud but daren't.

The constantly changing pace of the leapfrog was playing havoc with my body, meaning that I was never sure when to rest or to work. Drained of available energy my limbs felt like lifeless bags of heavy flesh, reluctant to move even the smallest of distances. By now my back too was affected, tired and aching from the strain of all those men pushing their full body weight down on to me each time that they had vaulted over me.

A half mile or so later, one of the staff shouted to stop. We knew that the word was not to be taken literally. Only the men right out in front were actually supposed to immediately halt, the remainder of us having to continue the back breaking exercise until we reached a position to form three ranks. As to be expected with my current run of luck, that command came when I was somewhere at the back. At least though, I could see the end.

Given a quick breather and allowed a sip of water from our water bottles, I inwardly rejoiced. But for the heavy rasps of strained breathing, we stood in abject silence.

The webbing around my belt was soaked with sweat causing it to shrink and harden. The catch over my water bottle jammed fast. Added to that, my fingers were throbbing with the heat. Desperate to accept the reward of a small drink of water, I struggled fumbling at the stiff canvas strap of the bottle carrier. Then just as I got my lips to the confounded receptacle, we were ordered to replace them back into their pouches. Cruel as this may have been, I knew that it had more to do with welfare than the sadistic nature of the staff. If allowed, some men would have drunk their fill greedily, but with the arduous tasks ahead, those soldiers would likely become unwell. Common sense told me that this was true, nevertheless, I was severely pissed off that all I had got was just a tiny drop.

Though still trying to regain some normality to my difficult breathing, the pace was set and we were running again. They said that the purpose of run 1 was to familiarise us with the local training areas. By the end of day one I didn't necessarily know every hill and ditch by its contours or its fauna, but I did know that I already hated them.

Trying their hardest to break us, the instructors relentlessly found hills to lead us up or even occasionally chase us up. As every twenty minutes or so passed the squad was halted. A loud reminding of our alleged and dubious beginnings became so normal that it meant nothing to me and certainly wasn't creating in me the reaction that perhaps the staff had hoped for. Still, there was no let up.

Both members of staff singled out soldiers and verbally attacked each one. One Corporal pushed his snarling lips so close to my face that he stole the clean air that my arching chest was heaving for. Instead all I got was a lung full of his foul breath.

At least though, the Instructors were consistent with their rudeness. We were told to never forget our origins. We were they said, the lowest of the low, the lowest form of life, a crap-hat! As for me and the other lads from the ACC, they quickly and repeatedly pointed out, that we were 'Hat-slop jockeys'. Corporal Ford warmed to the berating, taking joy in adding to the insults by shouting to all, that we were so low that even if we wore top hats, we could tip-toe under a shite house door.

Standing just one small pace away and fixing a stare on me, Corporal Ford filled his lungs and bellowed, 'Those that   want to jack, stick your hands up!' Jacking is a word used throughout the army, particularly by airborne forces and it means to give up.

No one jacked.

Reminded once again that we were all 'Hat wankers', I found myself running again. This time thank God, it was downhill.

Before another thirty minutes could pass, three men at different times and for varying reasons jacked in. Shame faced they climbed into the back of the safety vehicle, a land-rover driven nearby behind the squad. In effect it was a crude ambulance but it was known simply as the Jacking Wagon.

During one short break for water, two of our course fellows who were commissioned officers became the targeted delight of the tormenting instructors. For some reason which I can't explain, the Sandhurst men appeared to have had great difficulty either standing at ease or at attention. Both would unwittingly and repeatedly stand with crossed arms or instead place their hands on their hips like a girl. Both positions were considered to be outrageous within the ranks.

Fired with a healthy and perfectly natural dislike for commissioned officers and especially new ones, the staff found that they had a good excuse to award the subalterns plenty of additional press ups and the like. I thought it was great, not because I disliked these officers, I didn't, but it meant that every time the instructors were picking on the young officers I was being left alone. I was then able to take every advantage of their suffering so that I could claim any possible respite. By the end of the second day, both officers had learned their lessons well.

On our return into barracks we were a bedraggled shambles. The squad was halted at the footbridge and we listened carefully to the brief though booming lecture from Corporal

Ford. We were, he said, Pre-Para, something to be proud of. This enthusiastic moral boosting speech must have worked well because when we entered the camp boundaries we marched with a swagger, chests out and heads held high. Across the bridge we broke into a double but for the first time we stayed in a smart soldier like formation.

As soon as we reached our own area the staff once more delivered a huge moan telling us that we were definitely the worst Pre-Para course ever to have walked the face of the earth and then we were reminded loudly that the Bank holiday weekend had ended. Five minutes previously we had been given a very effective pep talk but now we were being put down. Any pride that any of us had felt was fast diminished. We fell out of our three ranks and were dismissed for the evening. The single lads went off to their rooms and the more senior ranks disappeared to their respective messes. Me, I had to walk home another two miles.

As I arrived home that evening to my quarters at Ramallies Park, there were two bangs. The first was me collapsing to the floor; the second was the door closing behind. Janet obviously concerned, asked how I had fared? I told her that I'd done it but I had desperately struggled during most of it and this had been only day one! I fell asleep on the sofa. Later when I went to bed, I was full of apprehension for what the next few days might have waiting for me.

The morning came and I walked nervously to the barracks ready for another day's hard graft. Once there, as per the programme I quickly changed into the army issued PT kit of red T-shirt and long uncomfortable blue shorts. With the others I paraded outside SHQ and managed almost immediately to inflame the dawning wrath of Corporal Ford.

I hadn't yet got my name on a piece of white material which was to have been sewn across the front of my T-shirt. I pleaded with the Cpl and promised to have it there by the end of NAAFI-break. For a while at least, I had appeased him and he left me alone.

Doubling around the Parade Square we deliberately kept the pace slow. Even so, beginning any exercise is often uncomfortable and on a cold morning it is even more so. I felt pretty miserable. A PTI walked out onto the centre. It was apparent that he was not in the slightest impressed with our lack of speed. He stood motionless for a minute without making a sound. Suddenly his voice burst into shouted angry instructions forcing us to speed things up. Following a routine of up-tempo exercises including side stepping, skipping and punching the air and others,our circulation was pumping.

Returning to a more familiar and faster double march the PTI shouted a simple command, 'Go!' This signalled the man at the rear of the line to sprint forward up to and then pass the man out in front. Soldiers in training as well sportsmen often use this little game. Intended to exercise heart and lungs and thereby increase aerobic capacity, it still remains an effective training method. It was fine but the change in pace was painfully hard. My heart and lungs didn't want to be exercised that morning and my will to force it through, was ebbing away.

After what seemed an age we were eventually halted. Everyone was panting like dogs on a hot day but before anyone could rest we were split into five small teams and started off on short races. First we were made to sprint across the square, touch the wall and sprint back to the next man in your team so that he could do the same.

Progressively the races got more and more difficult. We went from the fireman's lift to the human wheelbarrows and onto bunny-hops then baby carries. All were differing ways of manhandling a comrade and getting him from A to B.

Eventually those races did come to a stop and the last team to finish received its punishment of twenty-five press-ups for their trouble. I was simply glad that it wasn't my team. I took time out to recover, breathing in through my nose and back out through my mouth. It's an old trick, I don't know how or why it aids recovery, I only know that it does. The losing team having finished their press-ups re-joined the squad without having any chance to rest.

The staff had us running immediately around the square again and sprinting to the front man only this time it was everybody who had to run like hell to catch the front man. The fast runners really showed, but I was barely able to hold my own. I wasn't impressed with myself and I doubt that anyone else was either.

An hour and a half later and completely saturated in sweat I felt completely knackered. Just to make sure though, the staff finished us off with a warm-down which was just as bloody taxing as the warm up.

As always it was followed by a race to get to the showers. I pushed and clawed my way through for an early place in one of the only two showers available to the group of us. I hardly even had time for soap and completed my wash so quickly that I most probably still stank like a tramp. . The saved time was needed though to cut a piece of white material ready for sewing onto my PT-Vest.

I was still soaking as I rushed out into the room seeking what I needed. Of course nobody just happened to have a spare piece of white material hanging around and so, promising to replace it with one of my own from the married quarter, I persuaded one of the lads to part with his army issued pillow slip.   A pair of scissors to cut the cloth had to remain an impossible dream and instead I had to make do with a rough survival knife. I sat down and began to frantically cut out a rough rectangular shape then tacked it onto the front of my shirt and quickly wrote my name on it with a black pen. I had intended to finish the job properly at home. Right now I just wanted to keep the Staff off my back.

The break was all too quickly over but happily my temporary needlework passed its initial inspection. Without instruction the course quite naturally fell back into three ranks. Glad of the short rest and feeling rushed but refreshed we marched to the other side of the square. There, in common with everyone else, I was issued with a map and a compass and was sat down ready to revise the rudiments of navigation. To me, map reading has always been relatively easy so the physical and mental rest was now very welcome.

Of course the afternoon of day two continued with another squad run. As before, straight away most of us found it difficult to match the speed of the Staff and I found myself beginning to drag behind. About a mile and a half out of barracks we were brought to a halt at the bottom of a horrible looking hill. It was a squat lump of sand and flint gravel hidden in the heathlands of Aldershot. It had eight steep slopes, each of which led to a circular plateau. From above the feature appeared as a monster arachnid, hence the hills colloquial name, 'Spiders'.

Up and down its legs we ran, over and over again. At first our NCOs were leading but soon we were separated into lost individuals, each struggling as best as they could to catch the man in front. Short sharp steps were what were needed to climb the steep tracks. I dug in with my heels, searching for firm ground but mostly loose flint and sand just slipped away from under my feet making the going painful on my ankles and extremely tough on the calf muscles. Almost in a state of self-hypnosis I blanked the pain out from my mind. My head was down and my bum was out. I might not have looked dignified but it worked for me.

The new week started expectantly with yet another run. Though now we were to wear weighted packs for this and all future runs and marches. The packs weren't the Bergens of the Parachute Brigade but instead the old-fashioned 1944 pattern green canvas backpacks, which generally speaking didn't stay in regular service for very long.

Such kit was never issued to me so of course I didn't have one in my possession. Once again the Staff were unimpressed. It turned out that I was supposed to have collected one from the Squadron stores before the course started. Well nobody told me and now the stores were shut. Most of the Squadron was away in Kenya so there was no opportunity of getting one either. Remonstrating with the frustrated Staff I tried in vain to persuade them to allow me to wear my old A-frame, after all I had completed a fair bit of training with it. The trouble was though, the old A-frame may have once been army issue but it had long since stopped being in regular use. The '44' pattern I argued, was as obsolete as the 'A' Frame but I wasn't winning the argument. The answer was an emphatic 'No'. Instead the Staff agreed that I should wear my issued 1958 pattern pack. It looked similar to the 44 pattern but in reality, was a much worse design.

Each pack had to weigh thirty pounds exactly and the instructors checked this rigorously by weighing each one with a set of fishermen's scales and woe-betide anyone with even a fraction less than thirty pounds. It wasn't that clever if you were caught with more either. Viewed as a smart arse, the over keen soldier would still have found himself facing some horrible punishment.

Running with the dreaded 58-pattern pack proved to be an unwise manoeuvre. It's main supports were narrow bra like shoulder straps that cut into the thin flesh of my shoulders. The action of running caused the pack to jolt up and down in rhythm with my steps. To prevent this I tightened the straps but that in turn caused deeper cuts. To pile on the misery, the pack is further fitted with two steel 'D' shaped clips at the front, which were designed to fit onto a matching webbing set. Without this set though, the weight of the pack pulled the clips up and back so that they sat just inside my armpits, cutting and scraping skin as I went. In terms of running with it, a really crap design!

After another run some of the boys had suffered pretty badly with 'Bergen burns'; burns caused by friction on and across the wearer's back and by the constant rubbing up and down of bouncing backpacks. It seemed that the smallest guys suffered worst of all. I saw some with great sores of six inches across. Unable or unwilling to seek medical advice for fear of being taken off the course, treatment was administered by colleagues.

Men gripped the bed ends as they lay injured and writhing in pain, their knuckles glowing white with strain. In this case, the treatment appeared to be far more painful than the original injury for there wasn't any form of anaesthetic. Like a scene from old Hollywood western, each wounded man was given a stick to bite on. I don't know if it did any good or not but if they believed that it did, so it was good enough for me. A mate would administer the cure-all; usually surgical spirit or after-shave dabbed on with cotton wool and applied directly to the raw open wound. Despite loud gurgled screams of agony each time the stinging spirit touched the exposed nerve endings, men continued to queue patiently at the door, all waiting their turn for treatment. It was hoped and indeed believed by most that the spirit or the alcohol in the after-shave would both sterilise and harden the wound. Blokes who shared this common bond did it in good faith.

The afternoon brought a lesson in the 66 millimetre light anti-armour weapon and its standard operating procedures (S.O.P.s). The 66 was a slightly elderly but ultimately reliable, portable, folding and disposable missile launcher. Civvies often referred to it as a Bazooka, but in no way was it related to that even older weapon. I had never fired the 66 and so I was a little disappointed to learn that this lesson was only to be dry drills. During my basic training with the ACC we were only shown an explanatory film of the weapon. Since then I'd had to carry them and clean them, but never did I have the opportunity to actually use one. Still, it did round the afternoon off nicely and I went off to my home happy and smiling.

Panting wildly I found my mind travelling back to yesterday and wishing that I was still weapon training, but instead this morning I was standing with the others from the course at the M.V.E.E. (Military Vehicle Experimental Establishment). Pronounced 'Meevee' assault course. Situated near Wellesley Road in Aldershot the MVEE assault course had been abandoned for some years. Built during the Second World War, it still held some unique features, and some of its obstacles were not usually found on our more modern courses. This old and near derelict feature presented itself as quite a formidable and daunting obstacle. Four minutes was set as the maximum time limit for completing one lap of the course, but, as to be expected, we were first to run around it so that we could be shown exactly what was in play and what was not and then how each bit should be tackled.

A shrieking blast of an Instructor's whistle set us off sprinting across the open ground of bumpy unkempt grassland. As we raced to the first obstacle, a water jump, the squad stayed tight in a pack. The jump was a rectangular concrete construction resembling a fishpond, only about ten inches deep and about five feet across. It presented few problems and each one of us easily straddled the width in a single stretch of a running leg, then onto and through a small wooded area. Trying to keep my wits about me and never losing sight of my competing colleagues I ran on. Down a sudden and very steep slope I went only to find myself faced with the high wall of a tank stop, a three sided sunken concrete box with smoothed walls of around eight feet in height.

Faced with diminishing seconds I made the decision to fight my way through to the front. There were about a dozen men all scrambling at the wall. No words of command were given but the squad quite suddenly became organised. Years of drilling and working as a team were at last beginning to pay off. The fighting ceased and men calmed themselves, pausing to consider the best strategy needed to tackle this wall. One then two men slammed their backs into the wall pushing upturned hands down onto their braced thighs, queues formed instantly as men vaulted off their colleagues to reach the top of the wall but before they clambered over to disappear onward they waited. Those on top prostrated themselves and stretched an arm downward to assist the next man.

I was breathing wildly and never for a second allowed a thought of the physical strain that my body was going through. Instead, I was mentally alert, searching ahead for the next obstacle. A quick six yard dash took me over a near vertical climb across two parallel railway sleepers and then down the other side. At the bottom I immediately met a nasty looking barbed wire maze suspended about fifteen inches off the ground. I slowed fast coming to a near uncontrolled muddy skid. I dropped to my knees and pushed myself into a crawl.

Under the wire and being very careful not to get snagged on rusted barbs, I pulled my way through by my finger tips to exit and facing yet another wall. Once stood up, I traversed the five-foot tall obstruction of red brick. By now the squad had filtered out with me situated somewhere around the centre. I congratulated myself; so far so good.

Any congratulations though were premature for all of a sudden, the whole load of us ground to a halt. Coming from the next obstacle, a fast growing queue of impatient men sprouted upward. Immediately in front of me there were three other blokes. Frustration erupted inside me and I couldn't help bit spout loudly,

"Come on, what's the fucking hold-up!"

None of the others were listening to me, they too were also engaged in shouting abuse at the front. Ahead were three long telegraph poles, each spanned a three-foot deep trench of stinking stagnant water. One of the poles bore the evidence of years of exposure to the weather. Slimy green vegetation had crept around its uppermost curves. The remaining two poles stood proud, forming twin bridges over the concrete channel, but beneath them, algae infested murky liquid, fermented into bubbles like farts in a bath.

Already the poles were slippery, worn smooth and perfectly rounded by many years of constant tread. Now they were made yet worse as wet and muddy boots traversed their slicked lengths. Toeing carefully on the treacherous surface, two sometimes three men at a time tried to cross. Arms out widespread, they imitated circus acts on a tightrope. Some faltered, reaching the other side only because of luck and a good dose of determination. Others fell and found themselves submerged in the thick stew of foul smelling filth. Overcome with the cold stench of the wet algae the fallen men gasped almost silently, their lungs momentarily shocked into a paralysing inactivity. Eventually each scrambled out pulling themselves clear and onto the concrete bank ready to have another go. It must have looked pretty funny but no one laughed, nobody dared waste precious breath.

My turn came around quickly enough. Planning ahead was the answer. I hoped that a sprint over the log might give me enough momentum to cross even if my balance was to falter. Then again, perhaps a careful and steady balanced approach would be better. Decisions, decisions, in fact neither option would do. In a flash I had made up my mind. Instead, I would cross as prompt as I dare and wouldn't look anywhere except straight forward. No reliance on balance, rather I wanted to secure my stare on a fixed point dead ahead, only paying lip service to the perceived lesser worry of my footing beneath me.

I started well, reaching about half the distance across the log, but control left me suddenly as seemingly a giant invisible hand pushed my momentum and shifted my centre of balance to one side. I felt my waist buckle and my left shoulder fell sharply. I was falling. Quickening my pace I somehow and miraculously found firm ground under my feet. I had just managed to reach the other side.

Now in front was a sharp pyramid shaped slope of mud about eight feet high. Refusing to be beaten, I dug my heels in and easily flew over the apex but immediately lost my footing once on the other side resulting in a precarious slip down an equally steep bit of concrete going the opposite way. At the bottom a much worn track led the way to the next obstruction which sat at about twenty yards to the left. One of the instructors hovered over a small set of cement steps leading down to a man hole sized tunnel of old concrete drainage pipes. The lower steps were completely submerged in brown murky water which, now having been stirred by other feet before me, reeked of rotting flesh.

The instructor hurriedly and roughly heaved the sprinting men down and into the blackened hole. There was hardly a wait of even a few seconds before I too was thrown down into its entrance. Inside, the tunnel turned a sharp corner leaving me and everyone else in absolute darkness. There was no light whatsoever. I literally couldn't see the hand in front of my face. I was on my knees and soaking wet. The water was cold, very cold and every time that I moved forward, the sickening smell wafted up to irritate my nostrils. I could hear someone up ahead splashing and grunting and every few seconds a voice from behind shouted at me to keep moving but I couldn't see anyone. Under my hands in the freezing water lay about five inches of soft sludge fragmented only by occasional sharpened stones. Rotting leaves, vegetation and a whole host of tiny creatures worked together to create a mire of foul syrup which clung to my fingers wherever I tried to move them. By now my knees were getting sore and I could also feel the flesh on my hands becoming torn as I pulled my way through. Eventually, tired and hurting I could see the brightness bursting through misty corridors of light.

At the end of the tunnel, others were there waiting to help pull me through the last few inches. I was so pleased to see the outside that I became oblivious to the shouts being blasted at me. I remember being vaguely aware that some shouts were of encouragement and some were warnings but of what I didn't know and at that time I really didn't care. Only as I pushed a hand out from the tunnel and onto the first sunken step did I see what all the commotion was about. Half sitting yet half-floating was the badly decomposed rotted carcass of a small animal. It was difficult to tell what creature it was but I thought that it was once probably a fox. It was luck and not judgement that prevented me from pushing my hand right through the middle of this disgusting pile of skin and bone.

Free of the underground passage it was my turn to assist the last few from the exit then came my chance to run for the end. I could see the Land Rover, the Staff and those men who had already finished. A sprint led me to the lads who by now were calling wildly, shouting encouragement not just to me but those around and behind me. The Staff remained all the while silent. Motionless, they stood with their arms crossed pulling their clipboards into their chests. They watched and stared contemptibly into the eyes of the finishers, each trying to read their minds and challenge their commitment. I collapsed forward supporting my hands on my knees. Bright red skin radiated from my over-heated face and then my chest launched into familiar convulsions as I gasped for air.

The Staff didn't stop the clock until Private Elliot, another ACC chef and the last man, had crossed the line. As usual, none of the instructors appeared to be even slightly impressed. Though we had all managed to finish the circuit within the allowed time the staff were far from happy. There was no time for post-mortems they said and instead we were lambasted for being the useless wastes of airspace that we had undoubtedly proved to be. Around we went again. Then we went round again, then again and again, and then again until we were almost incapable of walking around it. I'm not sure how many times we went but it was at least ten times too many.

At last as I crossed the finishing line for the umpteenth time I could see that Corporal Ford had a smile on his face. He pushed a thumb over the tiny little button above his stopwatch and said something about our effort having finally improved. At last we were allowed a short rest and a water break.

From there we were formed into file and marched the short distance to one of the obstacles that had earlier been declared as out of play. The group was pushed into a rough semi-circle and made to stand under a ten feet high wall. On top and fixed into the brick work were two telegraph poles, each straddling a horizontal gap of twelve or thirteen feet to a near identical wall. From where the pole ends protruded out from the brick dangled a short but thick matted rope ending with a knot.

One instructor turned and spoke to the others. There was a slight giggle from some then one of them stepped forward. As Corporal Ford talked out loud explaining techniques and rules another instructor reached for the rope above and pulled himself up. Then, with arms out to his side he walked slowly and carefully over the log and then climbed down the opposite wall. Two at a time we climbed the wall and stood balancing on the logs awaiting the next instruction. When it was my turn I found what felt to be the best and safest position. I stretched my arms right out on either side and waited. There was a hold up; I don't know what but it was something to do with the other guy on the adjacent log. As each second of waiting passed my balance appeared to become more and more precarious and I could feel myself beginning to wobble.

An Instructor's voice interrupted any anxiety that I had, and I heard the command to start walking. Half way across the same Instructor shouted for us to stop. For just a second or two I stood perfectly still, tensing every muscle in an effort to keep my balance. I knew what was coming and I dreaded it. As anticipated, the Instructor ordered me to bend down and touch my toes. Of course I could easily reach my feet but I wasn't looking forward to having to retrieve my arms from their wing like position. Surprisingly, I had no problem bending and keeping my balance, nevertheless I was glad when I was allowed to continue and eventually reached the safety of solid ground.

Corporal Ford threw his clipboard into the cab of the waiting Land Rover, muttered something to the driver then he and it went off. By now we had guessed what we were to do. As a squad we simply fell into three ranks and started running. A part of me fantasised about being on that vehicle for the rest, but that was the jacking wagon and once in it, there was no coming back.

Each day of the course progressed with more and more difficult tabs, runs and other exercises. As we neared the end of Pre-Para there were just a few more events and tests to look forward to. One of the worst was to be a nine-mile tab. Nine miles is easy but this was to be no ordinary tab. On this one, much of the distance was to be completed whilst wearing a mark 7 respirator or 'gas mask' as most civilians like to call them. That would be bad enough but according to the programme, at the conclusion of the tab and once at Gibraltar Barracks in Minley, we were to continue onto the Confidence Course. Once completed, we were to immediately undergo the army swimming test.

Seemingly many pairs of feet pounded the road beneath. Webbing pouches rustled and belts rubbed the tangle of straps as they slapped the wooden hand guards of SLR rifles being swung in motion with the marching troops. The tab as expected was especially fast. The Staff, eyes flicking momentarily to tiny hands on their watches appeared anxious. Perhaps they worried about our apparent lack of progress on this rough country track hidden behind Aldershot's vast military town.

Marching through the wooded area near the M3 motorway the squad was brought to an abrupt halt. Already some of our number looked about ready to collapse. In recent days I had felt my own fitness improve dramatically yet I too was puffing like a dragon.

A shouted order came for us to fit respirators. Instructors rushed around hurrying the men but moans and groans were clearly heard and brought an immediately sharp response from the supervising staff. Once that we had our respirators fitted, rifles held correctly and large packs pulled tightly into our backs we set off again. Again, the pace was much faster than regulation double.

The earlier part of the tab had been particularly difficult. We had been wearing heavy equipment and had been running between six and seven miles an hour. I hadn't yet suffered as much as some but I was now sweating profusely and my body begged rest. Wearing this tight fitting rubber mask I felt nauseous and claustrophobic. Like most of us, I was ready to throw teddy out of the pram.

The Mark 7 has a side fitting metal drum filter, filled with meshed charcoal through which to breathe. The air doesn't simply flow into the mask unaided, it has to be drawn in with heavy breaths then blown out. Breathing in normal conditions with this mask is very restrictive and running simply amplifies those feelings.

My mouth was wide open, grunting and gulping at the thin air. Each breath into my lungs was like a contest. Suffocating panic was a mere nanosecond away. Terrified voices within my conscience repeatedly demanded that I jack. I began to wonder if death was just around the corner. I'm not sure whether or not I believed deep down that this was a real possibility, but I was scared and I believed that collapse was, at least, likely.

With each difficult gulp of air I tasted my own vomit and bile. My mouth began to dribble with excess saliva. Great rivers of sweaty moisture soaked my face and with nowhere for it to escape, puddles collected in the chin of the mask. The sticky liquid swilled messily about, splashing my mouth and nostrils. Things were getting bad, mixed feelings of exhaustion, claustrophobia and a natural urge to retch ensured that I felt near the end. I didn't want to throw up inside my respirator and I definitely didn't fancy collapsing but neither did I want to jack, I had to carry on! Thankfully my worries were sharply interrupted. Orders from one of the NCOs barked out and we were halted.

Sucking in hard deep breaths I strained to cope with the limited supply of oxygen. I blinked hard, trying to focus through the thick misted goggle style eyepieces I could see that one of the officers on the course was staggering about like a Saturday night drunk. A member of the staff ran over to him and ripped his respirator from his face and pulled it clear over the top of his very swollen head. The young officers eyes were shut, his face paled and drained of natural colour. He threw his head upwards arching his neck as he gorged himself on fresh clean air. Each gulp was accompanied with a harsh rasping from deep inside his throat. Someone shouted, "Jacking wagon!" and with that the stricken officer was led away. There was no resistance, not a word was spoken. It was kept to ourselves but everyone knew that each one of us was only a cat's whisker from the jack.

The Corporal's eyes caught the sight of movement at the other end of the squad and snapping angrily, he shouted, "Get that fucking respirator on your face, you hat bastard!"

In response a floundering soldier snapped to attention and pulled the mask back into place. His chest heaving as his lungs failed to adjust to the sudden drop in air delivery and then he just fell forward in a faint. Strike two for the jacking wagon. I never saw him again and often wondered what had happened to him.

We started off again. We doubled even faster now. I glanced behind. One lad who had dared to sneak a breath by partially removing his mask was now far to the rear and the gap was widening. Insults and orders aimed at the tailing soldier bombarded him but were to no avail. A hundred yards further on and he too was in the jacking wagon. Before we could reach our destination of Minley, three more would be keeping him company.

As we rounded a corner on the approach to Gibraltar Barracks, the few of us remaining on the tab responded to the command from the staff to brace up and get together. We removed our masks and each one of us drank in the sweet air. We paused long enough to form three ranks and as we did, Corporal Ford shouted, "Show some pride to these hat wankers as we enter the barracks!"

After a short march of a few hundred yards we took the opportunity to recover properly. We found ourselves at the Ariel confidence course. Essentially a series of ropes tethered to tall mature trees at heights of between fifteen to twenty feet. Looking around, I reckoned that much of it was reasonably simple to complete. At the start there were two horizontal parallel ropes stretched over twelve yards. Taking it in turns we went up. Each moved carefully and methodically. Nobody fancied a fall. From the next tree there led off another pair of ropes but this time vertically parallel. I held one rope and slid my feet along the other. Being an exercise that I've completed many times, it was easily traversed.

Only one part caused me a little trouble, a single rope which, set at twenty feet from the ground resembled a tightrope. None of us were circus performers so that meant we had to travel its length by swinging sideways and using only arms, a manoeuvre known as the monkey swing. I had done it before so I should have been confident but I wasn't. I kept looking down and twenty feet looks a bloody long way to fall. I swung across the thick fibrous rope trying my hardest to use the technique that I had trained with. The idea was simply to move the forward hand as the body swings and of course vice versa.

It was looking good and I anticipated getting across without a hitch. However once I reached halfway, one of the instructors shouted at me and told me to halt. For about thirty seconds I just hung there, motionless, limp and wondering what was about to happen. The strain on my arms was very obvious but at the same time, I took the opportunity to get my breath back. As the seconds passed, the ache in my arms and shoulders became more and more intense. The Cpl, whilst at the same time shouting at me, pointed his finger upward gesturing a somersault . He made it clear that he expected me to swing my body vertically over the rope. For a split second I wondered why on earth he had decided to pick on me but it would have been far too dangerous to voice any protest.

I knew that I would find this particular manoeuvre difficult. I was close to exhaustion. On top of that I was wearing considerably more than simple PE kit. In my head I had already convinced myself that I couldn't do it but I thought, what the heck? Forcing my arms to bend I pulled my weight up to the rope and lifted my knees to my chest. For just a fraction of a second I paused before violently throwing my head back in an effort to force my body round but it wasn't enough. I tried again and again and again, becoming more spent with each throw. Eventually the command for me to stop came and feeling somewhat relieved I continued along the rope. At that point I wasn't sure whether my lack of success meant a course failure or not. Even so, I remained severely pissed off that I seemed to have been singled out for it. Nobody else had to!

The last truly physical test of the course was the fifteen-mile tab in full battle order. The route of the march would take in some of the steepest hills of the South Downs. I had always considered the Downs to have a strange name because in my experience there seemed to be an awful lot of up and not very much down.

The severe pace of the 9 Sqn. Instructors had by now become fairly routine. I had even grown to expect it. So much so that when we slowed down, it pissed me right off. We hadn't been going for long when already some men dropped behind. Very noticeable was Jock Elliot, one of the other ACC lads. Throughout the course he had been seen perhaps unfairly, as a bit of a waster. He was generally weak willed and though his fitness was probably above average, he was, as far as the course was concerned unfit. Because he was so often unable to keep up he caused some resentment amongst us. It meant that we had to quite literally drag him along.

After only three miles and on a deep muddy path and parallel to a heavily furrowed field, Elliot began to drop further back until he was about the length of a football pitch behind the rest. Despite the verbal frustrations of the Staff he had been at the back from the start and had never at any point managed to claw his way into the pack. Shouts of encouragement from his colleagues apparently also had no effect then Corporal Ford, now red faced, short in tolerance and obviously bloody angry, bawled at Tom Onions and me.

"Walker! Onions! Get that Hat wanker up here! He's your fucking Corps, you keep him up here!"

There was a painfully obvious tone of deep frustration in his voice and either Tom nor I dared to hesitate or argue. We dropped back level with struggling Elliot. I cannot remember the exact words but both of us vented our anger severely, verbally and loudly at him. At that moment, if I had been told to beat him to a pulp, I would have, such was my rage.

With us on each side of Elliot, we dragged him along by the arms and by his webbing. Elliot seemed to take our efforts as a signal that it was all right to coast and amazingly he relaxed even further. For all of us, this tab was really hard work and we could do without this extra heavy burden. I shouted and I threatened. As I grew more and more angry, I could feel the temper inside me starting to swell. It was seriously in my mind to punch him hard in the mouth. I wanted to knock his teeth down his throat. I battled hard to subdue it but I sorely wanted so much just to beat his head in. I was working bloody hard, I reasoned, so why wasn't he? The more help he was given then the more he tried to lean on us.

Having been dragged unceremoniously back into the squad Elliot appeared to suddenly give up. It was as if he was drunk, hardly able even to lift his feet from the ground. His chin dropped to his chest and his eyes were barely open. To all of us it soon became patently obvious that he wasn't going to make it much further, and just a few tiny seconds later Elliot found himself back in the jacking wagon.

Despite my anger and frustrations with Elliot I was actually enjoying myself. Tabbing had always been one of my strong points and amongst the rest of my comrades I was shining. Only when we reached the beginning of a very long and steep chalky hill did I begin to experience problems. I was tired but comfortable and looking up ahead I could see the track disappearing into the sky. In quiet resignation I pushed my head down and my bum out then started the rhythmic march of many, many short steps.

I tried to think of nothing but the climb. I was succeeding too when one of the young Sappers, a lad called Smudger Smith called out. Smudger was nearing the end of his turn in carrying the LMG. As I drew level with him he seized the opportunity and correctly informed me that it was now my turn. I knew that at some time during the tab I would have to carry it but I really didn't want it right now. I couldn't see any point in offering an excuse so I shrugged my shoulders and reached out   to take the gun from him. Without slowing or stopping I slung my SLR over my shoulder and baby carried the bigger gun. The climb up this very long hill had just got harder. Before long   I was panting like a train but I desperately didn't want to slow down.

My saviour came about a mile later in the guise of another Sapper, Corporal Thomo' Thompson. He was a big lad, quiet and much respected by everyone on the course. Thomo' had recently been posted from the Sappers own Commando Squadron, 59 Commando, based in Plymouth. He caught up with me not long after I had passed over the top of the hill. I had thought that I was going to have to carry the LMG for at least another mile or so but the big man drew level with me and said simply,

"Give us it here, Chip".

I didn't argue, though I did enquire weakly if he was sure? Of course he was and I duly gave him the LMG. I don't know how he did it but he then tabbed away in front having left most of the others along with me behind.

On the last day of Pre-Para, washed and dressed in our smartest working uniform we sat patiently together. The remaining men, with the exception of just two who were absent through injury, waited on the first floor of the concrete barrack block. The atmosphere was tense and we waited in silence for our turn to be called to the Squadron office where the instructors would inform us of our results. Nine Squadron had an immensely proud tradition in their Pre-Para courses. In present memory at least, nobody who had completed and passed their Pre-Para course had ever failed P-Company.   The squadron was almost regal in the way it protected that tradition; they liked having the reputation for running the toughest Pre-Para and nobody but nobody would be allowed to dash that pride.

For me, acceptance from here to attend P-Company would be a huge boost to my confidence.

One by one each of the men returned to the block. All were immediately interrogated where upon they either confessed to abject failure or they were so elated it was difficult to get a sensible word out of them. My turn came near the end. I wanted desperately to know whether or not I would be joining those others in going down the hill to Browning Barracks on Monday.

I was, of course, a little apprehensive. Of my ACC colleagues I learned that Tom Onions had passed and that was perhaps to be expected. Jock Elliot had failed and again, that was surely expected. What lay in store for me I wondered? When my turn eventually came I stared straight ahead and avoided any eye contact. I marched in smartly. In close succession my gleaming boots slapped the carpeted floor in a precision halt. Uncomfortable and nervous I stood rigidly still and to attention. In front of me were two Corporals and a Sergeant, all sat behind a six-foot wooden trestle table over which was draped a grey blanket smartly pinned tight to the corners.

One of them called me forward and invited me to sit. Down at their level I dared a peek but was astonished to see that all three of them appeared to be reading and did not look up. *Surely there cannot be that much written about me?* I thought. As if on cue the three stopped what they were doing and together raised their eyes to focus on me. The Sergeant spoke first,

"How do you think you did?"

Steadily and cautiously I answered, explaining that I felt that I was ready to go down the hill and that I knew I had got off to a poor start but that I had consistently showed good improvement. I further emphasised that whilst there had been times that I had fallen behind, I never once gave up nor did I ever fail to reach the given objective.

"If I was told," I said, "to run up a bloody great hill, then run up it I did!"

The short speech hit somewhere because all three men of the tribunal smiled and then turned to each and spoke in whispers.

A few more questions later and I again sat back waiting for something to be said. Finally Corporal Ford stood up and said,

"OK, you'll do. Don't let us down."

The smile on my face threatened to tear my cheeks apart. All three of the NCOs now stood and each offered their hands in congratulation, adding a simple but most welcome,

"Well done."

CHAPTER NINE

SELECTION

Sunday evening soon came around and I arrived at Browning Barracks early dragging my old army issue suitcase and Bergen along with me. This was the home the Parachute Regiment and Airborne Forces.

At the barrier I paused to ask a young soldier where I was supposed to go. Remaining expressionless, he pointed me off to the CQMS store inside one of the ugly square concrete blocks that made up a large quadrangle. Built during the late Nineteen Sixties, they represented fairly typical barracks within the garrison.

Once at the stores I found myself in a long queue of waiting soldiers. I looked about, searching for any familiar faces. I saw some that I recognised from years before when I was attached to 7 Para RHA, but before I got a chance to talk to them, the queue moved and I found myself standing at the entrance to a first floor storeroom. The CQ inside looked at me impatiently. I wondered if he was waiting for me to do something. Guessing well, I stood to attention and called out my regimental number followed quickly with my rank and name. Examining a list, the CQ flicked his pen down the side of his clip-board before offering a tick beside my details. Assisting the CQ was a thick set Corporal who immediately started to shout out listed items of kit and simultaneously throwing the objects in my direction;

"Airborne helmet, Bergen, OG top."

Then he picked up a camouflaged cap known derisively as a 'Hat, Camouflaged'. The stores Cpl though, revelled in his position of authority over us and instead called it a,

"Hat stupid!" before throwing it at me.

It was cramped and rushed as I frantically gathered the loosely piled kit, shovelling it into my Bergen just as the stores Cpl began throwing kit toward the next guy. With my bags filled, I went off to find my allocated bed space.

Even though I had a wife and family already living in an army house situated only a mile away, I was nevertheless confined to barracks. Regulations stated that this was a residential course.

The course planner displayed on a large felt covered board inside the block showed that first up we had, 'Course intro' and then 'admin'. Very soon we were outside, formed into three ranks and were marched over to the gymnasium. Being careful not to trip over the coarse grassy matting protecting the delicate gym floor from our boots, we filed into neat rows of orange moulded polypropylene chairs.

On a platform in front I could see a number of Sergeants, all were wearing the blue serge tracksuit top of physical training instructors. I instantly recognised one as an old acquaintance from 7Para, Sgt Steve Ryder. Also there but not sitting with the others was the Recruit Training Company Sergeant Major, Ernie Rustell.

He gave a sharp shout.

"Sit up!"

Instantly the CSM had us sitting with our backs straight and facing the front in time for the OC to walk nonchalantly in, tossing his beret onto an old military desk as he passed. Even before he had reached the desk the Major spoke loudly to introduce himself as Major Kennett. Standing in front of us, hands draped lazily into his trouser pockets he went into a well-practised speech. He warned that we were entering one of the hardest selection courses to be found anywhere in any army in the world.

"Many would fail, but this was not to be seen as a disgrace."

He went on to say that some amongst us would attempt the course again and again. Then stifling a chuckle he called out,

"Where are you Cadbury?"

A thinly built black lad wearing the cap badge of the RAMC snapped to attention.

"Ah, there you are." The Major confirmed.

"How many times is this Cadbury?"

The young medic hesitated before replying,

"Er, six Sir."

"Good, good and are you going to pass this time?" Cadbury smiled and confirmed his eagerness with a resounding,

"Definitely Sir!"

Murmuring spread quickly around the hall as soldiers uttered their disbelief that someone would put themselves through this for a sixth time.

The Major finished his speech and the CSM took over. Reading out names from lists attached to a clipboard he detailed the men into large groups of about twenty. These groups were called syndicates. Every few seconds he would pause to look around. It must have been an unusual sight. This, I was told, was the largest selection course for many years.

I too glanced around and was amazed to see the huge array of different cap badges. This was the All-arms course. Men from all of the different Corps and Regiments which make up the units of the Airborne Brigade were represented here. Also included were newly commissioned officers of the Parachute Regiment, Two Sappers from 59 Commando, a Royal Artillery Lieutenant from 29 Commando, and, hoping to transfer to Para' Reg', was an SAC from the RAF Regiment. Most surprising of all to me was the attendance of a Naval Seaman who as a radio operator was hoping to serve with the one of the Independent Commando Units

I wondered how well we would all do? I couldn't help but think of something a Para had told me years before. That P-Company is the only course in the army where the instructors actually want you to fail. The logic being, he explained was that way the Brigade only gets the very best.

Despite its official title of 'Pre-parachute selection', it is not a course to select people who can parachute. After all, teenage girls and old women parachuted with the Red Devils display team on many warm Sunday afternoons down on Queens Avenue. Instead the course was designed to test courage, aggression, determination, leadership and both mental and physical stamina. Only if a soldier passed all the tests would he be considered fit enough to start parachute training and then eventually be able to serve with Airborne Forces.

The standards are of course high and they should be. The Airborne Brigade is different to any other in the British army. In times of conflict, it would expect to be left isolated with little or no air cover or armoured divisions. Paratroopers train to fight with and utilise only what they can carry or scrounge.

The rest of the morning was taken up with the usual course admin; names taken for a nominal role, bed spaces allocated and the like.

After lunch we found ourselves parading for the first time in our syndicates and we marched off towards the small square in front of the gymnasium but behind the company HQ. Shouting the orders of the day as they jogged toward us, the instructional staff emerged keen and boisterous from their offices in the gym.

The BFT was to come first. Dressed in routine boots and denims with a red PT vest we were turned about and as a company we marched away at the double through a side gate out of the barracks and along the path by the Farnborough Road in the direction of Northcamp.

Shortly before we drew level with the Wavell school, the Company were wheeled round and onto a sandy track across the Queens Parade playing fields towards the canal and the barracks.

Once we had reached a place not far from where had started we were brought to a halt and once again separated into our given syndicates. With gaps of one minute, each syndicate started their individual BFTs. The second and final part of this test meant going for the best and fastest run along a route which, would inevitably take us back to the square at Browning barracks.

Initially I found the run comfortable and I gladly stretched my legs gaining an even quicker pace and hoping to impress the staff by achieving a good time. I felt fine all the way round and when I could see the end with its member of staff holding his stopwatch, I drew on reserves of energy and finished in a sprint to the footpath between the blocks. As I passed the NCO he shouted out my time.

At the finish and whilst attempting to get my breath back, I stood in line with the other finished runners. An NCO walking down the line of men and carrying a maroon coloured clipboard approached. At each soldier, he paused long enough only to write their name and finish time. Without taking his eyes off his clipboard, he stepped up to me. Standing to attention and fixing my stare straight ahead I shouted,

"Walker, Staff!"

The NCO hesitated for a moment, before raising his eyebrows slowly. He stopped scribbling and demanded,

"Time?"

Embarrassment took over. I hadn't heard very well the time called out. I couldn't have asked the NCO with the watch to repeat it for me because he hardly had time to breathe before he was shouting the time to the next runner. Not only that but from the finish line I was herded away and into this line. Unfortunately for me, Major Kennett was standing close behind and must have heard. He side stepped through the line of men and leaned so close that I could feel his respiration on my ear as he growled, "What time did you get?"

I didn't know what to say but I had to speak. I could only offer a feeble,

"I don't know Sir. Nine minutes and something." Sergeant Ryder seeing that something was not quite right strode forcefully my way,

"Nine Fourteen!" He interrupted.

In my head I thanked him very much for saving my neck just there, but unluckily it wasn't soon enough. The Major pointed down to the cold grey concrete at my feet and commanded,

"Down twenty!"

Like a stone I dropped to the prone position and pushed out my press-ups. I hadn't got off to a good start. Now for the wrong reasons, Major Kennett had learned my name already.

The next time we paraded we sported our course allocated personal numbers. Using plimsoll whitener they were crudely painted onto the thighs of our denims and onto our long blue PT shorts and also onto the front of our helmets. Mine was number Twenty-three. For the next three weeks I didn't have a name and instead learned to be just a number. Whenever anyone asked who I was? The reply would be

"Number Twenty Three Sir!"

Paraded with my fellow syndicate members outside the barrack block on day three, we looked forward to the much wanted intrusion into the constant physical abuse that our bodies had been going through. It was photograph time. Each course was given the opportunity to pose for the camera in front of the old Second World War DC3 Dakota aeroplane, which was parked for display at the entrance to the barracks. To me it appeared a daft time to have a course photo. Already we had lost several people, mostly through injury, but some had voluntarily gone too. At the time it seemed more sensible to have a photograph taken at the end. Then it would show all those who had stuck with it. I thought that to be far more appropriate.

Thankfully we were given permission to remove our hated head-dress. Nobody wanted to be seen in the photo whilst wearing the dreaded Hat Stupid. That day, a gorgeous sun filled spring afternoon, had us balancing precariously on thin wooden benches set out in rows to accommodate all of us. The photographer, a civilian contracted from an Aldershot studio waved his arms about like a madman, gesturing us into an ever-tightening bunch.

Three clicks later and we were running back to the block to fetch our Bergens ready for another tab.

Two weeks passed much like the previous weeks spent with 9 Para. The only notable differences included the carrying of the much better SAS style Bergen, which we had to carry each and every day. This was a very welcome change from the atrocious 58-pattern pack. Also we now carried a rifle wherever we went. Not the SLR that I was used to but its elder cousin, a Belgian FN that had been captured from the Argentine Forces during the Falklands war. These rifles were now deactivated and were used solely for training. It's a little ironic that these weapons had been used against the Parachute Regiment but were now used to help them.

Correctly so, the Sergeant Major insisted that all rifles stayed in the hands of their users. At the end of tabs, before even any first aid could be administered or any refreshment was taken, the rifles were stripped, cleaned and checked. This allowed CSM Rustell to practice his catchphrase. He would strut about shouting,

"First my weapon, then myself!"

It soon prompted imitations and mimics from all quarters. I remember more than once the impolite suggestion that he recited this phrase to his wife.

I soon learned that for those who were further up the promotion ladder, this course was to be even more difficult. Senior NCOs and Commissioned Officers in particular were not expected to just be fit and keen, but also to be able to lead. On any squad run or tab, the easiest position by far was to be right at the front. SNCOs and Officers though had to ensure that they stayed at the rear, pushing and encouraging the weaker members of the squad. Proof was needed of their leadership skills; simply wearing the rank wasn'tgood enough.

Major Kennett, the course OC, demonstrated an unashamedly and distinct dislike for his fellow officers, in particular those of his own Regiment, but all of the officers were frequently given a hard time.

On one especially arduous tab we were in the middle of Long Valley. When dry, the valley is a dust bowl and when wet, a mire of soft sinking sand. This day it was wet. The Company had been halted at the bottom of a gruesome gravel hill track. Along with the others I stood perfectly still, not wanting to attract any attention. My face by now was severely reddened and my heart was pounding. I could feel myself listing to the left as my feet sank ankle deep in the thick goo of saturated silt. I feared that I might topple over, thereby winning myself some terrible punishment for daring to move. Some found it too difficult leading to NCOs darting about screaming shouts of, "Stand still!"

Over their voices I heard the OC asking one of the subalterns to produce for inspection, his white handkerchief. Baffled by the odd request the young lieutenant shrugged his shoulders and answered that he didn't possess a white hanky. The Major feigned shock and disbelief adding,

"All Officers carry white hankies!"

In a tone that could be mistaken as invitingly friendly, the Major calmly and softly asked the subaltern to run to the top of a far off hill and wave. Without a moment's hesitation the young officer darted from the ranks and commenced the sharp climb.

No doubt just when the other officers were thanking God that the OC had not singled them out too, he picked on another subaltern. Once again he demanded to see the officers white handkerchief. Told in a repeated reply that there was no hanky to be shown, the OC snapped! He now demanded that all of the officers should run up to the top of the hill and that they should also overtake the man now a third of the way up, or suffer the consequences.

Throughout this time I was of course simply glad of the break and I tried hard to take full advantage of it, using the time to steady myself and to regain my composure. There were plenty of similar incidents during the course and they only made me very grateful indeed that I had never taken the Queen's Commission.

One Officer, a doctor and a Lt. Col. of the RAMC struggled from day one. He was an odd looking man, slightly built and wearing thick lenses in National Health style spectacles. This man had great difficulty in passing the initial BFT so he stood little chance of getting through P-Company. He was a nice bloke I'm sure, but he was never going to make the grade as an airborne warrior. None of us could figure out why or how he had come to be here.

Rumours spread that 23 Parachute Field Ambulance was desperately short of a particular type of doctor. There were apparently no volunteers so this man had been persuaded to give it a go. Most of the men however, including those instructors willing to lend voice to their disapproval were unhappy that commands from high above had declared that no matter what, this man will pass P-Company. I witnessed first-hand some of the staff pleading with him to self RTU, only to be told that the upper echelons want him there and that he will pass. Eventually he did drop out. I don't know what happened to him after that.

Long Valley became a regular venue for our course. As another day came we halted with all the syndicates reunited as a Company. The senior NCOs were ordered to chase and catch the Officers in front as they ran in a circular route round a steep knoll. *Time for another breather*, I happily told myself. Once that the staff became bored of that game though, everyone was suddenly ordered down to the ground and to adopt the press-up position.

Just as with most of us, my forearms immediately disappeared, sinking fast up to the elbows in wet sand. I knew it was coming but I had hoped against hope that it wouldn't, and then it did. Staff screamed the order,

"Down!"

Bending at the elbow I dropped my chest to the ground, attempting to complete the first half of the press-up. My face and chest did a Titanic and became submerged and I could feel my wrists beginning to freeze in the cold and foul smelling mud. Someone shouted for us to rise up and then straightening my arms I pushed myself out of the sand and sucked hard to replenish my aching lungs with new air, just in time to hear the repeat order of, "Down!" The commands kept coming until the staff were completely satisfied that everyone had had a good ducking.

There were some who, when told to do their press-ups, luckily found themselves on an island of drier gravel. Luck was not with them for long though, for as soon as the instructors saw this they set about moving them until they too had that sinking feeling.

Finishing our now very routine daily BFT one morning we were quickly doubled away to change from our boots to regulation issued black canvas plimsolls. It took but a few scrambled mad seconds and we were back outside and forming a long line queuing to the gym. On the floor inside were placed blue and red exercise mats. All the mats had been carefully placed to form a large horse shoe shape. At the open end of the horseshoe was situated a single mat.

Once inside we were paired off. One of the instructors paired me with a lad that I knew from Pre-Para, Kenny Turk. Kenny was a Plant Operator from 9 Sqn. RE, an athletic bloke and quite distinct with his incredibly short crew cut blond hair set off against a deep bronzed tan. He had been with his Squadron for some time but because of overseas commitments he had not before had the chance to attempt P-Company. Each pair of soldiers was made to stand at ease on a mat.

With crossed swords emblazoned across his chest, the AI (Assistant Instructor, but pronounced ACK-EYE), cut a dashing figure as he effortlessly ran the length of the gym to take up position on the solitary mat at the front. As a Physical Training Instructor apprenticed to the resident staff of the APTC, the young Parachute Regiment Corporal looked impressively fit.

He shouted orders and at the same time he went into the routine of demonstrating some basic warm up exercises. Standing bent at the waist but with feet crossed I mirrored the Ackeye's stretching drill. I tried though not to think about all the nasty aches and pains that I felt whenever any of my ripped and torn muscles were stretched. Despite my best efforts, each movement forced a gentle moan. Seven or eight other exercises followed in quick succession.

He stopped, and then assumed the standing position of an accomplished gymnast. The Corporal swung his right hand out in front, traversing the braced men on their mats.

"You, out here!"

He had picked his volunteer, army style. The chosen one, with a nervous smile which failed to disguise his obviously worried face, sprinted to the NCO and stood in complete silence.

The volunteer had plenty to fear. The instructor, a bloke with so many muscles that he looked like he had sneaked cricket balls inside his skin, was there to revise us in the art of self-defence. A lightning flash later and the poor volunteer's legs flew upwards as the young man's wrist was suddenly bent double. It looked painful and judging by the agonising cries

The Devil Wears Maroon

136

from the volunteer, it was. Now more than ever I prayed that I would not be chosen as the next volunteer.

Continuing the movement, the Ackeye picked him up. Using just one hand, he pulled his victim upright. The victim showed visible relief as the pain began to subside but his reprieve disappeared when the instructor began a slow time repeat. He took us through the whole procedure again only this time allowing for pauses so that each technique could be explained. I found it difficult to take my eyes off his guinea pig that by now was obviously concerned to see that his wrist was now a very different shape.

The instructor demanded,

"Now you do it!" adding, "And go easy!"

There were immediate grunts and cries of pain followed by bodies landing heavily on the mats in an ungraceful thump. All around there were men wrestling across the floor. I felt sorry for the lone instructor who having realised that he had unleashed a wave of violence struggled to regain control. Screaming at the top of his voice he bellowed, "Take it easy!"

A more senior instructor on hearing the commotion left his office and entered into the fray shouting,

"As you were!"

Instantly the course stood still. Order was returned.

Both Kenny and I agreed that neither of us wanted broken bones and neither should we be as stupid as some of the other blokes had just been. We practised the movement fast and efficiently but when either of us felt any extra resistance to the technique, we released the pressure. By the sounds of pain elsewhere I don't think many others kept to a similar pact.

Time passed quickly and half way through the course when returning from a long hard tab, we inexplicably went straight past the entrance to the Barracks. Experience told me that this was probably a sickener, something done to test resolve. We tabbed and ran along the towpath of the Basingstoke canal and then onto Laffans Lane adjacent to the Army golf course. There, spanning the murky still waters of the largely disused canal, was a large steel girdered bridge. Typical of War Office design, it was somewhat box shaped and with its huge grapefruit sized rivets, it resembled a giant tunnel made from Meccano.

On the gravel across from the bridge we were halted in our syndicates and were turned about. I searched the surrounding area for any clues to what was coming next and I wondered what on earth they had in store for us this time?

The syndicates were quickly shoved closer to form a gaggle of soldiers on the bank. Thoughts of dread inside my head were repeatedly interrupted as loud voices from the P-Company staff went about separating the syndicates into two groups, which were then formed into file on either side of the bridge.

Horrified, I watched transfixed as the first man from each group was sent monkey fashion to crawl up the giant girders. Once up on the top some twenty feet above the road they were told what they should do next. Spanning the two main legs of the bridge were a number of much smaller girders of only around four inches across which then criss-crossed over each in a lattice.

On the shout of, "GO!" The two men slowly walked forward and crossed from one side of the bridge to the other and then back again. As those men progressed down the length of the structure the next pair was set off and so on. I could only watch mesmerised. I wondered how I would fare. I've always had a fear of heights. I know it sounds daft but perhaps surprisingly, there are loads of Parachutists who are awfully worried about heights and some too who hate parachuting.

My turn came around far too fast. An old enemy, the lump that forms in my throat then in my stomach when I'm scared, was back. My knees began to shake. I tried to force my legs to stay still but they wouldn't. I placed both hands onto the cold steel girder and paused. I felt as if everybody was watching me and was whispering about me. I looked up. I could see men all over the place and the one directly before me appeared to be in difficulties, which drew angry roars from the staff. The shouts aimed at the frightened soldier got louder and more intense but they failed to budge him from his perch.

I climbed up toward the stuck man. I looked down and it seemed an awful long way. I suppose that when my body height is added to the distance between my feet and the ground, it really was a long way. I stopped and looked past the roadway and down to the surface of the canal, it looked twice as far again. An instructor's voice boomed, waking me from my temporary trance.

"Right. Number 23! Move yourself!"

I asked myself that if the girders were on the ground would I have any difficulty in traversing them. The silent answer in my mind was a resounding no and so I convinced myself that this was not really any different from walking at ground level.

One part did cause me some concern, though I was careful not to show it. As I slowly stepped over one of the diagonal struts I came up against the bloke who was frozen with fear. He had sat down with both of his arms stretched forward and with whitened knuckles, gripped the metal supports. I was aware of the shouts from down on the road, which were aimed at the petrified soldier but up to then I had managed to shut them out. I was far more worried about my own precarious position.

Obeying a loud command meant for me, I stepped over the stricken man's arms, changing route to return back to the   side of the bridge where I had started. I was convinced then that the frightened man would suddenly reach up and make a grab for me sending us both tumbling to the road below. Fortunately for me, he stayed frozen to the girders. I continued over all the other girders and back again without displaying any problems.

Once down and back with the others who had by now also completed their bit, I turned to watch the strangely entertaining spectacle of the stuck youth. I was very surprised to learn just how many men had experienced such problems. Most were ordered to climb down but the one who had frozen in front of me had to be fetched by staff. Three instructors climbed up and gently manhandled the youth, coaxing him down.

Off the other side of the bridge and standing ready for whatever would come next we were pointed in the direction of the hilly training areas behind Aldershot. All the way up to and on the hills the instructors kept up their severe beasting. We were forced up and down the hills in sprints, hops and anything else considered to be competitive. Then we entered into a fast non-stop run back the way that we had come. I hoped very much that this spurt of madness by our instructors was just a temporary thing for us before we returned to barracks. However, I was wrong.

Our speed was slowed as we returned to the bridge that had caused so many problems for some earlier. We dropped down to the water's edge and waited underneath the bridge. Following instructions I removed my Bergen and joined a queue lining up with the others below one of the four giant girders spanning the canal. A shout from somewhere forced the line to split, producing four new teams and each placed below a girder. The task was to race across the canal by swinging like an ape along the steel girder.

The teams didn't start together. One started then with moans of, "Unfair!" the rest of them got started. Hanging at arm's length from the rusted iron, I threw my whole body into a pendulum motion. Everyone was to get to the other side. Perhaps surprisingly after what we had already physically completed that day, we were all successful.

Undaunted by our apparently unexpected success the staff simply turned us around and sent us back again. This time some of our course didn't make it all the way across and ended up with a ducking in the water. One by one soldiers disappeared into the dark stinking water to resurface coughing, spluttering and scrambling for the sandy bank. Getting filthy wet was bad enough, but there was also the embarrassment of having everyone else laughing at you which, in some way, felt far worse.

The exercise was repeated again and again until we few remaining, on seeing our wet but resting colleagues, realised that by far the easiest option was to let go and drop into the canal. I had originally wanted to beat the staff at this game. My confidence was high but it soon became obvious that no one was going to win. The Instructors would ensure that any survivors continued until they simply couldn't go on any longer. I was satisfied though that today I had scored some points with the staff.

My grip relaxed and I dropped the few feet into the water. The depth of the water was probably only a few feet but beneath that lay several more feet of rotting vegetation and silt. Without trying I managed to swallow plenty of the canal's foul liquid. The bitter taste jolted the back of my throat and at the same time I had this horrible feeling of freezing water spilling inside my clothes. It was a great relief for me to reach the bank where a couple of the lads took my hands and pulled me out. Nobody laughed this time, the joke had worn off. Everyone now was thoroughly cold and miserable.

I collected my Bergen, I was tired, dripping wet and smelled like rotting manure. My trousers were heavy with mud and being soaking wet, they clung to my legs, restricting any movement. We each had to find even greater strength just to move our legs. The syndicate began to move off further down the canal path and then instantly broke into a double. Being saturated I felt as though I was tied up. I had to force my legs to carry me through the awkward motion of bending my knees.

Each evening I made my bed into the neat regulation style and set about polishing the floor around my bed space so that it would be ready for the daily Barrack Room inspection for the following morning. Fortunately I had been detailed an easy Block job. All that I was required to do was empty the dustbins, wash them and then ensure that the area immediately surrounding the block was completely free of all litter. This included cigarette ends and matchsticks

P-Company was of course strictly a residential one but, as there weren't any attendance checks being made during the night, it was easy for me to sneak away and spend the night with my wife at my married quarter in Ramallies Park. Returning to Barracks each morning at about half past five when the others were just getting up meant that I was rarely missed.

One night, at around half way through the second week and whilst I was deep in sleep I was jolted awake with a hurried shaking from Janet. Through sleepy eyes I could see her leaning over me. Calmly but urgently she told me that her water had broken and that labour contractions had just begun.

Janet was well prepared. Everything that she would require in hospital was packed in a suit case and ready to go. In anticipation of just such an event my daughter had been allowed to stay with her Grandparents. I threw a dressing-gown over my shoulders and ran the short distance a little way down the road to the nearest telephone. An ambulance was sent for and Janet was rushed off to the Princess Louise Margaret maternity hospital in Aldershot. Once there, our unborn baby decided to take a rest, and nothing more happened for several more hours. By the early hours of the next day, the contractions had started again.

As I had done previously at the birth of my daughter, I stayed with my wife through her long painful morning, watching fascinated as my new son Terry entered the world of light and noise. Mother and child were fine and as well as could be expected. Not long after, both were exiled to a ward for some much earned rest.

Not owning a car, I was forced to run the two miles home to get washed and changed then with no time to spare I ran the next mile or so to the barracks, arriving slightly late. On entering the square I was just in time to see my syndicate parading for the daily roll call. As soon as the parade finished I marched up to my syndicate leader, Sgt Steve Ryder and quickly shared my good news then accompanied it straight away with the bad news that I had had virtually no sleep and more importantly for me, I requested some time off to be with my wife and son.

Naturally Steve congratulated me on the arrival of my son and then to my horror he turned to the syndicate waiting close by and told them of my news and that I would buy them all a drink. The lads cheered loudly but I said nothing. Turning back to me, Steve said that if it were up to him I could leave now, but the decision was not his to make. The CSM was the only man who could give authority for me to leave the course albeit temporarily, and he wouldn't arrive till nine.

I fell in with the others and went off to compete in the ritualistic daily BFT. On returning from the test and before going off to get changed, I snapped to attention and called to SGT Ryder. I never got the chance to ask him my question because he pre-empted me and sent me off without haste to the CMS's office.

CSM Rustell was liked and respected in the Company. He was a hard but fair man who also shared a keen sense of humour. He was famed amongst this course not just for his catchphrase but also for his apparent fascination with Hitler's military bodyguard.

One time when we were collapsing from exhaustion at the end of a hard day's forced march, he strutted amongst us, insulting and damning our very existence. That day and according to him we were unlikely to ever become paratroopers. He continued his tirade, telling us that we were the worst soldiers ever in the history of the world. Then he paused, took a breath and shouted a question, "What is the most effective fighting force ever known?"

Some of us, including me tried to impress by shouting the obvious answer,

"The Parachute Brigade Sir!"

To my surprise he suddenly and tersely disagreed, "Idiots! I meant the Waffen SS!"

He walked away seemingly further disappointed that we didn't know it.

I waited outside his office. When he arrived he glanced only very briefly in my direction. A scowl grew across his face as he sat down and called me in. By his expression I guessed that he was not at all pleased to see me. He likely thought that I was about to jack, asking for voluntary RTU. Inside, he sat quite still while I related my story so far. Interrupting close to my finish he stopped me and sent me outside to the corridor to wait for a while. All alone, I reflected that I was very unlikely to be given any time off. Hurtful as that was, I did fully understand why.

Steve Ryder came jogging along the corridor by the office. Without introduction the Sergeant Major demanded that Sgt. Steve Ryder inform him on how my progress had been on the course. Steve, with perhaps a little exaggeration, replied that I was well above average and that anything that I miss today could be made up later. With that the CSM called me back in. I could, he said, have the rest of the day off but he then went on to warn that I had better be back on time for tomorrow morning.

I went straight back to the hospital to be with my wife and baby. I needed transport quickly so that I could visit and then later on collect my family, so later on, I visited a dodgy second hand car dealer in Northcamp and managed to get talked into buying a heap of junk in the shape of an Austin Maxi.

The following day I returned to the barracks tired but ready. I came armed with cans of beer and packets of cigars for my mates in the syndicate and one or two others from different groups. I hadn't forgotten the favour that Steve Ryder had done me so I made sure that he was first in line for my gifts.

No sooner had I distributed the beer and smokes and we were off for our normal wake up jaunt of the BFT. Try as I did my time had barely improved since day one. I still couldn't break my target time of less than nine minutes. I was truly annoyed with myself because in Cyprus I was regularly running BFTs in under nine minutes.

Having earlier left our plimsolls in neat soldier like lines outside the gymnasium it was an easy guess where the next activity would take place. We lined up in the order that we finished the run and then the course was separated into halves. One half disappeared around the corner whilst we were turned to our right and were marched through the opened double doors of the gym.

The gymnasium was set out like an obstacle course or a training circuit. We lined the rear wall in two ranks and watched inward as one of the instructors explained today's exercise. There were ten sets of apparatus or stations where specific physical exercises were to be carried out. As one instructor talked, another raced from point to point pausing only to demonstrate each activity.

Then detailed into smaller groups ready to start on designated stations we stood patiently, waiting for a whistle blast. Each exercise was to be carried out and repeated as fast as possible for two minutes exactly. After the two minutes there would be a break of thirty seconds to recover. Then the whistle would be blown again and we would sprint to the next apparatus for a full two minutes of that activity's incredibly tiring work. The promise was that, provided we work hard enough, then the duration of each of the following exercises would decrease whilst the restful thirty seconds may increase to a whole minute. Needless to say, none of the instructors seemed convinced enough that we were working well. So the exercises got longer and the breaks got shorter.

Through every sweat producing, muscle aching, agonising exercise whether climbing up ropes, doing squat thrusts or even those damned burpees, there always seemed to be an instructor barely inches from my face screaming some sort of abuse. They insulted me, they called me disgusting names and that made me angry. I am sure now that, that was exactly what they had wanted. They were good; because of their treatment of me I worked bloody hard. I wanted to show them that they were wrong and that I was better than they were.

At the end and dizzy with a lack of oxygen the activities stopped. A lone PTI said calmly,

"Well done."

Then we and the other squads were back outside the gym in double time. With no time to shower, no time to even talk I changed into boots and webbing and pulled my Bergen onto my back. With that I fell in outside with the rest. We were off for another run.

After lunch we once more went out as a complete course. Out into the training areas we stopped on top of a high ridge behind Caesars Camp. Off the ridge were a series of seven sandy tracks lined with gravel. Each sloped downward for about fifty metres and descended to a track in the valley below. The tracks have taken the name of a set of hills on the Downs. They were known to us as, 'The Seven Sisters'.

CSM Rustell obviously feeling pretty fit, challenged the entire course to race him up and down all seven of the sisters. Down the first then up the next and so on until the end then a quick turnaround to do it all back again. Any of us, he said, who could beat him back to the beginning would be excused all duties for the rest of the day. Suddenly he was away. Determined to stay with him I stuck at his heels, running hard and forcing my legs apart to take uncomfortable strides up hill.

Before the end of the second sister most of the blokes were gone already, having fallen back behind. I gritted my teeth. I was still there as were several other lads, including two from 59 Commando. At the fourth sister I found myself reluctantly dropping back. Only a few yards at first but the gap was slowly widening. The Commandos and a small group of others were still up there with our sprinting Warrant Officer but as I finished the climb on the sixth slope I annoyingly passed the Sgt Major coming down the other way. By now nobody was even close to him. He eventually finished clear ahead of every one of us. Nobody had earned their day off. I was later informed that Ernie Rustell was a man who liked to run up mountains for fun.

After breakfast on the next day the syndicates were dressed in red PT vests and blue thigh length shorts. The roll was called and we comfortably doubled away to the playing fields behind the barracks. Two men arrived dragging with them huge nets in which were a number of medicine balls. The strangely named balls were made from softened leather and were around three times the size of a regulation football but at about fifteen pounds, they were much heavier.

As dictated by one of the instructors, several men scurried away trying frantically to grab a quota of balls and deliver them at intervals along different imaginary lines. After a quick shouted order I raced to join some others to stand adjacent to a solitary ball. Paired off two to a ball we shoved and pushed our way through to get as near as possible to a ball. Having reached one I grabbed it up from the ground and turned inward to face my partner.

The exercises included throwing the ball to each other as fast as our arms would allow and woe betide the fool who dropped his ball. Holding the great ball to our chests, each of us then had to sprint down to the end of the long line of soldiers in and out of the stationary men who had by now formed a slalom on the grass. Once at the end, an identical journey back again was made so as to be able to pass the ball to another ready for his turn.

After half a mornings work with the big brown ball all but one of them was scooped up and replaced in the nets. The four syndicates were then merged so that they could split again, this time into two large groups. On the football pitch the next activity to was to be Murder Ball.

An easy definition for the game Murder ball would be a game played indoors or outdoors by at least two groups of men. The objective is to score points by getting the medicine ball into a goalmouth by employing any means possible. There are few if any rules.

The two sides stood opposing each other at either end of the pitch. Some were obviously a little apprehensive whilst others still seemed quite excited by the prospect of imminent yet apparently legal violence. A solitary ball was carried into the centre of the pitch by one of the instructors. He looked all around to ensure that both teams were properly behind their lines. As it fell from his hands the great ball fell thudded to the damp ground, the game was on. More than eighty screaming men with blood in their eyes erupted into a maddening sprint for the ball. Adrenaline surged through our veins like high octane fuel. There's a fear in this game but God, I loved it!

A bloke from the other team got to the ball first. With great skill he scooped the ball up to his chest and charged right through the few men who initially stood in his way. Hardly had another second passed and he was down, trapped under a tangle of crashing bodies. With fists and boots flailing about it was a dangerous place to be but each man that could get a hand on the ball then fought bloody hard to keep it there.

Through the maddening crowd I could clearly see a patch of unoccupied earth which exposed the precious sight of leather. For the first time since the game had started, the ball became visible to me. In a dive that James Bond would have been proud of, I lunged towards the ball, reaching then clasping my hands around its bloated shape. Unfortunately, though I didn't originally realise it, several others from both teams shared an identical idea, which ultimately led to the same lack of success. Underneath the wrestling men above, a three-way tug-o-war ensued. With both of my hands dug firmly into the leather of the ball I pulled with all my might. I had a real chance to be part of the game and come what may, I wasn't about to give that up easily.

Instead of the ball coming to me, I found that I was being dragged along with the ball and was sliding through the muddy turf. In a desperate effort to reverse momentum I drove my toes into the churning green but it was all in vain. I pushed and I pulled then suddenly I was there right over the ball and there was absolutely nothing between us. I dragged it in, hugging it tightly. Hardly believing my good fortune I attempted to stand ready to run for the goal.

I could feel men from my own side pulling me away from the crowd and towards them but at the same time others were grabbing at my hair and my clothing. I was trapped in a sea of hands. I looked up and as I did my eyes just caught a lightning fast glimpse of a massive fist as it came hurtling down to land squarely between my eyes pushing the bridge of my nose completely flat. As the punch landed a flash of bright light stunned me and at the same time a deafening crack thundered through my head. Pain seared upward travelling like electricity through the bones and formed tiny agonising whirlwinds around my eyes. Tears of stinging torment poured from their ducts and I tasted the warm salty trickle of blood leaking from my nostrils.

The puncher had forced me to let go of the ball with one hand. In a combination of trying to keep my grip on the ball and instinctively reeling from this ferocious attack, I found myself down, on my side and sliding backward but somehow still with my prize. Involuntarily I brought my legs under my chest folding up into a protective foetal position. Realising that if I stayed where I was there could only be more pain and certainly no chance of scoring, I threw my body forward and upward. Once on my feet I began to run, at first it was anywhere just to get clear, then I focussed and ran for the goal.

I held the ball rugby fashion, fending off attackers with my free hand. I was *enjoying a truly great adrenaline high. This was brilliant. Sadly though just when I* thought that I might take the opening points, my glory came to a sharp and abrupt end. Sheer weight of numbers swamped my progress and once again I was forced to the ground. With more misfortune than luck I fell onto the ball in a surely misguided attempt to keep hold of it. This brought a frenzy of instant violence and all of it aimed at me. For a while I may as well have been the ball. Pulled, kicked and stomped by the countless legs of the mob I was obliged into differing and awkward positions. The ball was all too soon violently wrenched from my arms and I never saw it again.

Throughout, the game was abruptly halted as angry staff remonstrated with the over keen soldiers. "Murder Ball is the name! It doesn't have to be the game!"

An exhausting eternity of running, wrestling and thumping eventually passed and the game was brought to a calm and satisfactory end. Neither team had managed to score but everyone, including me and my sore nose, thoroughly enjoyed it.

From outside the army, Murder Ball doesn't immediately conjure up all the right images but there is a very real value to this game. Such activities allow young men to rid themselves of pent up aggression and at the same time, our trainers get the chance to see who might display courage along with physical dexterity. And if nothing else, it's a good stress break.

It was toward the end of the initial two weeks that besides our daily BFT, we were to be pushed into the first real test. We were often assured, 'Everything is a test' but this test set a rigid standard. The Two-Mile Combat Fitness Test (CFT) was strangely peculiar to Airborne Forces. Basically a fast race of two miles whilst wearing full Combat Effective Fighting Order (CEFO pronounced Seefoh) which comprises combat clothing including the wearing of a parachutists helmet and a full set of webbing complete with respirator, water bottle and all accessories. Of course this test must also include the carrying of the soldier's personal weapon. Usually this would be my SLR but in common with the rest of the course, I was to carry an Argie' FN.

The entire course of men were marched to the back gate near the bridge over the canal. We were lined up and told that a PTI would be waiting opposite the Queens Hotel and he would be the half way mark where we would be turned around to run the return trip.

An air horn blasted and suddenly we were away. Other than long distance, the initial part of any race is always the most difficult for me. My legs and lungs let me know of their struggle to cope with the dramatic increase in demand by wheezing uncomfortably for more air. This race was no exception. I was wheezing like an old man.

A time limit had been set for the test at fifteen minutes. Most people or at least those who run any distance regularly may think that completing a distance of just two miles in under a quarter of an hour should be a relatively easy task. In reality, having to wear heavy and clumsy clothing strapped to your body would be bad enough. Add to that a rifle weighing in at twelve pounds and long enough to require both hands to hold it, anybody would be slowed down. This test is run as a race and it's very bloody hard! I got to the turn-around point in under seven minutes and though I was physically wrecked I nevertheless remained confident of achieving a pretty good time. The return mile saw me passing several other men, some of whom had all but given up and were now walking, foolishly trying to convince themselves that they could still achieve a good time.

As I approached the gates searching my veins for a reserve of energy, I pushed my legs hard. I had squeezed that last drop of stamina to reach what I thought was the end, but when I got to the gates, the perceived finish, an NCO instructor directed me further on. I rounded the corner, hoping that the finish line was surely going to be right there but once again I was to be disappointed. A different instructor ushered me on again this time toward the barrack blocks. At last the end was now in sight. It was only another few hundred yards but I was already exhausted. I had to keep going. All of a sudden, it was there and I crossed the line triumphantly and with a respectable time of thirteen minutes and forty seconds.

I was happy with that and I was even happier to see much of the course behind me but still coming in.

It was late afternoon on the second Friday and it was nearing our going home time. Course personnel were allowed to leave the barracks on weekends providing they hadn't pulled a guard duty or similar. Standing at ease in three ranks outside the accommodation block we listened as the syndicate Sergeant called the nominal roll. My name was called out and I instinctively snapped to attention and shouted,

"Sir!"

This was an acknowledgment that though Steve was a SNCO he called the roll on behalf of the OC. Quickly completed, Steve pushed his worn card clipboard under his arm and squeezed his hands tightly together. Glancing up and down as he walked, the Sergeant casually inspected the men in his charge. All of us were dressed in smart civvies ready for our excursion home. The Regiment no longer demanded that its personnel wore a collar and tie but they did however insist that everyone was clean and tidy. After all, they reasoned, these men when outside were ambassadors for the Parachute Regiment and the Airborne Brigade.

In common with most of the blokes I was in 'Airborne Uniform'. Almost obliged to wear it, I wore fawn coloured suede boots known colloquially as 'dezzies'. Along with the dezzies I had straight cut blue jeans and a maroon T-shirt. Most of us were near identically dressed.

In the rear rank though, one bloke stood out like a sore thumb. John Dyer was an ex-civilian Police Constable who joined the army in search of adventure and was now serving with the RMP. He was a Corporal hoping for a place with the small but semi-elite Para Provost. This big fair-haired man gazed from behind thick rimmed sunglasses at the front ranks who in turn arched their necks to stare at him.

John's glowing white arms shone lamp like from the sleeveless brightly coloured Hawaiian shirt that he proudly wore opened over his chest. Its multi-patterned material disappeared into the tops of his cut off and frayed surfer shorts. Under his exposed feet he displayed open toed red plastic flip-flop sandals.

Looking like he was about to have an epileptic fit, Steve Ryder pointed a shaking finger at the young Corporal before tersely asking where it was that he thought he was going and especially dressed like that? Corporal Dyer replied in a calm, almost laid back tone, "What's wrong with it?"

Loud roars of laughter erupted first from the syndicate and then it spread to the other syndicates standing close by. Giggles and shouts from all directions filled the air.

A Sergeant Instructor from the REME who was in charge of another syndicate came over. Bent nearly double and with a grin which threatened to split his face, he slapped his palms onto his knees. His mouth stretched wide open as he let slip an earth shattering guffaw. Trying to straighten himself the REME Sergeant momentarily pointed at Dyer. He attempted to say something but was quickly overcome with hysterics and he creased up once more. By now the laughter had spread right across the course. Dyer though remained unmoved. He attempted a smile, trying hard not to burst out laughing with the others.

John Dyer had dared to do something which at that time just wasn't done, he dressed like a civilian and in our little world it was not only unacceptable, it was hilarious. In the Brigade, such clothes were known as 'Fuck off' clothes simply because if you ever wore them near an airborne soldier, you were quickly told to fuck off.

Sensing the approach of the CSM, Steve Ryder snapped out an order bringing the syndicate to immediate control and to attention. The other syndicates swiftly followed suit. The Sgt Major stood everyone at ease and so that he could address them all he bunched the four syndicates closer. CSM Rustell paced up and down along the front ranks watching the ground and only occasionally glancing upwards. Then returning to find some centre ground he went into a lecture which warned soldiers that if they were to be in trouble in Aldershot that weekend, whether or not it's their fault, they should expect military discipline procedures to follow. Worse than that, they should also expect an immediate RTU! The consequences being that a troubled soldier would not be allowed to complete the course.

CSM Rustell turned, feet apart and faced a central point within the paraded men. He had barely finished his sentence   wishing us a good and happy weekend when his attention was drawn to the rear rank. Something that was just not quite right. He spun on his heels and instantly confronted Corporal Dyer.

"Where in God's name do you think you're going?" He demanded! Pulling his arms tightly into his sides, the hapless Corporal replied,

"Into town Sir."

There was something in his tone, which questioned the CMS's authority. Reddening with rage the slim Warrant Officer shouted sharply, then comparing him to a Californian beach bum, ordered Dyer to change out of his awful coloured rags. Corporal Dyer now quite embarrassed at being the star of such unwanted attention and fearful at receiving the wrath of the mighty CSM, squirmed uncomfortably, wishing that he could just slip away somewhere unseen.

"I haven't got anything else", Dyer pleaded softly. Without a change in expression the CSM promised,

"Outside my office in half an hour dressed suitably or I'll find you some work uniform this weekend!"

The course was dismissed and several of us rallied round to support John Dyer. Everyone thought that he was a bit of a twat to try a stunt like this but that was just him. He was still part of our course and our syndicate, he was one of us. I was not unique in offering John the loan of some clothes to get him out of the pickle that he had landed himself in but he refused all help insisting that he could find something of his own. I didn't see John again during that weekend so I trusted that he knew what he was doing and that he did indeed have an alternative dress. I've never forgotten that day and in a way, I quietly admired John.

Chip Walker

Having been told to relax and be ready for Test Week on Monday and before the course was allowed to fall out, a hand went up and from one of the other groups, signalling a need to speak. The hand belonged to a SSGT of the RAPC. The Sgt Instructor there called to him, asking what he wanted. Everyone looked over wanting to know who was holding us up now. The Pay Corps Staff Sgt then said, "Is it ok if I run a marathon race on Sunday?" For several seconds, there was just silence as nobody knew what to say. Eventually, the Instructor simply said, "Fill ya boots." Murmurs flew around the men, 'Cocky bastard!"

During that weekend whilst off duty, several course members including some from my own syndicate got a little drunk and had ended up in one of the town's tattoo parlours. All of them had got themselves adorned with one or another of the embellishments representing airborne forces. More than one at least had the winged Pegasus tattooed on his buttocks.

As a proud soldier from the skies a keen young soldier may well be happy to show off his badges and might even want it tattooed right across his chest in great big letters, but what would happen, I asked, if they fail the course?

157

CHAPTER TEN

TEST WEEK

Here at the beginning of Test Week, the third and final week of the course, each soldier or student as they became increasingly known, is started with a set amount of points. A perfect student could theoretically finish P-Company with maximum points remaining intact. Of course there could never be any such thing as a perfect student. Everybody loses points somewhere along the way. Certain standards, both physical and mental, and deemed vital to Airborne Forces, are set and anything, which even slightly deviates from those standards will result in a loss of points.

Throughout the course instructors had been closely monitoring our progress. Some soldiers had already failed but didn't yet know it. For the rest the next few days were crucially important. There was no further training, now came the time to be counted. Dropping out of any activity now for any reason would mean an instant RTU and with that would come deep shame.

Monday morning started with the Milling. To the uneducated onlooker Milling was a barbaric act that served no purpose other than to feed a primitive blood lust but, to the military, Milling is a most valuable test. Once common throughout the British Army it became an almost exclusive event to the Airborne Forces. In a one minute bout fought between two soldiers of roughly equal size, Milling resembles boxing. Both soldiers would be wearing heavy sixteen-ounce boxing gloves and though welcome, the object is not to display skill and prowess inside the boxing ring but to show a good measure of controlled aggression and enough pure courage often in the face of certain defeat. At the end of what seems the longest one minute ever a winner is chosen. He needn't be the true victor. It could be that the fighter who received the most blows displayed the finest qualities and therefore could be chosen as the winner.

We were paraded as a course then we entered the gymnasium in syndicates. From the press-up position I tried to keep rhythm with a bellowing instructor,

"Down!...Up!...Down!."

It was repeated through a good number of press-ups. This was nothing completely new but I was beginning to wonder just what exactly was going on? After several minutes of activities and whilst still down in the press-up position, a command came for us to stop and to stay still. One of the staff shouted his instructions explaining that we must remain in this position with arms properly extended. Just then most of the staff casually left the room. I didn't know why we were left there or for how long we would be expected to stay like this? *Was this a test?* I couldn't answer any of the questions racing through my head. I made up my mind to treat this as a test, thinking, *I'll stay here until told different.*

After a couple of minutes of silently remaining in the position, the strain on my arms became quite painful. Forcing my elbows to lock tight I tried desperately to focus my thoughts elsewhere. All around me blokes were breathing noisily, grunting with great effort and though clenched teeth. Repeatedly my mind's attention returned to the difficulties that I was then experiencing. I knew that the worse thing to do was to dwell on the pain; instead I concentrated intensely on other things. Selecting a single thought I focused on films that I had recently seen.

In front of me and from another syndicate, squatted a black bloke. I didn't know his name; I'd just seen him around. He had a fantastic body being built just like Frank Bruno the boxer. He had arms, which were about the size of my thighs, but it wasn't his build that attracted my attention though, he was moaning loudly. In an apparent effort to shift his burdening weight he kept fidgeting. He shifted his hands around first this way then that way but all of it appeared to be in vain. From beside him I heard a comrade daring to break the strict silence by whispering some encouragement, "Keep it going Mate! Come-on!"

I too was anonymously urging him on when quite by surprise, this wonderfully sculptured man became the first in the room to collapse into an exhausted heap onto the wooden floor. Part of me pitied him while another part of me now saw him in contempt. I looked at him and hoped sincerely that I drew him as an opponent in the coming Milling. Anyone, I figured that gives in that easy couldn't be anything for me to worry about.

As more lengthy minutes passed by, more bodies crashed. I had to keep going. I told myself that only the weak would capitulate.

Looking down I could see that a large puddle had formed beneath my head and chest. It was sweat; it was just sweat but loads of it. I was then foolish enough to relax my guard and had allowed my mind to think about the situation. My arms and shoulders immediately began to twitch in agonising spasms. Voices from my inner self screamed surrender but voices of equal resolve convinced my warring conscience to stick with it. I knew that this test, if that was what it was, could not last much longer.

Ten immensely long minutes went slowly by before the instructors returned and allowed us a rest. Of the entire course of still more than eighty men only about twenty of us had managed to remain in the press-up position. One member of the staff made an immediate beeline for our syndicate and announced triumphantly that we were the best for we were the group with the fewest number of drop outs.

Some men were detailed off to assist in the building of our make shift boxing ring. They used four long wooden benches to mark out a square. At one end of the wooden square were pushed two large vaulting boxes, these were to be the judges chairs occupied by the Major and his cohorts. Surrounding the ring were placed additional rows of benches ready to sit the waiting fighters.

A command was shouted, "Tallest on the right! Shortest on the left!" In a moment of organised chaos the large group of men suddenly broke formation and began to swarm about, apparently disorientated. Taking control, an NCO physically took hold of the easily found tallest candidate by the shoulder and dragged him over to the far wall. Pointing sharply to the floor and at the gangly youth's feet the NCO snapped, "Stand there! Right, you lot! Fall in!" There was some hesitation, "Sort yourselves out!" Within seconds everything was as if the men had followed some great plan. The entire course stood in a single line with the heights of the men's shoulders getting higher until they reached the stationary tallest man.

Responding to the instructions the right hand man shouted, "One!" The fellow on his left then returned a "Two!" The next man in the line repeated the shouted number one. This continued until every man had shouted out either a number one or a number two. Those who had become number twos were told to stand immediately behind their adjacent number ones. The pairing off appeared complete.

In front of me stood a young lad from 7 Para RHA. Smiling to myself I thought this encounter to be a lucky one. My number one, though the same height was really skinny and he was wearing thick plastic rimmed spectacles. I didn't know him but he looked a bit of a wimp. My confidence soared.

The CSM walked up and down inspecting the line, visually weighing up each pairs. Selecting and swapping, he constantly moved men about until he felt happy that there was an even match. He approached me. I shut my eyes and like a small child I willed him to ignore us. I was whispering inside my head that this was indeed a good pairing and that he should leave us alone! To my great despair my number one was taken away and placed further on down the line and matched elsewhere. At six feet one, I was one of the tallest in the room but at that moment I tried very hard to look small. I wanted the CSM to find me someone who looked an easy victim. I waited with trepidation to get a look at the new number one but as he got closer, dire realisation sank heavily to my stomach.

The bloke who now stood before me, I swear, looked evil. As a Craftsman in the REME he was only vaguely known to me. I didn't know his real name, I'm not sure if anyone did. We simply knew him as 'Animal'. He looked much like a young Charles Bronson complete with black hair and a Mexican style moustache. His face was taut, almost expressionless and across the tops of his eyes protruded a Neanderthal ridge of hard bony flesh. I studied my opponent's well contoured body. It rippled with rock solid sinewy muscle and great blue veins
stood proud along the length of his huge biceps. I swallowed hard and quietly wished that I were somewhere else.

With my best efforts to show, 'Little boy lost' eyes, I looked pleadingly to any of the staff who happened to glance this way and telepathically begged someone to find me a more suitable partner. When one of the staff started to approach, I thought I had struck gold. Words raced through my head as I planned what I would say but when the instructor reached the front of the line it was not me he spoke to but instead turned to my number one and enquired, "Alright?" With the slightest of movements accompanied with a simple grunt, my partner simply nodded and the instructor sauntered away listlessly. Telepathy is fine I thought but next time I should be sure of the wavelength.

Together in our pairs we were squeezed onto the low benches forming the square. Remembering an old boxing maxim that many a fight was won in the dressing room I turned to my rival and with a psychological act that would have impressed Clint Eastwood I whispered,

"I hope you know a good plastic surgeon".

I waited for a second, anticipating his reply then with the rest of his body remaining motionless the man's head ever so slowly turned until his eyes met mine. His mouth stayed virtually closed so that only his top lip moved, commencing a curl upward to bare teeth. He said nothing, there was no sound. Then just as slowly, my angered challenger looked away. Telepathy was working fine now. It was easy to understand that I may have just made the mother of big mistakes.

Further down the line some of the staff were openly congratulating those soldiers who had been given the opportunity to fight a commissioned officer. They were being encouraged to be overzealous in their task whilst staff explained that they may never again in their career get a chance to strike an officer legally.

The OC effortlessly vaulted onto the box and sat down. Legs crossed he addressed the waiting course. The rules he said were simple,

"No Biting, Head butting or kicking!"

He added that he wanted to see a good fight.

"There must be no crying and no stopping unless the latter was by my order."

He went on to explain that if any of us failed to impress him, then the fight would continue until he did become suitably impressed.

"Those sitting down having finished their bout or waiting for their turn must shout encouragement!" With that he sat back and motioned to the staff on the floor below him to carry on.

The first two stood up. Either side of a Sergeant, they paused to face the OC. Major Kennett nodded his head and the opposing fighters were dispatched to their relative corners. A blast of a whistle followed and out they came, fists flying. In seconds one had dropped on all fours. The downed soldier shook his head trying to clear the sudden fogginess that now clouded his brain and unconsciously sprayed blood from his wounded nose over an eager audience.

Angry shouts from the course staff stung the man and he struggled to raise himself. The crowd hadn't for a second let up in their cheering and in doing so offered support until, feeling battered he clambered to his feet. More shouts followed, "Punch him!" "Kill him!" A repeat blast of the whistle signalled the fighters to continue. Having gained a quick and powerful victory the strong attacker leaped forward for the kill. The other bloke, now bloodied, bowed his head, closed his eyes and went in to meet his foe. In the time that it took the men to close the distance, the losing soldier sustained another ten or twelve blows about his head. The attacker realising that his rain of punches had not yet achieved the desired result changed tack, throwing jabs at the poor man's undefended torso.

164

The weaker of the two swung his arms around his opponent's waist and hugged him in a misguided attempt to find shelter from the unwanted onslaught. A blue sleeved arm belonging to a Sergeant reached in and prised them apart. A pace was set between them then the Sergeant turned to the battered fighter and insisted, "Keep your head up and fight!" Both men raised their gloves and the Sgt stepped clear. The whistle was blown again and a fighter went instantly crashing backwards. A shock stare of disbelief beamed across the ring. The man who had just now been the battered and sorrowful victim had seen the overconfident exposed chin of his rival and even before the Sgt had forced a sound from his whistle a fist was already flying upwards finding contact with a perfect target. Soldiers squatting down on the wooden benches pushed violently at the stunned fighter, forcing him back into the ring again where both men met and exchanged further blows. Finally the whistle went bringing the bout to an end. Silence descended and both men stood side by side awaiting judgement.

An NCO took hold of the men's wrists and turned to face the Major. The OC eyed both men, then with an outstretched hand, pointed to the lad with the bloody nose. With his hand held aloft, a roar of approval from the floor brought the victor into a bewildered smile.

My mate Tommy Onions was paired with the Pay Corps bloke who last week had astounded everyone by asking for permission to run a marathon just before the start of this special week.

Tommy recounted, "I looked across, eyeballed the twat for being so fucking cocky, The Boss picked up the Bell....Ding, ding. I literally sprinted across the floor bringing my left arm backwards in what seemed like slow motion, as we came together I swung it round like a classic haymaker. In my mind the fist was going to make contact smack bang on his chin, but he made an extra step on me, instead of his chin my left inner forearm crashed into the right side of his skull. He went bowling over the mats onto the floor. Watching the entire inside of my arm instantly turn purple, I screamed in pain. I turned to look at him, he stood up, wobbling as he did so. Then he started to shuffle over to me once more.

Then it began. Swipe after swipe from each of us. What seemed like an hour of smashing the shit out of each other was only in fact about 15 secs. Those 16 oz gloves all of a sudden weighed about 5 lbs each. The desire to beat this cocky tosser gave me the inner strength to push the pain from my left arm and to try and beat the shit out of my opponent. Arms became weak, I tried to use uppercuts to reduce how high I had to raise my arms. I needed to hit him, once, twice, three times Staff shouted at me to lift my arms. Then, like Big Ben going off ....*Dinga ring a ring*. I was pulled off him, my nose balancing on his right shoulder, I was snorting something, couldn't work out what until I brushed my right glove over my nose....It was blood, although I didn't know then whether it was his or mine.

Staff pushed us to each side and grabbed my left wrist and turned both of us towards the God of Bosses sitting in their all-seeing positions. All three of them looked at each other and then after what seemed like an age, the Major looked directly into my bloodshot eyes, paused and said "Skins". It didn't initially register, I looked to my left and saw the Pay Corps Knob jockey drop his head, I had won, I had beat this guy. I had won my bout and the elation was beyond words.

Each pair of men rose in turn to do battle. Some proved to be quite skilled in the ring, easily overpowering their opponents. Others offered a fight more suited to a pantomime. Such fights were halted and the soldiers warned of the consequences. One bout lasted three times as long because the OC was unhappy

166

with their weak effort. He described their attempt at combat with a single word, "Pathetic!"

The first of the bouts to involve an officer brought louder than usual cheering from the men on the benches. The staff sported broad grins as a young subaltern stood next to his given partner. Both men were fairly well built and were obviously strong and fit. In mutual respect each man eyed the other's brawny body.

Once that the fight had started both men exchanged heavy blow for heavy blow. The young Lieutenant was swiftly caught unawares and a strike to his forehead sent him staggering uncontrollably backwards. Undeterred, he went straight back, wading in with arms flailing about. His opponent, temporarily caught in the middle of this wild onslaught, was unsure how to cope with it and tried desperately to avoid the threatening shower of punches. In less time than it took for him to take two paces back he regained his fighting superiority over the officer and fiercely jabbed at the young man's head.

His fists were raised but he was no longer throwing punches, the officer must have been praying for the end when thankfully the sharp screech of the whistle blast ended his painful punishment. He fought well but to the delight of the baying crowd the fight went to his jabbing rival.

The spectacle staged before me had kept me entertained, so much so that I had quite forgotten that I too faced imminent death at the hand s of the beast they called 'Animal'. As the pair of men next to me stood ready to fight I felt the unwanted but familiar pangs of anxiety begin to ripple through my body. Through the corners of my eyes I studied my competitor searching for any sign of weakness. Instead my eyes bulged and my chin dropped to the floor. His veins really were pulsing! I could see them pumping up and down.

Together we walked into the centre of the square and turned to face the Major.

"Number twenty three Sir!"

I blurted it out using a volume far greater than was actually required. Animal followed suit by shouting out his number in equal volume. Our Sergeant Instructor stood between us forcing a safe distance. He wagged a finger like an angry teacher and warned us to fight hard and to give a good show. I turned to face my temporary enemy and managed a weak begging smile. He however remained expressionless.

Chaperoned to opposing corners we turned ready for the start. The whistle was blown and I went for him. To my horror he was already steaming full ahead and almost on me. His nostrils flared and in that instant I took several well aimed punches full in the face. Launching into an instinctive defensive attack I became a fighting thresher with arms powerfully swinging through great circles in the air, daring Animal to interrupt their flight. Unfortunately, he did.

Finding this animal just a little too dangerous I protectively raised my arms and backed off trying very hard to put some distance between us. To my rear some spectators stood up and pushed me forward and back into the path of the beast. Quite accidentally my legs got tangled with his and in his haste to restore some independent mobility he lost balance and fell backwards, landing on his arse with a resounding thump. Presuming that Animal was floored because I had knocked him down, the audience let rip with a massive cheer and for the first time I could hear chants of my name. Fortune though was not yet ready to smile on me as without even a second to check his condition, Animal threw himself into another frenzied attack.

For a few long seconds we stood with feet firmly anchored to the floor, simply exchanging blows. I knew well when I got hit, each time there was a flash and my mind registered the fact but there was no pain. I didn't lose my temper, I was in control and fully mentally alert throughout but I didn't have a plan and I felt like I needed one. Every time one of my punches landed, a point was notched somewhere in my brain. The welcome sight of redness as blood trickled slowly from Animal's mouth boosted my confidence fuelling my determination. Pumped with the success of first blood I increased the tempo of my still uncoordinated and fairly wild punches.

The bout should last for only one minute but already it felt like that minute had long passed, I was wishing it to hurry up and end. It was as if time had somehow become suspended. My forearms in particular appeared completely drained of all energy and I could barely find enough strength to even lift them. Subconsciously, a hardened will to protect myself took over and seeking respite I instinctively hugged my opponent. A Sgt quickly stepped in to prise us apart but without a moment's thought I found myself again closely bear hugging Animal. I was aware of a shout from the Major's box though it didn't immediately register. We were halted and pushed towards the fuming commander. He bitterly warned me that I must keep my head up and to stay a respectable distance from my partner, otherwise, he explained, he would have me stay in the ring until I did so.

The prospect of staying in the ring for any longer than was absolutely necessary must have done the trick because as the whistle signalled recommencement, I viciously attacked my bewildered opposite number. The fury of my sudden assault clearly shook him, as the man who had just now nearly frightened me to death started to back off seeking sanctuary from his corner. The bombardment from my fists was perhaps unguided but it was working and I continued to thrash Animal to the edge of the square.

Thankfully the final whistle was blown before Animal could recover and once more we stood separated by our Sergeant and ready to receive judgement from the OC. I was panting wildly just grateful that it was at last truly over, but then I started to worry and in my head I questioned what if the boss decides that he still isn't happy and that we should continue? There was a pause, and then the OC nodded his head approvingly and pointed to Animal. I was happy with that, he was the deserving victor. My colleagues cheered and clapped supportably and I returned to my seat where several of the blokes congratulated me on the fight. They were convinced that I had at least put up a brave fight against a man who was considered to be a fearsome adversary.

Later, Animal came over to speak with me. We shook hands and gladly agreed that there should be no hard feelings. Realisation forced me to accept that Animal was after all an ordinary man. As we spoke I studied his face for signs of any injuries. I felt rather proud to see that his lower lip was swollen and red with congealed blood coating its small but neat tear. There were other lumps too so obviously caused by the beating he had just sustained. When he left I went straight away to the toilets to seek a mirror where I could examine the extent of my own injuries. Much of my body was now very tender to the touch and over my right eye I sported the tell-tale signs of swelling and blackening bruises.

After the last pair had fought their bout, a lone Lieutenant got up from his seat. The course now had an odd number of soldiers and this resulted in having one man left over after the earlier pairing. This subaltern had not yet been given a partner. Some of the staff turned to face each other, smiles widening their already happy faces. Like boy scouts excited at their first jamboree, they scurried about searching for the soldier best suited in their view to be this officer's combatant.

Fingers pointed and some comments were made and quickly discussed. A big man with closely cropped blond hair was brought to his feet. I didn't know him but I did recognise him as a man that earlier had sent his Milling partner crashing to a rather nasty defeat. The imminent prospect of this man beating the patiently waiting officer obviously pleased the men of the course. Smiles led to cheers and whoops of joy as the rank and file got firmly behind the chosen candidate.

The formalities were completed quickly and the bout was started. The blond skinhead ripped mercilessly into the unprepared young Lieutenant. A vicious upper cut slugged the officer's jaw. Even sat where I was in the audience I clearly heard the satisfying crunch of bone as a heavy glove exploded on the man's face. Reeling, the officer bounced away backward in a half somersault. He crumpled to the floor in a semiconscious lump. The men shouted loud undisguised approval. Through the crowd, the MO ran forward and immediately began pulling the Lieutenant into the recovery position. Major Kennett looked down to the MO for confirmation that his charge had not suffered any serious damage. He had in fact sustained a fracture to his cheek bone and a mild concussion. He made it though and he was later back with us.

At the completion of each P-Company test an award was made of a pennant mounted upon a lance and given to the syndicate that the staff agreed had contributed most to or had done the best. I'm not sure who won this one but I do know it wasn't my syndicate.

The ten mile tab started off in packets of half syndicates with each being led by a member of staff. The staff, all wearing identical maroon coloured sweatshirts topped with their cherished berets looked comfortable while we were feeling definitely over dressed in our heavy helmet, combat jackets, PT vest, Boots and Denims and at the same time of course, we also had our FN rifles, webbing and Bergen.

The pace was fast. A Corporal from the Depot staff was out in front leading the way. His natural gait as he stretched his forward leg was strangely very wide. He had his head down and his arse up and with both hands gripping its stock he swung his rifle in motion with his steps. Attempting to use his experience I mimicked his action and matched each of his movements with one of my own.

The tab was a fifty-fifty mix of fast marching and running. After a couple of miles had passed, our syndicate became fragmented and spread over a distance of about a half a mile. I though was in my element; I loved every minute of it. I had learned from a long time ago that the best place to be in any tab was right up there in front. Whenever a gap is allowed it becomes twice as hard to make up the distance. There's nothing much worse than being placed at the back of a squad with the result of having to work much harder than I would otherwise have to.

The tab took in much of Aldershot's familiar landscape of heathlands, which are sandwiched between the towns of Aldershot, Farnham, Fleet and Farnborough. Imposing in the centre is Flagstaff hill, the highest point on the training areas. Its slopes took a devastating toll on our marching men. The hill has a murderously steep narrow track up to its summit and it completely wrecked all but a few of the men as they set about running it.

Enjoying the high of an adrenaline buzz I felt almost relaxed, I truly felt really great. To me the time taken to complete the tab flew past and very soon I found myself approaching the finish. Beside myself there were just two others who had managed to keep up with the leading Corporal. The absolute time limit set for this tab was two hours but the expected and accepted time limit was just one hour forty-five minutes. I was pretty pleased to note that my time was less than one hour thirty.

Some people didn't make it. Failure to get in on time meant a complete course failure. There was no room for error. On reaching the end we were met by a Sergeant who recorded on a clipboard the names and times of those that crossed the finish line. Afterwards we were given permission to remove our restrictive and close fitting helmets. I fumbled with the awkward buckle then releasing the straps, I raised the protective dome from my head. Cool air filtered through to my scalp bringing instant and refreshing relief. Unless you've sweated bollocks in one of those things, you'll never understand how great it feels to lift it away.

For the first time since the tab had started, I reached down for my water bottle. A few gulps of warm water swilled around the inside of my mouth before I spat it into my cupped hand to splash it onto my sweat soaked forehead. I did it again but this time to wash away the crisp dried saliva encrusted around my mouth. There had been other opportunities to drink but I was determined to stay up at the front and I didn't want to waste a single second. Of course I was thirsty but it wasn't an uncontrollable urge. Some of the blokes behaved as if they had tramped through the searing heat of an African desert and had been deprived of water for days. They had used up their own supply of water quickly and when it was kindly offered by those who were more cautious with it, they grabbed at it greedily like dying men.

Having finished, we were allowed to change our sweat-drenched vests. It was a lovely feeling, releasing the buttons to my DPM jacket and opening my soaked torso to the cool breeze. Refreshing air rushed in to wash away the trapped heat around my waist sending uncontrollable shivers up my spine and making the tiny hairs in the back of my head stand erect.

"Quickly sort yourselves out!" came a shout from one instructor then without any prompting, loads of the blokes replied in chorus, "First my weapon then myself!"

Stifled giggles of self-congratulation spread quickly to rowdy laughter.

I continued to wriggle free from my equipment and dropped my Bergen to the ground ensuring that my helmet and rifle lay close by and being especially careful to balance my weapon on my helmet keeping it off the ground. I knew that being caught with a rifle lying discarded on the ground would bring about swift punishment.

Scrambling at the ties which fastened the top of my Bergen I reached in and removed a clean PT vest and rapidly changed my clothes. Hoping for as much time as possible, I stretched the DPM Combat jacket thinly over the ground in a desperate act to dry some of the sweat from it. At the same time I took hold of the dirty PT vest and with both hands squeezed it tight, freeing much of its moisture. Much to the amusement of Tom Onions, salty urine scented perspiration poured through my open fingers. Tom, who was by now sat squarely on top of his Bergen, with his boots of and was busily examining the fluid filled blisters on his toes laughed out loud and shouted at me. "Walker! You're such a minger!" He didn't stand a chance; my wet PT vest jetted to him, slapping him hard and fast before wrapping itself around his face. It was a brilliant shot and I laughingly shouted at him to shut up! In mock astonishment Tom fell backwards kicking his feet in the air as he toppled off his bulky Bergen. He let out a giggle then pulled my shirt from off his head and promptly sent it back again. Unfortunately

Tom's retaliatory action was spotted by one of the Cpl's who had led us on the tab.

All Hell suddenly broke loose as Tom instantly became the target of more than one angry Instructor. Down he went grunting his way through thirty punishing press-ups. He didn't moan though; one instructor threatened that as Tom obviously had plenty of energy left he could do the whole ten miles all over again. The threat was taken very seriously.

On either side of Tom, a member of staff stood counting press-ups and every time that he lowered his body to the ground his mentors cautioned that he had not got his chest right down to the floor, therefore that press-up didn't count. Tom must surely have believed that no matter how many he completed, the count was never going to get past five!

I was by now feeling pretty guilty and just when I thought that things couldn't get any worse for him, they did. One of the Instructors pushed the flat of his boot trophy style into the centre of Tom's back, and pushed him flat to the ground. Ten press-ups later and the exhausted prisoner to bad timing was thankfully released, warned of his conduct and then allowed to continue his unfinished chiropody. Tom looked up at me and silently and slowly mouthed filthy insults at me. All I could do was whisper, "Sorry Tom."

It took a while for all the others to finish the tab and I was glad of the opportunity to rest. The test admin' was completed and another syndicate claimed ownership of the prize pennant.

I was never privy to the workings of the points system involved throughout Test-week. I did know though that each event was worth a maximum of ten points and that points were deducted on a sliding scale. Everyone started with their points intact and each time that a student failed to produce a perfect show then points were lost.

With everyone back together, the men were moved a little way and situated inside the woods nearby. The CSM brought everyone close and addressed the whole group. We were, he said, to accept the scenario that we were now at war. As a company our task would be to defend this hill from a threat to the East. Shovels and picks were distributed and we were then detailed off into pairs.

The Officers and SNCOs of the course set about deciding the location of our defensive positions and issuing instructions regarding arcs of fire. The men, some of whom because of a shortage of digging tools had to scrape at the ground with their bare hands, set about hastily digging fire trenches into the hillside. As the men dug into the hardened flint filled ground, instructors visited each site and added to the scenario further. Our Instructors told us that the trenches must also have cover from overhead and that this cover must at all costs be able to withstand the weight of a vehicle being driven across the top.

We were given dimensions for the fire trench that we had to try very hard to keep to. The trench was expected to be six feet long by two feet wide and at a depth of about five feet.

Tom Onions and I were partnered together and I was pretty glad of it. I'd got to know Tom reasonably well in the last few weeks and I was happy discovering that he was a bit of a grafter. Tom started digging whilst I disappeared to make a quick scavenging trip in search of any useful materials such as timber, logs or corrugated tin.

About six or seven minutes had passed before I returned dragging two large pieces of rusting corrugated tin. Interrupting Tom's frantic digging I called to him mockingly,

"I bear great gifts Oh worthy one!"

Without acknowledging my proud achievements he nodded his head to one side drawing my attention over to his right.

"Look at that Prat!" He scorned, continuing, "Didn't have his gat!"

I followed Mick's gaze and saw a bloke from 7 Para RHA on a return trip back up the hill. Even from this distance I could see that the physical strain was clearly visible by his contorted expression. Carrying his rifle high above his head, his tensed arms shook with fatigue. As he got to the top of the hill an instructor shouted something and sent him back down again. This was a display for all to see; this is what happens if you're more than just an arms-reach from your weapon. I felt some pity for him, but most of all I was just glad that it wasn't me.

Digging through roots and loose rock the progress was painfully slow but eventually, close to exhaustion, we completed our architectural task. Our hard work paid off and as darkness fell over us, both of us collapsed into the bottom of the trench.

The rest period was short lived because from outside a member of the staff suddenly and very loudly reminded us that the roof needed to be stronger. With a heavy leap he threw himself recklessly onto our roof causing it to instantly buckle and bend in the middle. Dirt and rocks rained down inside the trench. It wasn't good enough so we had to get started, building it up again but this time better.

Using some old discarded house bricks and a few logs we elevated the tin sheeting to about six inches above the top of our trench and then in an attempt to camouflage the entire structure, earth and debris from around the digging were thrown haphazardly onto the roof.

Feeling mighty proud of ourselves, we crawled inside the tiny vertical hole leading to the darkened inner sanctuary. Then, sitting on the damp ground at the bottom, we examined the walls and over complimented ourselves on how clever we had been. On a small shelf that we had earlier dug into the trench wall I placed the serrated edge of one of our folding mini-stoves. It was time for a self-congratulatory brew.

Black soot burnt hard onto the base of the polished aluminium mess-tin as two pairs of eyes longingly willed the water to boil. It had been some time since we had been given a warm drink so now even the mere thought of a hot mug of tea caused the glands in our mouths to salivate, filling my throat.

Just as the water was about to boil there was an abrupt scream from outside the trench,

"Onions!"

This was followed immediately with the sound of girlish giggles. Both Tom and I were curious and looked out from one of the slits that we had built into the side of the trench. Right in front of us were two pairs of muddied DMS boots beneath legs, which stretched up beyond our field of vision. Around us and to the rear I could hear further footsteps of fast approaching men.

"What's his name? Onions?" A voice jovially enquired.

Raucous laughter broke out from a number of unidentified voices which were all coming from somewhere above us.

The questioner continued, "What a name for a Slop! That's brilliant!"

The owner of one pair of those boots ordered us out of the trench, then shouted a question.

"What the bloody hell is that?"

Before either of us could answer, he began to kick violently away at some of the roof supports and demanded to know from us just how we expected this structure to stand up if it was the target of a fire fight. Bravely if not stupidly leaping to its defence, I argued that I firmly believed this to be a very fine structure indeed. I added convincingly that it was strong and well-constructed that, had I been an estate agent, I could have easily sold it!

Still, this particular instructor wasn't interested in buying and it was all he could do to counter with, "Bollocks!"

He paused for a moment, "If you think it's so bloody good, stay there."

I didn't like the sound of that but I knew I had probably talked myself into a tricky corner. Tom and I slowly looked at each other, sharing the same doubts. I couldn't refuse the challenge. Having loudly and readily sung all of its praises, how could I now not be prepared to prove its worthiness?

There were two terrific crashes as two instructors simultaneously jumped up and down bouncing on our make shift roof. Muck and grit rained down threatening to bury the two of us in dirt and woodland garbage. Finally the jumping came to an end. The Instructors became bored and our trench had thankfully held up. Dirt had spewed through dozens of newly created holes and cracks but overall the structure remained sound.

The Instructors had not left completely though, I could hear two of them talking amongst themselves. They were openly disappointed that their efforts had not brought about the collapse of our roof and one then suggested that further assistance would be required. Agreeing with each other, they enlisted the help of another and then all three instructors laughed when as a team they uniformly jumped onto the roof landing flat on their feet. Still the structure held!

Even more frustrated, one of the Instructors leapt from our roof and like a small boy made machine gun noises whilst at the same time kicking bricks and logs away from under the

179

crinkled metal ceiling. Great turves and lumps caved inward falling down over our heads. On the roof, the punishment continued as the other two men crashed about bouncing and shaking the covering above us.

After what had seemed an eternity, silence fell again. The sounds of the laughing tormentors could at last be heard moving away toward the next trench. Damaged it most certainly was, but considering the battering that our trench had just taken, it stood remarkably well. We probably deserved a slap on the back but there was no time for that, as repairs had to be carried out urgently.

As darkness fell into an eerie stillness the course began normal field routine. In anticipation of an impending attack by some imaginary enemy the Company was brought to a high state of alert known as 'Standing to'. For over an hour and a half each pair of men stood in their trenches and as the Company prepared to defend itself from attack, the soldiers peered over the tops of their rifles and focused their attention, studying the foliage concentrated within their arcs.

After the stand to, the men in near silence and hidden in their camouflaged slit trenches relaxed and got down to the immediate basics of weapon cleaning and personal admin'.

The cold night air slowly crept in replacing the warmth of the day. Icy wind began to bite through the flimsy lightweight uniform of green denim bringing dull damp aches to my beleaguered knees and ankles. As some men were hurriedly donning their thick green NATO style woollen pullovers, their efforts were interrupted with urgent whispered messages filtering down through the trench positions. "Kit on! Light Order."

A few NCOs ran around cautiously gathering groups of men from their trenches and forming them into sizeable fighting patrols. The patrols were to reconnoitre the surrounding training areas. There would be, according to our Instructional staff, a live enemy. In other words there was someone out there to test us and to muck us about so watch out.

A real operational fighting patrol engaged on a hostile mission would usually be fairly small in number but for ease in this training environment the course was roughly divided into two groups with just a few men left over. With a bloke from 7 Para, RHA I was detailed off to stay behind on picket, a sort of guard duty. At first I very much welcomed that decision for I reckoned that there was a fair chance that I could grab myself some undisturbed sleep. However, as the night wore on it proved that such optimistic hopes were not to be matched by reality.

There were plenty of mostly young local civilians who knew only too well that soldiers on night time exercises on these army training areas might often leave stores and other items of kit hidden, perhaps camouflaged but nevertheless unprotected whilst off on patrol or engaged in some other manoeuvre. Thieves had been very busy in recent months stealing all sorts of clothing and webbing. For that exact reason all the blokes had to bring their Bergens over to me where I had taken control of a large trench which had been built into a natural ground depression.

One of the Staff quite bluntly warned us two guards that if even a single item of kit went missing it would be our fault and that we would receive the full blame. We would, he said, have to explain any loss to the CO on a formal charge of neglect. I was absolutely petrified that some thieving toe-rag of a civvy would somehow sneak into our camp area and nick something without even noticing. My new comrade and I decided to accept no risks and so we stood to, staring outward, examining every tiny movement or sound from both sides of the trench throughout the remainder of the night.

When morning came and reveille was sounded I'd had only about two hours of sleep. Then ordered to fill in the trenches, we set to scraping the earth back into where just twelve hours earlier we had so carefully removed it. Once the area had been inspected to make sure that no one had left any litter or kit we were simply left idle and with nothing to do, including me. Most of the men crudely propped themselves up against their Bergens and tried to grab some sleep or as it was known, to push out some zeds.

CHAPTER ELEVEN

EVERYTHING AT SPEED

Shortly afterwards, our temporary slumber was awakened by the deep throaty rumble of an arriving four ton Bedford truck. Its clanking payload rang out as the truck's driver struggled to negotiate his vehicle around the coarse open ground. Two men from the staff climbed into the back of the truck and began shoving out six-foot lengths of steel pipe.

These pipes had been welded to two sides of a strip of metalled tank tracking, the sort that's put down on the ground to form an immediate but temporary road surface. Other staff on the ground busied themselves lining out the nine steel stretchers. Each stretcher, a heavy one hundred and eighty pounds of inflexible solid lumps of metal was to be used to simulate the evacuation of a casualty and his equipment.

More staff ran in tight little circles hurrying the course members, detailing men away to fill water bottles from a portable bowser and at the same time telling everybody that we should drink plenty of fluid because today was going to be a hot one.

Things settled down quickly and we were divided into teams of eight men. The course was brought back together and as a whole we were marched into an open area fairly near to the Garrisons Driver Training Area. Here we were once more separated into the teams of eight that we had earlier been placed. I was pretty happy because Steve Ryder was given the team that I was in. He pointed to a tiny single track which disappeared tunnelling into the thick woodland up ahead and urgently advised,

"The first team through there has the edge 'cos' it's bloody difficult to get past for ages!"

Our Sgt quickly went through the rules of this next test. Our twelve stone metal frame stretcher was going to be carried by the team over a course of quite rough terrain and for a distance of more than seven miles. It was of course a race and therefore was to be completed in as fast a time as possible. We all hoped and aimed to be quicker than any of the other teams.

Steve said that four men were to haul the stretcher on their shoulders with the remaining four carrying all the rifles. We were allowed though he explained, to change places as often as we wished as long as the team stayed together and that no one dropped out. Sgt Steve Ryder went on to say that unfortunately, he could not and would not take part in the race and neither would he tell us when to change places, though he would shout encouragement. His task, he pointed out, was one of supervision and to ensure safety and that was that.

With no time to waste, we set to, organising ourselves into pairs of roughly equal size. We then decided who was going to go where on the stretcher and who would swap with whom. It felt like we had taken no time at all when suddenly the booming voice of the CSM cut short our chatter and brought us to the start. I was to take the back left on the stretcher. I held it with one hand and with my other hand I tried desperately to adjust the loose helmet strap dangling beneath my chin.

The CSM reiterated the already clear rules then ordered that each team should place their stretcher back on the ground and then turn around. Each team was marched about fifty yards over to another Sgt who said nothing but held his arms out making a cross and guiding the teams onto an imaginary line level with him.

I heard the whiz of an ignited thunder flash and I knew that a big bang was coming but when it did, it still made me jump and caused my eardrums to whistle.

Responding to the start signal I turned swiftly and sprinted fast towards our team's stretcher. I was pleased to see that all of the team got there in good time and more or less together. Already there were screams of haste coming from Steve Ryder. I didn't have time to listen to him as I threw off my loosely slung rifle and shoved it in the direction of the smiling Able Seaman to my rear that eagerly grabbed it from me.

Reaching down to the stretcher handle, I glanced over to the man opposite, a stockily built Signals Sergeant with a large gap of missing teeth in the front of his mouth. Instinctively, we both cast eyes away and to the blokes at the front of the stretcher. As if it were well rehearsed we simultaneously shouted, "Lift!" and in one swift movement the scaffold stretcher was firmly bridging our shoulders. We started to run, running like our lives depended on it.

Someone, I don't know who, was calling out the step, "Left, Right, Left...Left, Left!" Trying to get a rhythm going but nobody was paying any attention. We sprinted hard, almost oblivious to the heavy weight pushing us down. The team worked as one and just went for that gap, desperate to get through it before anyone else could.

Feet pounded the hard earth as adrenaline flowed through veins pumping hearts at ever-faster rates. At that time I could barely feel the twelve stone of metal on my shoulders; I pulled it in tighter.

Through my peripheral vision on my left I could see that at least one other team was beginning to nose its way forward and all the other teams, who were still very close to each other, funnelled into the tiny track leading through to the gap. Sensing that already my fellow team members had realised the dangers posed by the other team and in particular the one that was so close to my left, I fought hard to push the stretcher and the team with me. We had to reach the point of the wide triangle in front.

Our nearby rivals found more speed than we could muster and disappointingly, they edged ahead. First into the track, they pushed their way through, forcing us into second place. But we were still there and at their heels. The path twisted wildly occasionally opening onto a brightly coloured carpet of heathland heather. Each of us searched for any possibility for a pass. Pushing first to one side then to the next we explored every option to make the overtake. I felt that our team was faster but only if we could find the space to get in front.

As the frantic minutes passed, the unrelenting weight of the solid stretcher poles thumped down onto my right shoulder. In an instinctive and reactive effort to purge the pain from my mind I shook my head violently and screamed out loud. Still pushing, puffing I was so short of breath, *God it hurt!* Glancing sideways, I could see that the toothless Signals Sgt opposite was also feeling the strain. He was sweating profusely; staring ahead with a horribly pained expression stretching across his face. I was determined though that no matter how awful I felt I was not going to be the first bloke to crack and come off this stretcher.

In my mind, and despite my determined ambition, I prayed for a change to come soon. *Let one of the others take over, please!* Though the thoughts were inside my head I screamed them so loudly I was sure that everybody had heard. From behind I could hear that perhaps my prayers were being answered

186

because I heard a shout of "Change!" I knew that us two at the back couldn't wait for much longer.

Without stopping and with their legs pumping like pistons along the uneven ground the two spare men ran slightly forward of the rear bearers then pushed themselves under the arms of the steel stretcher shouting "Go"! They were now in control and taking the lead. The passage of the heavy stretcher faltered only slightly; for a second it wobbled, threatening to pitch itself over as the fresh men adjusted their grip and the worn men loosened theirs.

I was glad to see that a change had taken place and I had wished with all my heart that it could have been me, but it was not yet. All I could do was to carry on.

A few yards up ahead, as we ran the increasingly steep hill, the track came to an abrupt end. A wall of thick sandy coloured mud and shingle shot away upwards taking the path up to an uneven but higher level. The leading stretcher team went headlong in to tackle the false plateau in front of them. Their front man attacked the metre high precipice but the guy on his left stumbled badly, falling backwards. Their heavy burden listed sharply to one side, then unable to control the rapidly shifting weight, the leading man fell also, crunching painfully to his knees. Disorganised and leaderless, the team lapsed into a chaos of noise. Their guiding instructor, a Sgt from the REME, screamed orders at his stricken team but momentarily at least, they were lost.

Our team had seen this golden opportunity and none of us needed further encouragement. We ran for all we were worth, skirting around to their right and biting into the deep ledge. With one bound I was up and landed unceremoniously in a crude squatting position but still on my feet. The pole had slipped down level with my thigh. Steve Ryder screamed, "C'mon! Keep going, don't lose it!"

The muscles above my knees ached painfully as I struggled to stand up. One of the blokes at the back of my team was on his knees dangerously trying to push our stretcher up hill. There was no prompting but acting as one; the two weapon bearers positioned themselves on either side of the weighty steel stretcher. Straining, they lifted the bars high into the air awarding the two men at the rear the chance to clamber up the ledge and take control once again.

We were up and going, there would be no stopping us now. It felt really good to be in the lead. Sergeant Ryder was clearly ecstatic. He hadn't actually stopped shouting since we had started but at least now though, he appeared to be pleased. It's difficult to describe how seeing that the Sgt. was happy could have made much difference to us but it did. It made us want to work even harder. We wanted to please him more.

A second later and our nearest rivals had regained their composure and were quickly closing the gap between us to just a few inches. They desperately   wanted their lead back.

The bony part of my right shoulder was threatening to fracture under the prolonged battering. I tried hard to keep the stretcher pole tucked hard into my shoulder but that didn't work, then I tried pushing my fingers under the pole as it bounced onto the bone, but all that did was bruise my fingers as well. Exhaustion too was beginning to catch up with me. My lungs were fit to burst; I felt that couldn't wait much longer. I don't know where it came from but somehow I managed to summon a blast of oxygen and let out a piercing cry, "Change!" Almost   straight   away the Signaller Sgt. opposite had copied my initiative and before I could manage another three paces a young medic from our team pushed his way in front of   me.

Chip Walker

Two hands clasped the warm sweat-drenched pole in an over hand grip and pulled it away from me. The Medic grunted as he took the weight and in a barely audible cough, wheezed, "GO!" Satisfied that he had full hold of the stretcher, I reached for the three rifles that my colleague was still carrying, slipping them from his left shoulder and dropping them into my arms. Forcing my legs to accept the smallest of respites, I fell back, tucking in just behind the stretcher.

Our route climbed up through a path known as Windy Gap and then beyond. Anticipating the next change I made sure that this time I was on the other side so as to spare my battered shoulder. If there was a knack to carrying a hundred and fifty pounds of metal, then I can honestly say, I never ever found it.

On the stretcher once more, I needed to pull the pole hard, forcing the weight tightly into my shoulder. I at least wanted to spare the agony of another near non-stop thumping on the protruding bone of an already sore shoulder.

At about half way through the six-mile route we sadly lost our comrade from the Medical Corps. He fell badly and though another colleague immediately took his place, freeing him of the stretcher burden, he was still unable to keep up. Every now and then I sneaked a quick look behind to see if my medic friend was still with us. He had somehow managed to maintain a followed distance of about fifty yards but seemed unable to make up the gap.

With a team of seven instead of eight, things became more difficult. We were not able to change places as often as we would have liked to. The combination of extremes of our activity and the sun's hot rays beating down ensured that everyone remained very uncomfortable.

For some, the heat had become quite unbearable. Having dropped out they found themselves the victim of what looked like a panicked attempt to revive them. NCOs just inches from their faces shouted and screamed their names then forced them onto their feet before pouring cold water over their heads. Those with apparent heat stroke struggled like drunks just to stay conscious.

On, on we went. Agonising cutting pains thudded through the uppermost bones of my shoulders, constantly reminding me of how rigid our weighty stretcher in fact was. I reckoned that I was in an unlucky spot by being one of the tallest in my group and definitely bigger than my opposite bearer. With me holding the stretcher high above my neighbours shoulder it meant of course that the metal poles landed firstly and more heavily on my shoulder. That would be bad enough but because of my rather thin build, there was hardly any flesh to provide protection by covering the bone, just a thin layer of skin. On that day I really envied the fatter blokes.

The pain was bad, but to compliment it there was still, of course, the pure physical exertion of this race. Wearing a combat jacket, which was designed fundamentally to keep men warm on the central plains of Germany, had quickly become a bad idea.

Very soon after the race had started, I, like probably all of us, had become intolerably hot and had sweated buckets. My combat jacket acted like a sponge and just soaked it all up, becoming heavier. After a while and with repeated movement and repeated sweating, each time I moved an arm inside the jacket the drenched material would stick, rubbing away the top layer of skin creating stinging friction burns.

As we neared the top of a monster known as Hungry Hill, the pace was as hard as ever. Underfoot our boots kept sliding on the loose flint that lined the path and for a while it seemed that for every inch that we went forward, we then slid several inches backwards. It was obvious to everybody that the four men on the stretcher were having immense difficulty climbing the final yards of the steep and narrow path leading to the summit.

Someone shouted, demanding a change and I gratefully passed a handle onto a willing comrade. Apart from me there were now only the four men with the stretcher. The other three had all gone. One was in the jacking wagon and the other two were plodding along somewhere behind. I was determined not to join them; I had to stay with the stretcher.

The steep slope brought the team to an abrupt and grinding halt. With knees bent the men pushed and pulled but gritted determination was just not enough. The heels of our boots dug desperately into loose gravel, kicking up huge chunks of sharpened flint as each of us fought for a foot hold. Seeing the team and its litter uncontrollably sliding backwards I bent forward into the hill forcing my chest over and in front of my toes.

Falling forward, the leading bearer on the left-hand side pulled the whole load down to the ground with him and, as he struck the dirt, he let go of the stretcher. It slid clumsily away down the rivulet of moving stones. I grabbed the unattended pipe and pulled with all my might. My knees were bent and turning to face the remainder of the team I started to chip rearwards up the hill.

At the apex and freed of its invisible tether of gravity, the sheeted steel stretcher suddenly found momentum and shot forward. With the load easier to move, the carriers marched swiftly and in unison striving for the next summit. Stretching my painful worn out legs I tried hard to set a faster pace from the front but annoyingly whilst we had been sorting out our problem on the slope, another team had managed to get in front. They were now surging ahead increasing the gap to around twenty yards.

Other members of staff appeared as if from nowhere and joined Sgt. Ryder. They too shouted, trying to spur us on. I was still on the front of the stretcher but when I looked behind I discovered that there was only the four of us left in this team. Me and one other bloke still had hold of all the rifles also. I really wanted to give them to someone else but there wasn't anybody left to take them. Though I was strangely aware of the screams aimed at my team mates who were now behind, I could do nothing so tried to ignore them. The shouts ordered the men to catch up and relieve us of the rifles but none did.

The path leading the way down the hill was even more treacherous than where we had come up. Barely wide enough to accommodate a grown man, it twisted and turned sharply through extremes of declivity. The entire path downward was a dry water fall of small stones which rolled away beneath our feet and threatened to carry us away.

Occasionally I saw tree roots criss-crossing in front of me, cruelly daring to thwart any would be traveller. Either side of us, a sheer bank of compacted red sand and wiry brushwood stood proud, forcing the runners to remain within its confines.

Mixing weighty momentum with a total disregard for our safety, we launched ourselves downward. Once started, we were committed to travelling down the slope at speed. The velocity accelerated and then we had huge difficulty in just staying upright. Almost every pace was lost in a hole or slipped on gravel. I tried hard to counter by searching in the split second before my foot impacted with the ground for firmer footing but then lost it on the next.

As if some invisible person had pulled giant curtains apart, the strict imprisonment of the track suddenly unlocked the way into an open stretch of land. Rows of old disused butts of a rifle range appeared in front of us with giant sandbanks sloping away. We could easily see our rivas in front but this time the gap had closed to only ten yards.

"Last half mile! C'mon, you can do it!" Someone, I don't know who, belted out more encouraging words.

A minute later and we were on the metalled road, which ran alongside the hundred yard firing positions on the range.

All of us were gagging for relief from the stretcher but there was none to have. Knowing that just made us even more frustrated and angry. In my head my battered body was begging for mercy. As always, there was a part of me that wanted to give in but a stronger part argued. I was not going to jack!

As we ran along the comfortably level road we saw a very real possibility of not simply catching up with the leading team but even pipping them to the post. Adrenaline had fuelled our pumping muscles and from deep inside, our battered and tired bodies somehow found more. We were all thinking the same and as I accelerated into a near sprint, the others in the team, without encouragement, kept pace, matching my speed.

The burden carried on my shoulder became almost unreal, like it no longer existed. I had become oblivious to its presence. Emotion swelled from deep in the pit of my stomach erupting up into my chest and inside my head causing the tiny hairs on the back of my neck to stand to attention. I was on the highest of emotional highs. The thrill of the chase was beginning to get the better of me. I could feel my eyes puffing up as tears threatened to burst in excitement over my face.

The rival team, feeling the pressure pushed even harder. The gap between us was fast closing. Still I wasn't sure if there was enough time left to make up the crucial distance. Through every swift but agonising step, the four of us still on the stretcher were moaning loudly, each gasping noisily for air.

Ahead I could see a parked Land Rover. It was pushed right over to one side, almost in the ditch. Behind it there was the four ton truck but with nowhere to go, just straddling the road. Near the Land Rover there were a few Instructors standing in a huddle around another man who held a clipboard and a stopwatch. I was aware of shouts encouraging us on to a faster finish but I don't know who did the shouting or where it came from.

In one neat movement my team went to the right. This was to be our final chance to pass the others and finish in first place, our last hope of victory.

Alongside the other team we were unable to even glance in their direction for fear of slowing down and losing the tiniest fraction of a second. We each looked straight ahead and aimed for the finish. Breathing powerfully in a noisy but controlled rhythm I swung my free arm in long arcs from front to back: grabbing at the air: pulling and clawing my way to the front. I could feel warm air as it whistled through the straps of my helmet and caused a loosened buckle to flap annoyingly from side to side, stinging my cheek with persistent tapping.

Out of the corner of my eye I could just see that the other team were still neck and neck with us, worse still I could hear the loud arrival of yet another team literally at our heels. Fighting hard and running bloody fast I was so very disappointed to see the parallel team just inch in front to take the winners pennant.

The momentum of our run and the weight of our stretcher meant that we needed several yards before we could finally stop. I was almost overwhelmed with the desire to simply collapse and die. My lungs were heaving up and down, trying to find enough oxygen to satiate my tired body and though the race was over, we were not yet allowed to put the stretcher down.

Keeping the stretcher at shoulder height I turned in quiet interrogation of the others in my team. The expression on my face asked the question. Where did we go wrong? But there was no answer.

Small consolation I know but I did feel better once that I had seen my team comrades looking far worse than I actually felt.

Right behind us on the finishing line was another team and just slightly behind and to one side of them was yet another. With them was one of our strays. I felt no anger; instead I was simply pleased to see that my team mate had finally made it.

An Instructor approached and told us that we could ground the stretcher. In what must have seemed like telepathy the four of us turned inward simultaneously and started to lower the litter but before we got it to below waist level another NCO ordered all the teams to push their stretchers onto the four tonner. It felt wonderfully free and light to suddenly not have that heavy chunk of metal banging at my shoulders. It was like walking on cushions of air.

Lining the roadside we all applauded and cheered the last teams as they raced for the finish. The atmosphere of great achievement was so brilliant it was almost visible and so thick that I could almost taste it. We had worked hard: given a fine account of ourselves and we rightly felt good about it.

Under the cooling shade of a mature silver birch and once that the last teams were in, the whole course formed a queue. On the ground and placed in a neat row was a line of hay-box containers. The big green tea-chest sized insulated steel flasks held the hot breakfast that had been earlier prepared by the cooks back at Depot Para. The saliva in my mouth started to thicken as I fumbled eagerly at my water bottle pouch to get at my one-pint plastic mug. It was housed over the top of the bottle like a lid. Yanking it free I turned to a mate and got him to remove the two aluminium mess tins from my kidney pouches worn on my belt.

Permission was then given to remove our webbing whilst we ate; I took hold of the webbing yoke and gently eased it over the smashed tissue of skin and flesh covering my shoulders. My right shoulder in particular had swollen to half its size again. Hardened blisters taut with fluid sprouted up from the bone to form a bubbled surface on the reddened skin. It was extremely sore to the touch, I wondered for a while if I had in fact fractured the bone? The left side was not so bad: tender but just bruising really. Either way, there didn't appear to be much that I could do about it without jeopardising my chances of passing.

Breakfast was wonderful. There was; sausage, bacon, scrambled eggs and fried bread all washed down with a generous pint of hot sweet tea. The food and drink sunk immediately like a brick to my stomach and warmed my aching muscles. For a short while at least my whole body felt revitalised.

It probably wasn't very long at all but after all that rushing around, the break for breakfast seemed to last forever. Just when I was beginning to wish things on a bit there was a sudden snap of movement and members of the staff were busily shouting orders. Waving their arms around like mad men, they sent soldiers first here and then there. I wondered if this was deliberate to provide some stressful harassment or were the staff simply disorganised. I may have wondered, but I daren't ask.

With the heavy hay-boxes closed and sealed, they were each lifted onto the back of the truck and taken away.

Order was fast restored and the course was once more formed into three ranks but again separated into their syndicates. The pennant was awarded to the winning syndicate whilst the rest of us stood by and clapped. The soldier designated as the recipient marched forward collected the prize and returned justly cock-proud to his comrades who were by now cheering ecstatically.

From an almost formal parade atmosphere of the award ceremony came a whirlwind of chaotic commands. It was all a rush as we scrambled to obey the orders which hurtled in from all directions. Webbing was on then it was off, until finally we were told that we must place all the webbing and our rifles neatly onto a four tonner. Two men, failures from the earlier race, clambered up and into the truck. They were to be the escorts for the rifles and other equipment.

As a company we were then marched off from Caesars Camp along the Aldershot Road and into the thick woodland situated behind the Royal Officers Club.

The CSM's voice boomed across the training area. "Company will advance! Right turn! Stand at ease!" The Company paused. I let my eyes gaze upward to the dull grey scaffolding sprouting from the ground and, which then stretched into the treetops at heights varying from twenty to fifty five feet. We had arrived at the feared Trainasium.

This oddly named contraption of aerial obstacles was designed to test a soldier's agility and his head for heights. Perhaps more importantly, it measured pure nerve. For me, the Trainasium was the one test above all the others that really did give me cause for concern. I had already gone some way in proving my fitness, now I would have to overcome my fear of heights and demonstrate my bottle.

Because of its large size the Company was separated into three groups. Each group was then positioned at differing parts on the Trainasium ready to start. The group that I was with ended up being pushed under the shadow of a tall tower. Draped over one side of the tower was a roped scramble-net. The pattern of heavy woven squares hung limply from a wooden platform set at about forty-five feet up. Reaching skyward from there for another ten feet were a set of poles rigged like a ladder which in turn led to two parallel bars of around eight feet in length.

A SNCO instructor wanted to start but a PTI warned everyone to wait until an ambulance from 23 PFA had arrived. The waiting was short.

As we were being briefed by the PTI on the importance of safety, we were interrupted abruptly by a top-heavy Land Rover. It was painted out in familiar camouflage of green and grey but each side sported a large red cross on a white background. The noisy vehicle slued to a halt, just yards from the gathered staff and, before even the engine could be cut, the side doors swung open and from inside two airborne medics jumped out and skipped around to the rear. Opening the doors one disappeared inside. The other dropped to his arse and sat on the raised steps protruding at the door.

Major Kennett pivoted on the balls of his feet and holding his hands firmly clasped in front of his chest he asked, "OK?" One of the medics waved his right arm and answered, "Ready Sir."

The OC turned to his front and nodded approval to the PTI who in turn nodded permission to the lower ranked instructors. Another SNCO instructor standing adjacent to the tallest tower called out for everyone to pay attention to his brief lecture on safe use of the tower.

He sent a young Cpl of the Depot Permanent Staff swiftly up the scramble-net. At the top the Cpl. stood to attention and awaited the next command. Told to mount the shuffle bars (the two parallel bars) he quickly shinned up with practised efficiency and again stood still. Balancing on the two galvanised steel pipes he remained upright, his arms held out to his sides like a circus tightrope walker. Throwing his voice up into the air the Instructor shouted to his subordinate, "Forward". The young Cpl. his eyes never once changing direction from straight ahead, shuffled forward in fast but smooth slides of his feet. The demonstration was quickly completed and I couldn't help but think that it all looked quite easy. I wondered, *"what was all the fuss about"?*

The Cpl. slid, fireman's fashion, effortlessly down the vertical pole to the ground. From there he went about traversing each and every obstacle along the Trainasium. Throughout the practical demonstration the SNCO continued his talk explaining each time what it was that they the instructors would be looking for. The whole demonstration probably lasted only about ten minutes.

With slight trepidation I watched anxiously as the first three blokes ran towards the net. Each selected an individual rope to help guide their way up and like spiders on a web they raced to the tree-top high platform. Forming a small queue they stood patiently underneath the shuffle bars and awaited their turn. One man climbed up and after calling out his number went proficiently through the routine without a hitch. The next quickly followed. A little more cautious; he didn't display any problems. The more that I watched, the more that I became worried.

As a kid I had often suffered silently with a terrible fear of heights. I still don't like heights but I had recently learned how to control that fear. Now though, I wondered if I had nerve enough once more to defy those rising fears. Ten minutes of intense spectating passed.

With a sleeve wrapped around his clipboard to protect the paper from light rain, an NCO fervently scribbled our names and numbers across the dampened page. My turn arrived. Pushing my left foot into the square hole, I jumped hard upwards reaching successfully for a thick strand of rope which hung invitingly in front of and just above my chin. Gripping the rope hand over hand I climbed step by step up the net. Skill and agility were what I was looking for at this stage but I don't think anyone here could resist the urge to treat the ascent as a race. Two of us leapt ahead of the third man and together we clambered upon the wooden platform below the shuffle bars. Our eyes met and slightly short of breath we smiled silent acknowledgement of each other's achievement and an event well raced. The last man just a few seconds behind grunted his way between us and onto the thick wooden planks.

At the ladder I watched nervously as the bloke in front progressed slowly and laboriously. It took an eternity before he had managed to successfully traverse the bars and reach the other side. I looked down, *Christ!* I thought. *This is bloody high!* Thoughts of horror invaded my head. Helmet or not, I didn't fancy my chances if I fell from here.

Then it was my turn. At the top of the ladder I rested for a second. With nowhere left for my arms to pull upon I searched for a way which, felt safe for me to get on top of the bars. Time was against me. I straightened my back and keeping my hands free I very carefully stepped up to the top wrung. Having to lift my right foot another twelve inches onto the wet and slippery scaffold pole and with no way of anchoring my weight with my hands, I leaned to my left to counter balance. My body weight shifted uncomfortably as the centre of gravity in my chest altered. I wobbled then instinctively threw myself forward catching hold of the horizontal bars with each hand.

"Get off there! Stand up!"

I knew that he was shouting at me. I suddenly felt very guilty having annoyed the man who was actually engaged in marking my performance. Pointing my toes outward I pushed the heel of each foot firmly against the poles and dared to let go with my hands. For a second I remained in an unconventional squatting position, just concentrating on my balance. Again I heard an angry shout of "Stand up!"

I forced the shaking muscles of my tired thighs to straighten and raised my sweating torso. In something of a star position with locked knees and arms held pointedly out to my sides, I waited.

He pushed his beret slightly further back on his head then using the cuff of his blue serge tunic, wiped from his eyes the tiny droplets of rain that had settled on his face. He looked first at his clipboard then up at me. Finally he snapped, "Next!"

Instantly replying I called out; "Number twenty three Sir!"

"Go on!" He instructed.

Hardly lifting my boot, I shuffled it along the slippery pole feeling every fraction of an inch beneath my foot. Trying desperately not to over extend my reach I moved along the bars using just one foot at a time. Near halfway across, I responded to an order to halt. For a few brief seconds I stood perfectly still, staring directly ahead and only occasionally stealing a quick glance down to the ground below. To test my nerves the Sgt instructor asked for my name and number.

"Walker, number twenty three Sir!" I shouted somewhat agitated. There was tiredness in his voice as he lazily countered, "Touch your toes!"

Fright gripped my whole body and shook it. Beads of pearly sweat mixed with the rain as it ran down my face. Visions of my feet slipping away with me and tumbling fifty feet to the earth flashed in my mind's eye.

I shook my head and concentrated on what was being asked of me. Bending at the waist I pointed my fingers and stretched both arms down to the scarred toe caps of my smooth worn DMS boots.

"Go on!" He ordered once more. I straightened up and dragged my feet with me as I reached for the end.

Not quite opposite to each other but shackled onto the bars were a pair of scaffolding brackets. These two relatively small protuberances may have been only three or four inches in height but on a shuffle bar fifty feet up in the air, they may as well have been a six-foot wall. If I was to have any chance at all of getting past these brackets I was going to have to remove one foot at a time from the much needed sanctuary of the pole and I definitely didn't want to do that. The idea of being one footed on a slippery pole and this high up was at best, unappealing.

The surfaces of the bars dripped with rain water and had fast become as slippery as ice. Every now and then my boots slipped a short skid along the pole and caused me even more worries. Gently I raised my right foot, my weight shifted to my left but my right foot probably only just cleared the steel bracket. It must have looked like an exaggerated slow motion karate kick from some corny martial arts movie. But I successfully manoeuvred the hindrance, allowing a big sigh of relief to escape from my lungs. I shuffled forward before easily repeating the exercise on the opposing bar. Climbing off the bars I rushed to the fireman's pole and swiftly slid to the

Chip Walker

ground then ran around the corner to the next part of the test: the Standing Jump.

In common with the shuffle bars this obstacle carried a high failure rate. The start for this test was a simple board of eight by twelve inches suspended at about eight feet up on the platform. From there, soldiers stood very still then on a given command would be expected to jump without any hesitation onto a mesh covered plank set at six feet away but two feet lower. This provided a mental as well as a visual illusion of being much further than it actually was. From the ground the feat appeared hardly daunting. But from the platform and with the additional height of the jumper's eye level, the prospect of leaping into thin air with the hopeful intention of landing on a thin plank of wood some six feet away seemed very difficult indeed.

There were two such standing jumps set alongside of each other, allowing the testers to process me two at a time as we in turn tried to prove we had a bit of bottle. I looked over to the tiny landing area and felt a shiver travel shakily down my spine.

It didn't take long for my turn to arrive. Imitating a monkey, I ascended the framework of cold steel bars and, leaning back on the main supports, I eased my feet forward and down until I was able to stand unaided on the tiny jumping step. Preparing myself, I scanned the landing area. A single plank just eight inches wide and eight feet long sat suspended out to the front and below. It led away from me before reaching a gap, and then there was another similar plank.

My stressed heart was busily pounding the cavity in my chest as blood drained from my face and leaving me with a distinctively odd feeling. I didn't fancy this much at all. The man with the clipboard wrote my number on his sheet and

203

spoke with control but softly, "Ready?" I kept my gaze on the target ahead and shouted, "Sir!"

With both knees slightly bent I pushed my arms behind adopting the stance of a sports diver. "Go!" The instructor spat gruffly. Before he had the chance to close his mouth I had gone and was flying through the air. In a resounding crash that reverberated through the apparatus I touched down. Keeping my knees and feet tight together I caught hold of the plank as it rushed up to me. Momentum carried my body still further forward and in an effort to halt my trajectory I pushed both hands downward to grip the thin plank beneath me. We had been warned not to do that but it was somewhat instinctive. The problem was that all the planks were covered with a sort of metal mesh like chicken wire but instead it was made from quarter inch steel. Both hands slipped along the edges of the meshed plank and as they did so, skinned the flesh from inside my thumbs. In stung like Hell! In a jerky, perhaps awkward but continuous movement I ignored the discomfort then righted myself to run along the platform, make the next jump and off the other end to reach the ground.

Just a few yards away I climbed the next phase of the Trainasium. As was the rest, this part was constructed largely of long grey scaffolding poles and topped with wooden planks. Apart from some short gaps between planks which required not much more than a good skip to get over them the run appeared easy enough. The gaps were designed only to serve as nothing more than interruptions and to restrict the soldiers speed. The real frightener on this part was what lay waiting at the end.

Required in this test of bottle was a mammoth leap of around twelve feet into a loosely slung scramble net, which was screened across one end and was suspended vertically from the ground. In writing I know that twelve feet doesn't sound too bad, after all there are school kids who can long jump further. However, because the planks are set apart with gaps of three feet, the men could move only at a jog. They simply would not be able to build up enough velocity to make a jump easily and below this particular long jump was a drop of around another eight feet.

No one waited for the command. Once up onto the initial platform I watched for the man in front to produce a reasonable gap between us. I braced myself ready for the start. Having judged the distance to be about right I kicked my legs into action and ran the gauntlet of broken bridges. It took but a few seconds to reach the end where I steadied myself for the leap but before I could jump there was a startled scream of

"Stop!"

It brought me to a wobbly but sudden halt.

"Stand still everywhere!" commanded a very worried looking SNCO.

Like moths to a flame, men in blue serge tops sprinted to the net screen just ahead of me. Flicking my head around to follow in their direction I was horrified at the sight in the net. Men were scrambling up to reach a trapped being. Caught like a bug in a spider's web was a LCPL from 23 PFA. With his legs slotted through holes in the huge net, the soldier lay dangling and upside down.

It was strange but there was no noise, it was like watching a silent movie. The staff eased the man from his painful snare. Shattering the eerie silence the V8 engine of the land rover ambulance coughed loudly and spluttered to life forcing blue grey smoke to belch from its under belly. A door slammed shut and with its wheels spinning the heavy beast of a rover shot away backward bumping over stumps of long felled trees.

At the net the medics eased the stricken soldier down onto a waiting brown canvas stretcher. In seconds it was all over and he was gone. People looked around at each other, some asking, some telling but everyone was talking about what had just happened. He was a fit bloke who up to now had been doing really well on the course but now I heard that he had dislocated both of his femurs from their pelvic sockets.

If I wasn't apprehensive about this test before, I certainly was now. There is, I'm sure, an art to throwing your whole body into a giant net; perhaps a degree of skill is required if one wishes to keep his legs attached to his body: I reminded myself that I had already seen the proof.

During our earlier demo we were advised that the best method was to leap headfirst with arms uppermost and with fists clenched like superman. That way, we were reminded, you won't break your fingers. I suppose that it all made sense. If I could get my fists and arms through the net it will be only natural to pull myself into the net and grab it for all my life's worth.

It wasn't just the guy in front of me who had hurt himself, though so far he was definitely the worst. Several men told me of their own misfortune or that of another. Most, it seems, had hit the net with feet first. Commonly these unfortunates escaped with little more punishment than a short incapacitating dull ache as both legs shot through the ropes followed very quickly by twelve stones of hurtling man flesh only then to find a lonely static rope preventing any further progress as he slammed into the net using his testicles as fenders. Reason enough, I thought, to ensure that I went head first.

I could see the final plank as I fast approached and then it disappeared from sight into nothingness. I burst free of gravity sending my head and body up and through the air. Coming to a brutal crash I impacted hard into the tightly strung ropes. A blinding flash momentarily stole any concentration as the heavy fibres painfully whipped my nose and chin. Stillness revived me and I was quick to realise that just one of my arms had caught the net well. The other was awkward but at least it was still attached to my shoulders.

Speedy movement above my head attracted my eye and I shook myself from this self-congratulatory daze. Turning fleetingly, I just had time to glimpse another bloke as he leaped into space and jetted towards me. It wasn't panic but an urgent wish to get the Hell out of there that assisted my very hasty and successful retreat from the net to the ground.

That phase having been happily completed, I went back to the start and re-joined my waiting colleagues. As the last bloke on the net came down to us, the groups were reformed into three ranks and were stood at ease. Some of the blokes, still brimming with adrenaline recounted their experiences so far. Others more like me arched our necks, watching a soldier who was having some obvious problems on the shuffle bars. Over to one side three SNCOs clustered together as they jointly considered the young soldier's predicament. Occasionally breaking from their conversation they shouted encouragement and commands to motivate the man to complete his task.

Exasperated, the CSM shook his head and eyed the ground in frustrated defeat before spurting, "Get him down!" A Sgt. with hands placed on his hips shouted angrily at the man on the scaffold and ordered him to climb down immediately using any method that he can. The sick looking soldier slowly squatted to his knees and timidly climbed down. Feeling shamed and embarrassed he stood alone and away from his syndicate colleagues.

Witnessing the entire unnerving experience with me was a bloke that I vaguely knew as a LCpl. from the RCT, and he was to be the next man to ascend the shuffle bars. He was already anxious. He had told me earlier that he had deep worries about his impending performance. He had watched his predecessor wrestle with his fears, now it was his turn.

Following the loud shout of, "Next!" the twenty one-year-old LCpl. reached upwards and started his climb. Shuffling forward and unsteadily in exaggerated awkwardness he pre-empted the imminent command and stopped. Unperturbed the SNCO barked his orders,

"Touch your toes!" There was no response.

"Touch your toes!" He repeated.

Already suspecting the cause of the problem the instructor paused for thought. Never once removing his gaze from his young soldier the SNCO changed tack and altered his tone.

"What's your number Son?" Still there was no response; nothing to even indicate that the young driver had heard the softly put question.

Up above, the soldier had discovered that his most frightening phobias had come to greet him. Battling his nightmare, he bravely fought to squeeze the fears from his mind, daring himself to straddle the perilous structure at his feet. Forcing his heels into the cold grey bars he straightened his back refusing to allow his eyes to be drawn to the angry men nearly sixty feet below. Instead he fixed an icy stare on to the tree top in front. Stretching his arms he reached out to either side. He knew now that this was do or die. Near crippled with fear the sorry soldier was unable to spur his muscles to move. Paralysis had struck, locking his limbs tight.

Chip Walker

On hearing the pleading tone of the vexed Instructor the CSM, followed very shortly by the OC, joined their man on the ground at the base of the tower. Obviously concerned, they both watched the affected LCpl. mentally willing him on. Minutes past and the CSM could hold back no longer, taking a step forward he called up to the soldier and asked who he was. He too found himself without any sort of reply.

Numerous complications and considerations must have gone through CSM Rustell's mind as he wrestled his options. Obviously the bloke couldn't simply stay stranded up there forever. On the other hand there was the worry that the man's paralysis might turn to panic, therefore endangering his life and that of anyone near him. Furthermore, I'm sure that all the senior staff must have been concerned that this sad episode could have an adverse effect on course morale.

Instructed by the CSM and the OC a PTI ran around to one side of the scramble net whilst the CSM went to the other. They promptly scaled the chequered web of netting and in the time it took to look around, had positioned themselves at either end of the lofty shuffle bars. The CSM took control and spoke softly to the fear ridden man. It seemed an age with time apparently standing still, but slowly the brave Sergeant Major edged nearer. All those close to me who were witnessing the rescue let out a huge sigh of relief as the distraught youngster was gently coaxed down. He left straight away in the jacking wagon. I never saw him again.

Long instilled discipline ensured that movement onto the next phase of the revered Trainasium was swift and uninterrupted. Eager to be tested, we each queued for our turn. In hardly any time at all the call came for me and with the confidence of a man who had just completed the two most daunting tasks, I raced to the top of the steel frame. Standing to attention, I shouted my number. Under starters orders I watched fervently as an Instructor, different to the others in a faded maroon sweatshirt, pointed his chewed biro to the sky. Checking about him he nodded approval to an invisible friend and shouted, "GO!"

Twenty feet up in the air and running as fast as I could dare but not quite sprinting, I cut along the thin planks at tree height. Striding confidently over the three-foot wide gaps I paid no attention to the frightening view of the landscape and burst through the breaks in my path. Whilst in full stride I was confronted with a ninety-degree change in direction. This turn was awkward when running and when so high up on a wet wooden surface, was treacherous. I couldn't help but notice that there was a distinct absence of railings or barriers.

The aerial obstacle course continued to wind its way along, breaking into large gaps and tight corners. For me the Tilt-bridges represented the most formidable of coming impediments. Their see-saw planks balanced on a centre fulcrum before falling worryingly about twelve inches or so as soon as weight was put on it. I pounced and was instantly thrown off balance. Luckily, I remained travelling in roughly the same forward direction, and I was able to let momentum carry me over the centre and on to the other side. Of course I knew what was coming now and I was ready for the shift of weight to suddenly fall away under me. Flicking my right foot and extending my gait I managed to attain that extra inch so that I could use the flat of my foot to safely land.

Around the following corner I found myself stuck behind the bloke in front. The momentum of each soldier's initial run had bottle-necked abruptly at the Japanese Bridge. This bridge of ladder shaped steel poles curved upwards into a crescent and by now there had been many men who had already skipped across it. Wet muddy boots had deposited wet grass and slippery grey mud onto the straddling struts. This was having a slowing effect on the men now trying to cross so cautiously. They, knowing that a slip would mean certain injury or even death, were understandably taking great care. As I waited for my chance to cross, I weighed up the pros and cons.

Pre-Para. On the log with 9 SQN RE.

Pre-Para at the MVEE assault course.

The end of the tunnel at the MVEE.

*A quick break following many hard miles
uphill.*

Another candidate escapes from the filthy tunnel.

Tom Onions leads the pack, dragging Jock Elliot as he goes.

A slow and methodical approach would make the job of balancing easier but speed might pull me through. With all this mud around, I was no longer sure just what to do.

With caution thrown to the wind and my heart thumping hard enough to be heard, I launched myself up and onto the sloping pipes. On each swift step I could feel my boots begin to slide. Only the fixed moulded heel of my rubber soled DMS boots prevented disaster by hooking onto the pipes. As I found the solid footing of the adjoining boards, a wave of welcome relief swept over me. I had made it.

I continued on for a few more yards and found the next obstacle. This time a simple pair of parallel bars set like the Japanese Bridge into an arch, but this bridge hadn't any steps or struts. The only way to traverse this gap was to solely use hands and arms. The method demonstrated to us earlier showed the PTI hoisting himself up onto locked arms and then pushing down on the poles to bring him up to waist height then he dangled the remainder of his body free of the apparatus and through the gap. From there he walked his hands up hill till he reached the pinnacle of the arch and until he could swing his legs onto a safe piece of board.

It was here that having successfully negotiated my way through some of the most dangerous and scary parts of the Trainasium, I was quite unexpectedly attacked by old phobias. Fear struck fast at me and for a moment, I hesitated. Uninvited pictures of me falling through the trees flashed through my mind. Stepping up ready to the start, I wished that I didn't feel the things that I did. I fought the paralysing fears desperately, but still they gripped my whole being.

From below there was a loud shout. A Sgt. insisted that I move. Behind me I heard a colleague groaning his disapproval too, then urging me forward. Still reluctant I fidgeted with indecision. Looking for an acceptable way out of my predicament, the battle raged inside my head. Do I go on or is there an alternative? A voice from below broke my silent arguments and brought my attention to the origin of the sound.

The OC asked the Sergeant, who was holding everybody up? Once informed, he threw his undisguised frustration towards me. His middle class accent shattered the relative peace by bawling. "Who's that up there?" Quick as a flash I countered, "Number twenty three Sir! Walker Sir!"

There was the tiniest of pauses before the OC continued, "Well you wanker, get a fucking move on or I will personally come up there and throw you off!"

This was not the first time that I had incurred the wrath of the man in charge and I certainly didn't want to rile him again. Muttering something stupid I hastily pushed my way over the arch. On the other side I calmed and then got really angry with myself. Now completed, the task seemed incredibly easy. I could only ask myself what the fuss was all about.

A few feet further on and I was clinging to a small platform housed on a large horse-chestnut tree and built around its trunk. From twenty-five feet up I nodded readiness to the instructor below. In the same instant he cast upward a long rope, which had been fixed to some scaffolding above. Leaning as far as I dare and with my right hand stretched out, I just managed to catch hold of the swinging tether. Then, with it hooked into the fold of my elbow, I clasped it close to my chest.

The target, waiting for me to aim was a huge basket of netted ropes loosely slung into a sloping hammock. Like Tarzan I leapt into the air on the rope, swinging through green foliage. As I rushed to the net I waited for the rope to reach the maximum height in its trajectory and where momentum should carry me to my goal. Releasing a vice-like grip, I spun round uncontrollably in mid-flight before landing crumpled on my back near the top of the net. Urgently propelled by the sight of another man flying towards me, I straightened my body and rolled cigar fashion down to the bottom of the catch area. With a grin that any Cheshire cat would be proud of, I made my way triumphantly to the equally grinning course mates and who had already finished.

An adrenaline buzz filled our veins and without exception, we felt absolutely great. We exchanged excited stories of our successful and even some less than successful exploits in the air. After a few minutes, it seemed quite natural to turn our attention to the blokes who were still up there and being tested.

Now though, as experienced experts we considered some poor bloke's merits or more often, his lack of them and deliberated on his chances of passing. We were self- righteous idiots.

Having paraded in three ranks and our syndicates we were brought swiftly to attention then immediately stood at ease again. It was time again for the pennant presentation.

Out in front and to one side the staff members stood about in a huddle isolating the pennant bearing course Major. He glanced fleetingly at a piece of paper handed to him by the CSM, then taking a breath, he simply called out, "Number two!" Surprised but instantly recognising the number as that given to my own syndicate I quickly turned to my colleagues to confirm our success. Before I could say a word though, the syndicate roared into cheers of deafening approval.

Someone pushed forward and slapped our hysterically funny and very popular matelot friend on the back, insisting that it should be he who would collect our prize. At first he was reluctant but goaded on by just about everybody else, he shuffled forward of the group. Once clear he marched out, halted and in smart military fashion took the winners pennant from the tall blond major. Switching the lance to his left arm he tucked it tightly into his body then flicked a slanted Navy salute to the OC. The OC seemingly perplexed, returned a salute then spoke to our bare headed sailor,

"Do you salute without head-dress in the Navy?"

"Of course Sir!" The smiling pennant bearer bluffed without even a moment's hesitation. Overcome with doubt by the sudden and confident answer, the Major turned away, seemingly embarrassed and worried that he may have appeared a little naive. As he walked off, knowing sniggers broke out from the applauding course.

Formal saluting in any branch of the British armed services can only be offered when the complementing subordinate is wearing head-dress.

With our proud pennant carried at the lead, the company marched the short distance back to Browning Barracks for a much needed chance of a wash and to get some well-deserved scran down our necks.

Though the lunch period lasted for less than an hour, the admin period that followed dragged by slowly. Meals were scoffed energetically in about seven minutes and that included the time spent queuing. Our weapons were cleaned and handed into the armoury before going off to get into a change of kit.

In instant boredom, I sat idly on my bed before lazily looking up at the image in the mirror. I looked ridiculous. Agreeing with the mocking reflection, I studied the strange looking form which appeared in front of me. Huge size eleven boots, both sporting worn patches deep in the toe caps, were topped with folded down thick green woolly socks. Great milky white knobbly growths of legs pebble dashed with blue and brown bruises sprouted from the socks before disappearing inside a pair of very old fashioned baggy mid-thigh length navy blue PT shorts. From the waist up I had on a thick red T-shirt with my name emblazoned on large black letters against a white background across my chest. Bad enough I thought but now I was also wearing a helmet. I allowed myself a simple giggle; I looked and felt like a mushroom.

When the time finally came, we marched to the Paras assault course, not far from the Royal Officers Club.

We stood still in three ranks whilst one of the Staff briefed us, telling us what was expected and the rules that went with it. One of the PTIs then began to lead us slowly around, stopping only for a minute or so at each obstacle to demonstrate the best way to tackle it or to explain a technique.

The assault course was purposely built for the Parachute Regiment during the late 1960s. It comprised seventeen differing impediments and each was separated by yards of deep brown mud or energy sapping loosely laid shingle. Once around this course would perhaps be test enough, but the high standards demanded by the Airborne Brigade meant that we had to race around it three times without stopping. The whole company would have to fight each other for individual space. The qualifying time set for completing the three circuits was a startling seven and a half minutes.

In an opening amongst the birch wood we lined up ready for the off. A shout nearly lost in the thick growth of trees and shrubs let us loose on the assault course and each other. Within thirty seconds, a frenzied tangled mess of men pushed, shoved and wriggled their way over a two-foot high brick wall.

Separating only briefly over an eighteen-yard dash before once again forming into a large group, we came to a sudden halt at a six-foot wall spanning five yards and deliberately blocking the way. Some of the blokes were attacking others in frustrated temper, angrily cursing anybody deemed to be in their way. The sight of madmen frantically fighting on top of the wall jolted me to a decision. Instead of wasting precious time and energy fighting at the wall, I stood back searching, waiting for a gap. An instructor, likely noticing my apparent lack of enthusiasm blared at me. "Number twenty three! Get over that bastard wall!"

Disappointedly I had no choice but to revert to plan. I ran at the wall and instantly collided with several others but there was no fight. The soft shingle slowed my advance and sapped the energy from my clumsy attempt at a powerful leap up the wall. Somehow however I found just enough to get myself over the top and down on the other side. I went straight into a run; the first couple of paces though, quickly drained the drive from my legs.

I was in a long pit filled with tiny stones, which simply slipped away from under my feet. Running in slow motion I eventually got to the end of the pit and went straight into a twenty yard sprint. Barely interrupting my run and with some ease, I comfortably hopped over another short wall.

A little way past the wall and the surface changed to thick wet mud. It had been deliberately kept damp so that even in the driest of droughts, it stayed wet. Every time that I tried to take a step forward, my feet slid out to the sides. I was very careful to negotiate the approach to the next wall.

Hopping over it I was disappointed to see that I had landed in yet another pool of mud bringing me sliding to a skaters halt. Three paces later and I pushed a boot to the front and up a sloping ladder of galvanised scaffold pipes, which went up in a slope away and ahead of me. The loose set of metal rods set about one yard apart succeeded to a height of thirteen feet.

Because of the large steps between each pole and because the use of hands was not allowed on this apparatus, a slow climb was unwise, speed and momentum was the answer.

Slime-covered mud decorated the upper most part of each pole. The thought of slipping now sent shivers of trepidation to my tired body. Having to kick out uncomfortably upward and outward to reach the next bar I threw my arms out as a counter balance and locked my heel onto each slippery pole. I took careful but hasty steps, climbing as I went and quickly ascending to the top. At the summit I leapt fearlessly into the air to catch a Fireman's pole allowing me to slide speedily but unceremoniously to the earth before arriving in an undignified heap. I had correctly hooked my feet around the pole to provide stability in my descent. However I came down so fast that I didn't manage to uncouple them before I hit the Earth hard.

Subsequently I landed so awkwardly that I twisted an ankle. I wasn't exactly crippled but at the time, it bloody well hurt.

With delay now condemned as foolishness, I overlooked the discomfort and continued the sprint to the next structure, odd that it was. There were wooden boards built over a steep apex, much akin to a house roof but without any walls to support it. In a bound I was up and over the eight-foot high hindrance and hadn't experienced much difficulty, except perhaps the feeling of sheer exhaustion and the dull ache in my muscles, which never quite let up.

I scanned ahead and could see dozens of blokes following each other hastily over more obstacles, the view behind me held a very similar sight. As a course we had split up into gaps large enough to allow room for some manoeuvre but just one slip or hesitant step could mean a guy becoming an annoying blockage to over-stressed blokes rushing up behind him.

220

An easy run on a slightly descending slope of fifteen yards through small trees led us to two more low walls. One was about two feet high and the other a little taller. Both were built close together and therefore necessitating a step up rather than a simple hurdle. The twin walls were designed to offer no more than an interruption in a soldier's stride and with that, it ensured a change in muscle usage and when tired, that simply means more pain. It worked!

Over the second wall I landed in an unwanted six-foot long bank of wet and heavy mud. Trying to move fast, I pulled at my thighs bringing them through and out onto firmer dry land. Again I felt the energy being sapped from me. There was no option other than to continue. Into a clear sprint of twenty-five yards along the narrow wooded track, around a corner another two side by side walls appeared suddenly. Stepping over them in the same way as the previous pair of walls, I got ready for whatever might come next.

Turning sharply on my heels and to my left I ran to yet another set of scaffolding bars, these ones were constructed in a similar fashion as those that I had earlier met with the Fireman's pole. For the only time since the initial high wall I was suddenly aware of shouts of encouragement coming from some members of the staff.

The wildly spaced poles climbed in steps to two pairs of wooden arches made from old railway sleepers. Each arch comprised of two vertical sleepers topped with a third. The initial pair stood about nine feet up and seven feet long and as I reached the upper most part of the first arch, I was aware suddenly of another man parallel to me but on the other set of arches. Encouragement continued to be shouted at us. The arch disappeared from under my feet and for a second an illusion of height took my concentration. I glanced down from nine feet up and quickly surveyed the four-foot wide gap. I kicked hard and launched myself chest first over the space and landed a second later already running to the next near identical gap. Several paces after that I was back in the mud.

Exiting the deep mud, I felt stinging pains shoot up both shins. It was like knives piercing the very centre of the bone. To stretch the muscles, I leaned to the left and carried my hurting body around the tight left-hand bend. The ground thankfully became much firmer and I was able to push off a concrete step, leaping as far forward as I could so as to clear a six feet wide water filled trench. Returning back to earth I landed safely, though shakily. With only two yards to settle my lurching feet I confronted an identical water jump.

The assault course carried on relentlessly around another bend to the left bringing us round in a circle onto about thirty yards of mud churned ground. Straightening up I was glad to see the finish. Suddenly I didn't feel quite so alone, Staff joined alongside, shouting and yelling, most of it was swearing and fairly insulting yet still encouraging at the same time.

I forced my legs onward up onto the Log Bridge. The bridge was constructed from a long telegraph type wooden pole, which was secured across a deep pit of filthy stagnant water. Experience had already taught me to look straight ahead and to forget about balance and footing. It was easy and I reached the far end smoothly. A twelve-yard sprint led me to the top of a wedge shaped concrete slope. The very top of the wedge stopped at a very deep, very cold and very horrible water trench covering an expanse of twelve feet. It was going to be near impossible to clear it well enough to land on any dry soil. All I could do was hope that the launch had been sufficient to get me at least close to the edge of the water.

The jump wasn't quite powerful enough to escape the pond altogether. In the water I promptly slid backwards, out of

222

control and into the soup of brown stinking wetness. As if in slow motion the foul freezing water crept slowly up and into the inside of what had been till just now, warm clothing. Icy fingers of filth spread up my legs invading all my most vulnerable crevices and creases.

There was no time for worry nor even to shiver. Beaching my weary body I pulled myself onto the ground ready for the next seven-yard dash to yet another obstruction. Standing in my way were six railway sleepers, each set four feet apart and two feet above more cold water. I swept over the sleepers arriving briskly at the last one, then pitched my chest before me, throwing my whole weight into the air. Somehow my feet hit firm land, missing the deep-water trench, but momentum got the better of me and I toppled forward folding into a roll. I landed on my feet in a roll that any gymnast would have been proud of and probably, not one that I could have ever repeated.

Another five yards on and I attacked the large wooden gate. I pushed with one foot from the lowest log and pulled myself over the top in a classic vault. As my legs swung over the top I allowed my body to naturally fall the right way up. I landed well enough but facing the wrong way. I spun around quickly and raced straight through the next ten yards of puddles.

Eager shouts shrilled from the spectators standing in the breaking tree line. Adrenaline and excitement surged once more through my blood providing a new euphoria. The end of the first lap was at last getting closer. In terms of distance it was barely a spit away but there were still two further bars to the finish.

Hardly bending my body, I raced through two parallel bars and onward to the final obstruction. Two planks led to a wooden platform and on the end of that there was a sand pit.

Designed to slow the runner it was evident that avoiding the sand altogether had to be the best option.

With just one lap around the course completed, my poor body cried out for respite. Request denied. I gritted my teeth and propelled myself straight into the next lap.

Round and round we went. I miraculously found a reserve of energy to somehow finish with a sprint and completed the third lap feeling pleased, agony racking through my lower limbs.

A Sgt. stood at the end calmly calling out times and reading from a stop watch. I wanted to collapse onto the ground but the CSM spotted this weakness in me and some of the others. He bellowed to the troops to get into a single line! With the rest I joined those already forming a line. My chest was heaving, straining to breathe.

One bloke, who finished in front of me, was finding it difficult to cope with his uncomfortable and tight fitting helmet so to relieve the hot sweaty pressure he removed it. A Sgt. leapt over instantly to the exposed soldier, screaming obscenities at him. Under the tirade of abuse the soldier buckled, falling to the ground. But the attack continued.

"You Dickhead! You were told to stand fucking still!"

Eyes everywhere focused on the grounded soldier. His crime was simply being noticed at the wrong time. If it was sympathy that he was after, he didn't get it. Twenty press-ups taught him very quickly that it was not a good idea to remove his headgear without permission. Twenty burpees reminded him to never fall down until ordered to do so.

Looking up the line, I was immensely pleased to see that I was in the top fifteen or twenty of those to finish. I felt really proud of myself but God, I thought, it was bloody hot! Sweat cascaded from underneath the headband inside my helmet, forming little rivers running down in zigzags across my face, stinging my eyes and filling my mouth with salty moisture. Nervous spasms inside me craved for dryness on my skin and urged desperately for me to wipe the wet from my brow but, remembering the poor soul of a few minutes earlier, I made up my mind to not even contemplate removing my helmet or even daring to wipe my brow.

The OC announced his great satisfaction at our efforts and once again it was our syndicate that won the   pennant.

We marched back to the Barracks and paraded on the small square in the shadow of the large NAAFI building. The mood changed and Sgt. Instructors strutted around indignantly. One such Sgt. from the REME raised his voice warning the course of what he at least saw as our failures. He said that he and some of the other Instructors had been monitoring the standards of hygiene in the barrack blocks and that the standard was well below that which was expected at Depot Para. There was a tiny pause. He looked down to the ground in apparent disgust then, swinging back into action, he launched into a stinging verbal attack on the Officers and the SNCOs. Berating the seniors the REME Sgt. accused them of living in the comfort and sanctuary of the Messes when instead they should have been getting in amongst their men and sorting them out.

I was glad that for a change it was not me or those nearby who were receiving the worst of it but at the same time I knew that in the end it would be us who would have to suffer. Needless to say, our senior ranks and officers decided that the evening should be an In-night or a Bull-night as it was more commonly called.

As it turned out, it truly was an evening of bullshit and an awful lot of unwanted and overzealous supervision. Due to the

SNCOs and Officers having been embarrassed into doing something, they seemed to take their revenge by badgering and bullying the rest of us. It would have been fine if they had allowed us to get on with the job. Then perhaps they should have inspected the end result. Instead, Officers wandered about expressing a need to tell someone to do something even when it wasn't that soldier's job, resulting in a disorganised slow down and chaos. We ordinary ranks were gaining first-hand knowledge in the workings of that old cliché; too many Chiefs and nowhere near enough of us poor Indians.

Morning reveille brought a scurrying of frantic activity as we again swept, polished and swung the big bumpers around the floor. Happy that all was now complete, we stood by our beds while a strange procession of inspections got under way. First of all the blokes checked each other, their bed spaces and their block jobs. Then the NCOs (including me) looked over the smart crisp hospital corners and polished slate effect floors. With just seconds to spare there was a shout of, "By your beds!" Scooting off like frightened rabbits we all scattered back to our own bed spaces.

Our SNCOs accompanied the Course Instructors as they now went about in packs scrutinising every nook and cranny in their search for forbidden dust and dirt.

With that out of the way the course, now physically and mentally tired, paraded outside. The mood was low. In the meantime our Officers entered the block and began conducting a close and meticulous white gloved inspection of the accommodation. Waiting outside, it appeared to last for ages. Young men stood silently at ease, each bursting with the desire to fidget but not daring to do so or even to whisper for fear of immediate retribution. Sensing the discomfort amongst the men, one Instructor broke the disciplined trance by announcing a joke competition. Everyone in turn, he said was to tell a joke.

226

No joke, he warned, or even worse, a bad joke, would mean press-ups.

Some jokes were really good and roars of laughter demonstrated approval from the men. Some were nothing short of dire but it didn't deter. The Instructors had over the years managed to develop an unbelievably bad taste in humour. It seemed that the sicker or more insulting the joke then the more some of the Staff appeared to enjoy it, even if the rest of us had recoiled in disgust.

Giggles were still rippling through the ranks when the blond OC emerged expressionless from the weathered doorway. Fingers of morning sunlight forced him to squint before commanding absolute silence. Addressing the entire course he told us that the standard of cleanliness that he had found had barely met the basic requirement expected of his recruits let alone supposed trained soldiers.

Holding up for everyone to see, he showed off a greying white glove as rage burst from his fast reddening face. Showing his very obvious anger, the boss complained bitterly that under two mattresses he had found copious amounts of dust on the bedsprings! Only an incredible performance out in the field, he added, would save us from another miserable bull-night tonight.

Across the road from the Royal Officers Club, we were all laid down on our backs and on the grass with our feet towards the main Farnborough Road. As ordered, we kept our hands held clasped behind our heads and listened expectantly for the deafening boom of an exploding thunder-flash. For me it didn't seem to matter that knowing of an imminent bang, it still made me jump. The thunderous crack of the giant firework shattered the air around my eardrums, signalling the start of the next test; the dreaded steeplechase.

The steeplechase route was set in thick woodland situated not far from the Assault Course. A mile and a half of difficult water filled ditches, felled trees, heavy going moisture soaked clay entrenched pathways and man-made obstacles scattered across the trail, was all that we had to look forward to. Not just once but twice round and all of it had to be completed in less than nineteen minutes, otherwise no points and no points meant a big 'F' being written against your name. Hard enough in any condition but to my already tired legs and that the fact that I was dressed like a mushroom in boots, I was more than a little apprehensive.

Already orders were being barked sharply. Staff skipped sideways screaming at the sprinting men. There were nearly two hundred yards to go before we would reach the concealment of the trees and the real start of the steeplechase. Like the stretcher race before, it was important to enter the tree line as fast as possible, for here it too funnelled into a bottle neck and much valuable time would be lost by those forced into a fight for positioning.

Sprinting has never ever been my strong point, instead my running strength had been endurance, and I was a real plodder. I knew that I could keep going long after one of the racing snakes had dropped to their knees. Some blokes were disappearing into the dense greenery before I had even covered two thirds of the ground yet happily I still appeared to be in the thick of the crowd. The crowd though was thinning by the second as it herded into the tiny darkened entrance. Pushing to gain every measured yard, striving for perhaps even the tiniest of leads over any of our colleagues, we pumped our piston-like legs. As the tree line got closer, men disappeared like fish caught in a whirlpool, pulled into the ever faster swirl and swallowed by the sucking hole on the water's surface.

Inside the woods, despite my best efforts, the going immediately bottlenecked to a near halt. My mind's eye flashed to picture the sprinters, those who had got through the opening in the wood first. I knew that they must now be surging ahead. Instead of racing with them, I was jostling and exerting much more energy than I could afford, and all to merely pass colleagues in this dark channel. The track was purposefully chosen for all its sharp twists, which were banked heavily on both sides with stinging thorns. Nature proving that she too, could easily imitate the worst of man's flesh ripping barbed wire.

As the tempo of the race quickened I ran for all I was worth, holding my arms out as far to the sides as the creeping foliage would allow so as to maintain a good balance, however the trail soon became not much more than a perilous slide. This wasn't quite like slipping on a banana skin; this was like running on a whole road of rotting skins five inches deep.

On entering each corner I braced myself ready for the almost inevitable fall. At one particularly sharp bend in the path, my feet slid uncontrollably from underneath me, jarring my joints. I tried desperately to lock muscle with sinew hoping to prevent my unstable body from toppling over and somehow, I managed to stay up even when once, I ended up sliding into those who had already fallen and were now artlessly straddling the way through.

The difficult route persisted, taxing every muscle as we worked our way through mud filled trenches, mud that crept deep into the tiny openings of our boots. Cold wet mud oozed, infiltrating then crowding the little gaps between our toes. On the outside of my boots the soles were gripping great lumps of chewed turf and refusing to let go. Each raised foot felt like it was lifting an additional four pounds of mud whilst each plunging step only went to reinforce the already thick wedge of

Aldershot clay now firmly joined to the bottom of our boots. For me, I felt that I may as well run with buckets of cement tied to my feet.

I needed to rid myself of some of this extra weight. Looking for dry ground where I could wipe my feet, I tried in earnest to place my footing at the edges where the ground was slightly firmer and the mud not so churned by plodding feet. Here with my legs wide open I was not just running forward but adapting a somewhat weird position of a horseless rider, stepping from side to side.

Approaching a ninety-degree right hand bend, I leapt over the well-trodden swamp, searching for a firm base where I could land and then twisted my body through the turn. Instead a cold brown porridge of mud splattered my face as I hurtled downward and backward, striking the wet earth with alarming force. Above me I could see the perfect blue sky as it penned in the spreading tree tops keeping the air still and the humidity high. All around me there were boots and legs all kicking out, trying to find safe haven for their owners and all rushing to and fro' urgently aiming to avoid my sad prone body.

The firm ground that I had hoped for was not what it had at first appeared to be. Upright tufts of reed grass had given me the impression that the ground was virginal. Therefore, I had thrown my whole weight into the stride which should have taken me to drier and harder ground but rather than provide a platform for me to bounce from, I instead sank deep enough for the mud to completely engulf my ankles and reach up to the shins. The saturated and compressed clay under my boots caused my left leg to slip out of control and away from my chosen path. On a man-made glissade, my upper body begun its manoeuvre to the flank and with it, the heavy momentum of my shifting torso was being pushed away from the direction of that where my limbs were going. I plunged to the ground with a thud showering all those around me with fine globules of dirt.

Just in time to avoid a dangerously menacing boot I shook off the numbing shock of being decked. Lifting my fingers to my eyes I cleared my vision of wet filth but didn't bother with the speckles now garnishing my reddened complexion. I quickly rose from the mud bath and pushed past somebody on my right to continue with the chase. I was only too aware that the clock was now by far my worst enemy. Energy had been drained expensively from my muscles. Restricted by drenched taut denim PT shorts it was an effort to convince my legs that there was more to be done.

Opening out onto a short clearing the ground thudded with the sound of men running upon flint and baked sand. Ahead of me I could see a small queue of agitated waiting soldiers. They, seemingly nervous of some distraction, stood around just waiting. Off to the left and barring the way forward lay a steel-scaffold pole that was positioned three feet off the ground. From a drop of about six feet beyond and below the pole was what can only be described as either a deep pond or a bloody big puddle.

Men gathered impatiently around this difficult obstacle, only daring to tackle it one at a time. Each man in his turn took a great run at the horizontal bar, vaulting off it in a vain effort to clear the steep sided tank of freezing water. I watched as some got reasonably close to the edge but none managed to pass it. Everyone there ended up getting a soaking, sinking to slightly below waist level.

As I advanced on the small group of men I searched for a gap. My consciousness was flashing from one thing to another: I tried hard to make sense of what was happening. The pole at approximately eight feet was long enough for more than one man at a time to cross it. As everyone around me was already wet through there seemed little point in wasting more very precious time in a silly queue and even less point in spending so much valuable energy in some huge arrogant struggle to clear the pond.

The shrill voice of a thinly built Cpl. Instructor rudely woke me from my brief moment of contemplation. I don't know what he said but it was obvious that he too had seen the wasteful delay. Stopping for a moment, he paused to pull the zip of his jacket tight up almost to his neck then skipped expediently down the slippery slope and over to where we were stood. His frustration was obvious. No one, he said, had the luxury of excess time to allow the niceties of queuing. The veins in the Cpl.'s neck pulsed with rage before he let out a loud. "Get over that bastard pole!" As he got closer, his shouts progressed to threats.

Suddenly with a great crash, half a dozen bodies catapulted themselves over the barrier, before each in turn splashed and disappeared into the dark brown watery mess below. From the watery mire, I remember looking up and seeing another soldier plummeting toward me. I *was* trying to move quickly out of the way but the mud and water held me back. I could do nothing but let out a shout as thirteen stones of soldier landed squarely in my back, forcing me back under water. I was winded, the soldier himself escaped injury and together we untangled and climbed out.

The second time around seemed deceptively easier. Aware of each problem and now with more room for manoeuvre, we were able to run harder and more comfortably. This time I didn't bother to avoid the large puddles and chose instead to wade straight through. I was already saturated therefore I easily became disinterested with trying to stay dry.

It wasn't the wet that bothered me but the growing pain inside me. A knot in my stomach muscles began to twist. Deep pain had been racking my limbs and now I could feel its creeping presence deep inside. Nasty cramps attacked the flesh in my lower body causing a stiffening of my muscles but I dare not slow down or give in.

To add to my woes, I found that as I ran, my sides were being slapped annoyingly by the heavy drenched flannel of my red PT vest which had by now been stretched and contorted well out of its normal shape and size. I knew that I had to ignore it but still, the repetitive stinging was bloody irritating.

Up ahead, some men stood in a line, their chests heaving up and down, trying desperately to once again find some of their lost composure. By coincidence, as if in a practised movement of synchronised goldfish, a whole group of men raised their heads, holding them high as they gasped for refreshing cool air. Like always there was an Instructor with a stop watch waiting for men as they crossed the finishing line. This time though, the Instructor had the back-up of a partner and he held a clip board and recorded the soldiers finish times next to their names.

Deep inside both of my ears, there were strange gulping sounds as the air popped, attempting to equalise. I was suffering the dual combination of an inability to clear mud and debris from my face as well as my body's inadequate effort of taking in extra oxygen. The shouted time aimed in my direction as I passed was totally wasted. All I could hear were the echoes of my own thumping heartbeat banging away inside me, preventing any coherent sounds from entering. Gurgled voices bubbling under water were all that I heard.

Back in the billet it was a case of rush bloody rush. *Situation normal then.* There was no time for a shower or any other such niceties; instead there was time only for a very quick change of clothing. It felt great though to get out of the dirty wet kit. I knew that I wasn't clean, but I at least felt cleaner. Standing alone in the room and naked, I struggled to pull on a clean pair of denim trousers over my damp skin when just as I was in mid` hop, an SNCO entered the corridor from opposite my room. In mock screams of agony, the Sgt. clasped his hands to his throat pretending to choke. Straightening up and waving his hands underneath his screwed up nose he bitterly launched into a half joking complaint of the ineffable stench emanating from the rooms and in my direction especially.

He might have been joking but the smell was real enough. Permeating the fouled air was a toxic cocktail of composting earth, vile smelling sweat laced with gallons of stale booze and topped off with farts released straight from the arseholes of Hell.

We in the rooms could barely notice the smell but nevertheless, we all took great pride in both the sound and the strength of our farts. The more somebody could be seen to be visibly sick or annoyed, then the better.

With scran quickly thrown down our necks, we as usual paraded outside the blocks. The lucky or perhaps, the wise, had their spare boots on, ensuring that for most of the time, they would have another pair drying out ready for the next activity.

There was though, a problem with trying to dry out DMS boots and that was that they tended to dry hard, becoming rock solid and eventually they would refuse to bend. Creases in the parched compressed cardboard hardened enough to tear away at the tight skin over the bony parts of our feet. Still, I suppose that this was preferable to having to wear saturated boots or shoes which would always cause blisters no matter how toughened your feet had become.

Wet socks were just as bad. The army issue of woollen socks of the time were truly atrocious. When they became very wet as of course they often would, then they would slip down annoyingly inside my boots to gather inside the toecap in a screwed up bundle.

An unexpected tap on my shoulder followed by a gentle whisper warned me that the button on my trouser map pocket was undone. I nodded my head in grateful thanks to the comrade behind me, for an undone button could easily cost me dear in unwanted press-ups and burpees. Fastening the flap over the pocket in slow motion, I used my fingertips to search and examine my clothing. Not wanting to be seen moving and not daring to look down I felt for any hint of loose apparel, any unconnected fastening.

Hard green webbing once more bit painfully into my flesh. The stretched skin around my over prominent hipbones was once again the target of friction. Wincing, I pulled hard on the straps to tighten the pouches into me. I knew that before we were set off on yet another run, I had to restrict its movement. Happy with my check I flicked my arms back behind me and resumed the At Ease position.

It was around that time that I became aware of a dark shape fast approaching from my left. In the corner of my eye I could see that a nightmare was about to develop for the shadow was that of Major Kennett and he was heading straight for me. This could only mean bad news. The CSM followed close by.

Facing me from a couple of yards away, the OC spoke in a louder than usual pitch and with words which he pretended were for the ears of the CSM but were actually spoken so boisterously that the whole company could easily hear.

"Sar'nt Major! There's a man there who can't keep still. He has plenty of energy, perhaps he hasn't worked hard enough."

Suddenly the CSM was in front of me. His face was only inches from mine. The CSM, no doubt trying to make a point, made it abundantly clear to me that my life was at best, lowly and at worst, not even worthy of this mere existence. Down I went for the common ritual of twenty press-ups. At the same time I had to count the exercises out loud so that the OC could clearly hear my punishment.

With the cruel chastisement finished, I stood up, grateful that that was the end. The OC, who had by now turned his back on me and was chatting idly to the CSM, twisted at the waist and arched his neck to face me and   snarled.

"I never told you to get up! Down! Give me twenty!"

Biting my lip, I sank to the ground. I must have raised my eyebrows or something for the CSM noticed some change of attitude in me and curtly added, "Twenty-five! Before my punishment ended I had added burpees and sit-ups to the tally.

On the small sports field behind the main blocks of the Airborne Museum we broke into groups of around eight men. Earlier we had been shown how to prepare the telegraph poles, which we were to use for the log race. This contest had the dubious reputation of being by far the worst of all the tests. It was a fairly short route of only two miles and all of it completed in less than fifteen minutes. I had done loads of log races in the past, they were pretty strenuous but still it all sounded quite simple, after all there would be eight of us to carry it and the distance was only a couple of miles. I couldn't see what all the fuss was   about?

Each team went off with their log to the back of a four tonner and loaded them together. Once done, the teams assembled again and then we too were ordered onto the trucks. Shortly afterwards we arrived at the hilly training grounds. In front of us was a miniature desert of sand, which encroached onto   the golden basin of Long Valley. The ground appeared firm and flat and the sand glistened with recent dampness.

Half a dozen logs were disgorged forcefully from the truck only to dig their noses into the sand. For just a brief second, they seemed to have life, standing proud before smashing over the very ground, which had caused their birth. The Bedford truck choked and spat its darkened grey smoke in deep swirls then noisily and shuddering, it slowly inched forward, then it was gone.

For a few chaotic minutes there was an absence of leadership. Men just stood around, huddled in small groups and chatting idly in the sunshine. Already I was very hot, uncomfortably so. Pushing my forefinger up and into the lining of my Airborne helmet I begged for the relief of cool air, but there was none to be found and inside my helmet, I was sweating profusely.

Sweat should have been my saviour. As the body's self defence system against overheating, it was definitely failing. The salty vapour had nowhere to go; instead it collected in puddles in the gaps inside my helmet before flowing downwards in a trickle at first, then as I became increasingly hotter, it turned into sticky torrents down my face.

One of the Sgt. Instructors, sensing the lack of organisation abruptly took control. "Everybody down! Ten!" He demanded. No one seemed to make any objection. All of these little bouts of physical exercise had by now become quite normal, routine in fact. Behind the Sgt., as if not connected to us at all, other Instructors appeared engrossed in conversation, not even noticing the frenzied activity happening all around them. Perhaps they had just seen it all so many times before.

After what seemed a very long ten minutes, the OC and CSM arrived with the jacking wagon. An order was loudly shouted and the syndicate leaders (our Sgt. Instructors) barked out yet more orders. They pointed and waved wildly in frantic haste. Once that all the syndicates and their sub-groups (the log teams) were lined up, the PTI in charge explained the few rules to be observed during the coming race.

"This is a team event! Under no circumstances will anyone let go of the log! It is going to be hard. Fight for it and you'll be OK!" He went on reassuring, "Everyone here is capable of putting up a good show, otherwise you wouldn't be here."

Individual Instructors flew about between the logs checking that each log was in one piece and had been tied correctly with the rope handles. Steve Ryder, whilst going about the rigorous checks passed out helpful hints and advice.

It was near to the start and our last chance to sort out who goes where. Sailor was volunteered as the leading man. In front was needed the best, the fastest and the most reliable. Sailor was quick witted and gutsy as Hell. Our man had proved his worth over and over again during this course. He was the best that we had; it had to be him.

The weakest men went either side at the front of the log but behind the lead. Being considered to be one of the strongest, I was paired with another large chap at the back. Knowing how difficult it is to run blind at the back and that also, when running up hill, the men at the back quite literally shoulder much more of the weight, I became a little disenchanted. Seeing my disappointment, Sgt. Ryder gritted his teeth in false anger then came over to explain how important it was to have someone reliable and strong at the back so that they could push the weaker ones out in front. He was right of course but it still felt horrible. I was comfortably good at the front and I didn't want to be stuck at the back with no control over direction or speed.

All the logs and their teams were lined up level with each other across the sand. PTIs scurried from one to the other in an effort to ensure that all the teams were exactly flush and that no team could complain of any disadvantage. The teams with ropes in their hands sat down some yards behind their grounded logs.

A piercing shriek from a whistle blast gave us the off. I launched my body upward and into an instant sprint and arrived simultaneously with my team mates. I scrambled at the rope, securing it fast. With the rope tight I screamed for all I was worth. "Go! Go!" Eight pairs of legs pounded the firm wet sand as our lungs burst brusquely into life. Each one of us wanted to be the best and all of us sprinted as hard and as fast as our bodies would allow.

Like one or two of the tests that we had already encountered, the first team into the woods and onto the tiny track leading the way along the route would have an important advantage that could turn out to be crucial. Muscles in my neck strained as I desperately searched for the way forward, willing the team ever faster. But I needn't have worried, the matelot was good. He took full advantage of every rock and every twist. Sailor chose his route well.

Close to the woodlands entrance our team pushed to get in front and as we did so, we collided with a rival team. The opposing sides bounced violently as over a hundred stone of men and wood met with a great crash. Thankfully for us at least, the other team seemed to fare far worse and were forced to take several steps out to the side just to keep some balance. However, they very quickly recovered and fought back instantly but for them it was already too late. We were there first.

The gap between the teams spread a little but still the boys, who we had just smashed out of the way, were right up at   our arses. At that point, the other team was undoubtedly trying for the front position much harder than we were. Maybe their team was better than us, but we were in front and we weren't about to let it go easily. To get past us, they would have to fight for it.

Half way up a hill, the woods and gorse that had until now dominated the landscape suddenly went, clearing to reveal an area carpeted with the shocking pinks of wild heather. Seizing an unguarded opportunity, the close-by rival team raced up from behind, flattening the squat plants as they threatened to take the lead. Screaming my heart out, I urged my team onwards but one of our blokes was now dragging on the log. Before we could recover, the other team were squeezed into the front. Now it was our turn to fight.

Our leading man pulled bravely at the log in a determined effort not to allow an increase in the gap between the two log teams. The weaker men at the front had apparently all but surrendered. One, a Signaller was allowing himself to be carried along but at the hugely wasteful expense of his team mates. His arm dangled uselessly over the log and whilst he was for the time being able to keep up with the team, he was very obviously struggling. His feet were hardly clearing the ground; instead he skipped stiffly, wearied and exhausted.

Perhaps what his tired mind was not able to comprehend immediately was that with this lack of action he risked considerable double jeopardy. The spent Signaller faced the anger and frustration of his immediate comrades as well as the terrible wrath from the master of harangue; Sgt Ryder. The tall SNCO Gunner wasted no time and threw himself into a verbal tirade as he ripped into the struggling youth, tearing his soul apart with an expert use of disciplined command bullying. The straggler, aided with a hefty shove from behind, pulled himself along the pole to at least maintain his correct team place. He may not have actually been tugging the log but he wasn't holding it back either.

At the top of the hill there was a cut-out, a sort of short cliff of around four feet in height confronting the racers. Large lumps of grey and red flint cemented into the rusted orange sand glistened, daring the first man to contemplate climbing its banks.

With his left knee firmly tucked into his chest and his toes pushing on jagged rock, he forced his body weight through his lower leg. Lifting his right foot his chest began to rise. He could see the ground coming invitingly closer, then just at the right time he kicked forward, searching for firm footing. The leading man from the team in front was confident that he had found safety. But before he could take advantage of his success, the jagged rock cruelly broke away from its mud moulded housing, crumbling beneath him.

The doomed soldier, feeling his weight suddenly shift violently, tried desperately to compensate but the terrific dead weight of the massive log put pressure on his balance from behind and from below. It was too much, and their leading man went crashing down to the earth. The brutal impact jarred his back and like sweets in a kiddie's bag, shook his insides mercilessly forcing the air to explode from his lungs. Even before his cry of pain could be heard, his eyes were forced to involuntarily close, squeezing tight. A reaction from deep inside his brain tried in vain to force out the horror that his eyes could not now see but that, which his mind could not ignore.

The huge half telegraph pole plummeted down toward him and draped over its great wooden length was the taught petrified body of his terror stricken mate. With his eyes firmly clamped shut also in an attempt to deny the inevitable, the out of control soldier recklessly gripped the log to his chest in his panicky attempt to halt its tumble but it was all happening far too fast.

Sailor didn't dare to hesitate. He couldn't spare the time to help the opposing team or even to pay them more than passing attention. Selecting for us instead a safer route, he bounded effortlessly over the small ridge. Our log by now, was perilously almost vertical. As I looked on helpless, I could see the lads at the front as they struggled valiantly to keep the front end up. Sailor yanked hard at his rope, bending his knees and slinging the tether over his shoulder to form a makeshift yoke. Up and over it went, then it toppled, falling to our front, its momentum carrying it lazily forward.

At the back we pushed like fury, forcing the log through and along its uphill trajectory. The front men faced an opposite problem, for them the log was in danger of leaving them behind. The three at the front end scrambled awkwardly, stretching their arms up to keep hold of the flying log above. Then for a moment they too took off. Dangling from the pole as it levered its way over the rocky ridge, our front men empty pedalled at the air before their feet inevitably kicked at the sand and pebbles below.

Vision seemed to play in slow motion. I witnessed team mates at the sharp embankment falter one by one. Frustration coupled with an overdose of adrenaline, brought the abrupt pressure of angry temper up into my chest, threatening a loud eruption. Fortunately and before my legs could kick out at any one, the team was over. The men and the log righted themselves directly. Boiling pangs of madness inside me quickly subsided and our team was again hurtling forward down the skinny track. This time our team were the clear leaders.

The trail twisted and turned its way through the dense spring foliage, constantly climbing. Surprising ourselves, we continued to hold the lead. The other team, which had dogged us all the way was now so close and barging and pushing that we fought for space. Meanwhile we, in a near sprint, dragged our huge lump of wood between us. The thick fibrous rope handles tore into the fleshy parts of our hands as muscles and ligaments expanded down the length of our arms and threatened to wrench themselves free from their sockets. It felt like every sinew in our bodies was begging for fast relief.

Across my shoulders, the agony had never left. Every step that I took allowed the pole to swing in rhythm but the whole team had lost its unified rhythm and were all running independently, which meant that the pole swung awkwardly and erratically. I tried to pull the weight into me but in its loose cradle of thick rope held together with weakened bruised flesh, it rocked out of control.

Just as the fight was at its toughest, it was over. The summit of a steep hill was conquered and we started the descent. A third of a mile ahead and already clearly visible, were the trucks and the blue jacketed P-Company Staff. Some stood still, closely examining their stop watches, others were yelling enthusiastically, urging us on to the invisible finishing line.

The hill suddenly fell away to our rear and we found ourselves on the strangely unfamiliar terrain of flat ground. Between us and the small road which led to the Instructors and the wagons lay a dry lake, a hundred yards across of perfectly smooth yellow sand, interrupted only by the occasional sprouting of thick stemmed grasses.

Shouts were overtaken with grunts and the sounds of heavy footsteps from either side and behind. As the teams battled for superiority, others lurched ever nearer. Adrenaline, spurred on

243

by the sudden intensity of competition, flowed through our veins, oiling our tired limbs and providing much sought-after energy. Almost in unison our team pace quickened. The bloke next to me started to yell. "Com'n! In...Out! In..Out!" At first it seemed that his efforts to regulate our step had fallen on deaf ears, then one by one, the team responded, grounding their inward legs to the call of, "In!"

The shouts of coaching began to have an effect too. Fresh confidence filled our minds and as the finish drew closer, all of us shouted out the steps. The team with its log propelled itself amid the waiting staff. Sounds of claps and cheers filled our ears as we crossed the line. Adrenaline still buzzed around inside my body and I truly felt

Some roared their congratulations to us for being the first but I think that mostly it fell on deaf ears and was largely ignored. With the stopwatch now firmly behind us, some of the men clearly felt the need to simply drop the log and then collapse. Before we had a chance to do any more than think about it, a PTI pounced and ordered the log be taken straight onto the back of a waiting truck. Sailor, as ever full of energy, leapt up onto the dropped tail gate of the big lorry and as we pushed from below, he pulled the long obstacle into the darkened belly of the wagon. Sailor couldn't be persuaded down so we left him up there to assist with getting the other teams poles up there too.

That done, we stood in line fairly near to the positions where we had earlier started and watched the as the last few teams came in. When the OC presented the winners pennant it was Sailor who once again marched forward to collect it. My attention though, was somehow drawn to the smiling face of Sgt Steve Ryder. He was standing squarely behind the Major and grinning like a Cheshire cat. He was proud of his boys.

Chip Walker

Thursday morning broke with a totally clear sky. The sun had already begun to spread its golden fingers of bright warmth across the blue. Today I felt great and the prospect of the imminent fifteen mile tab held no fear for me. I was, instead looking forward to it. The tab was to take us back to the South Downs of Sussex.

In the corridor, bodies bounced up and down as they shuffled this way and that way with their heavy Bergen kit bags, all in an urgent effort to ensure that the big sack was fitted correctly and was as comfortable as the weight would allow. Once satisfied, last minute adjustments were carried out on their various straps and buckles of the sometimes confusing array of 58 pattern webbing. It was a buddy-buddy system, everyone checked everyone else. Once completed, the NCOs checked everyone again.

Everything was ready. We lined up the kit in a smart row and having left two blokes to keep guard, we marched over to the cookhouse for breakfast. Like most of the lads, I purposely forced stacks of food down my throat. I knew that though there was an increased risk of me needing the toilet, if I didn't eat more now than a belly full, my body's need for vast amounts of energy would soon confront me. Most of the men didn't really understand the theory of nutrition so instead compromised by eating everything and anything.

I don't have a particularly sweet tooth but I ensured that I finished off a bowl of cornflakes which had been densely coated with sickly powdered glucose and then I followed that with several fried egg sandwiches. It was an odd sensation this, having almost as much food as I could ever want. Ordinarily in a Cookhouse, portions were strictly controlled. This was apparently not so at Depot Para. Men attending P-Company courses were given near total freedom to eat as much as they liked and eating a lot was much encouraged.

245

Back at the block, I fitted my webbing, pulling tightly at the now supple canvas straps across my hips. In one smooth and articulate swing, the heavy Bergen slid up my back and over my shoulders. A few seconds later there was a shout and suddenly, we were marching at the double towards the little square shaped unit armoury to collect our Argentine FN rifles.

In a well-rehearsed routine and as soon as we had hold of our weapons, we immediately marched over to the small square in front of the NAAFI and then lined up in single file. Staff went about their familiar inspections, walking amongst the men, checking for loose straps and poorly stowed equipment.

Shortly after that CSM Rustell marched forcefully up and down the lines, writing each man's name and course number onto an unattached piece of paper, which flapped annoyingly about on his clipboard. Next to him, a Sgt. simultaneously held out the first Bergen to be weighed. He hooked the big bag onto a set of brass fisherman's scales and with two hands lifted the whole lot off the ground. If it were so much as an ounce less than thirty pounds, the owner would suffer immediate retribution in the form of severe physical activities.

A throaty grunt and an approving nod of the head told me that my Bergen weighed in at a little over thirty pounds and was acceptable. Shoving the Bergen unceremoniously between my knees, I clasped my webbing and hooked that onto the waiting scales. The requirement was for it to weigh at least fifteen pounds including the full to the brim water bottle.

The next check was of course the water bottle. Great practice had gone into refining the skilled art of filling an army water bottle. Earlier I had held the black plastic two-pint bottle under a sink flooded with cold water. As the final mushrooming bubbles of air burst to the surface, I pushed the half inch deep lid under the water and whilst still submerged, I sealed the container. Experience had shown me that when an SNCO removed the bottle cap, water spilled out. If it didn't, it meant that there was room for more.

Having weighed and checked absolutely everything in my kit and on my person, the last and most bizarre examination came from the CSM and which, literally shook us up. He gave the order for everyone to put their kit back on and jump up and down. This we did until he eventually screamed out to stop! I suppose that the object of that particular exercise was to ensure that nothing rattled or moved about on our webbing and at the same time the Staff could watch out for anything that might fall off. If that were to happen, then may God help the poor sod who had allowed it.

We had arrived at a muddy track, high up on the Downs. The clean country air filled my lungs as I breathed deeply, allowing my senses to feast on the unpolluted smells. I needed it for I had near choked with thick acrid fumes of diesel fuel on the way here. "Serves me right!" I muttered to myself. After all it was me who had insisted on sitting at the back, half-hanging out over the tailgate for the whole of the slow two-hour drive.

I felt pretty awful. I was determined though to shake it off. I knew that this is where I should be playing my trump card. Tabbing had always been my strongest skill in these tests and certainly, my fitness had dramatically improved over the last few weeks.

Resolutely, I convinced myself that I would do well. To pass, I needed to complete the fifteen miles in less than two and a half-hours. I know that that sounds quite easy but it must be considered that throughout the distance, each man wears a cumbersome airborne helmet, carries a minimum of forty five pounds of weighty equipment plus a further nine pounds of rifle. The soldier is then expected to climb some of the steepest hills in the country and after that, remain fit enough to fight a battle.

With all the Staff from the Depot, as well as several hangers-on who were here simply because they enjoyed a good tab, there were about a hundred of us. Too many to just march off and effectively take over a route, which after all was a public right of way, instead, we marched in groups, keeping a ten-minute gap between. As expected we set off almost straight away into a run. It was made only slightly easier than would normally be expected because the first mile or so was either downhill or fairly flat.

Some bright spark was shouting out the time for our pace but he may as well as not bothered because the pace was fast and each man was struggling enough just trying to keep up. It was nine or ten minutes before we calmed down and broke into a normal marching speed. By then I had suffered the now accustomed feeling of physical devastation. There had been no warm up, so sudden muscular fatigue had played heavily on all parts of my body. It was horrible but I knew that once my heart could adjust to the swift demand for oxygen and energy, my body would actually settle down and believe it or not, I really would enjoy it. However, settling down was made very difficult because of the stop-start nature of this particular tab.

Time passed quickly and I was soon in my element. I felt good. The scenery was great and it gave me something to concentrate on. Taking in the splendour of some of the best English Downs, I was easily able to forget the huge weight that I carried upon my back and around my belt.

The first five miles though were still fairly difficult. We worked closely as a squad and that meant staying as close as possible to each other and all the time remaining in three ranks. The awkward part was that nobody could march well at such a speed whilst carrying heavy kit and being in three ranks prevented us from swinging our arms or kicking our legs out to maintain a comfortable gait.

Personally I found that being in the front of the squad meant that the paces were far too short to be comfortable for someone like me with long legs. After a couple of miles of constantly and regulated marching to an unnatural pace, I always suffered great discomfort and eventually quite a bit of pain, especially at the front of my shins. However, if I was positioned somewhere near the back I knew that I would end up repeatedly sprinting short distances to catch up those people in front who were not keeping their dressing.

The squad stopped momentarily at a sharp point on top of a hill. Down below at the end of an apparently endless track, and completely dwarfed by a huge black Dutch barn, were the hard square shapes of the jacking wagon and a four tonner, both parked a little way past a farmhouse. By now Sgt Ryder was out of sight. Far behind us, he had been detailed by the OC to chase up any stragglers. Acting as our supervisor was instead a Cpl. from the Parachute Regiment. He was a thickset lad with a head that, due to the absence of any visible neck, appeared to just sit there on his shoulders.

Bunching us together, the Cpl. waved his arms in great big circular gestures then clearly exaggerating, shouted. "You can smell the tea from here, let's go!" No sooner had the words filled the air and he was gone, doubling away down the lane towards the vehicles. We in the squad silently looked at each other then, shrugging our shoulders, set off in unison after him. The slope fast became steeper so that in hardly any time at all, it was gravity that pulled me down the hill. My descent began to accelerate so much that I was struggling to stay upright.

From somewhere nearby there were cries of pain accompanied with a clatter of rifle and equipment as some hapless soul was sent sprawling across loosened chalk and flint. It provided me with a very quick reminder of just how fragile my own position was. Curiosity urged me to peek at the source of the crying, I desperately wanted to know who had just crashed but fear mixed with an awareness of my own precarious position ensured that my eyes looked nowhere but just one pace straight ahead.

Shortly before the farm at the bottom of the hill was a small freshly made tarmac road. Being one to never forget my Green Cross code in road safety, I felt ultimately obliged to look all around and check that the way across was clear. As it was, young Paras from the QM's department had halted traffic on either side. The quite sudden experience of finding flat and firm ground under my feet felt remarkably odd. So much so that I couldn't help but have my boots slap the road surface, both looking and sounding like a performing sea lion.

Forgetting my difficulties for a moment, I struggled to suppress a girlish giggle as the image of me waddling across the road and searching for my land legs appealed to my rather warped sense of humour.

Just a few yards past the farmhouse some of the others joined me and together we rounded a corner to find another group already prostrate and relaxing with mugs of hot sweet tea.

This location was geographically close to the actual ten-mile point for this tab, and had been chosen for its safety and shelter as a quick resting-place. At last we had the chance to sip at a welcome hot drink of NATO Standard, hot tea complete with sugar and tinned evaporated milk.

With the others from my group I skipped along to the short wheel based Land Rover parked nearby. A stainless steel   five-gallon tea urn was balanced precariously over the opened tailgate. Behind it we queued, each with one pint plastic mugs held firmly in our left hands whilst never taking our right hands from our rifles.

Some of the lads had obviously experienced problems. There were men scattered about all over the place busily checking their toes, holding them up in the air for easy inspection. One pushed his fingers into the bony ends and winced dramatically when it hurt. Others tore at their Bergens at the very first opportunity, rashly trying to make the straps even a little more comfortable. Personally, I felt all right. Obviously there was some tiredness and certainly, my shoulders were a bit tender, but there was nothing that would actually cause me any real trouble.

Finding a quiet corner with a grassy bank, I sat down. The angle of the ground meant I was able to sit slightly forward of my Bergen without taking it off, thereby temporarily removing its weight.

This most pleasant moment of day dreaming was rudely interrupted with angry shouts which were almost immediately joined with a chorus of other similar shouts. At first I was not sure just who had started the shouting but everyone's attention appeared to be aimed at a couple of blokes who were busy urinating against a short sandstone wall.

At first I reckoned that the alarm was because this display was being conducted only yards from a large window of somebody's farmhouse. I shook my head in disbelief and attempted to continue my rest. As I turned my head, I caught a glance of a shiny engraved plaque, which was cemented into the wall. It was a memorial to a little girl who had been run over and killed just a few years before. I, too, then joined in with the loud chants of disapproval. The two blokes were just bastards. The rest of us left them in no doubt of that.

Time disappeared and soon there was a long thin line of green clad soldiers snaking their way up a narrow tractor lane which led steeply up the mighty Chalk Hill.

Starting afresh at the farm, the men were in confident spirits as the order to go was given. We had started off in small groups to tackle the climb but fairly soon the hill had begun to take its toll. In only about five or ten minutes, the groups had split up to form a rag tag trail of ambling wanderers.

My mind flashed back to a time, years before when a friendly QMSI told me that the best way to tackle a difficult hill was to get angry and attack it. He advised then to fight your way up and keep going till you've conquered it all.

Chalk Hill was not going to beat me. Reciting to myself a silly army dictum; "Head down, arse up and brain in neutral", I powered my legs up and through the steep rough track.

Occasionally I passed a breathless colleague stopping momentarily for a rest. As each of them fell behind me, my self-esteem and pride grew tenfold. I glanced behind. The glowing white track was disappearing into the vastness of the distant valley. Now that I was near the top of this monster hill, it seemed difficult to believe that I had covered so much ground in so little time. Unashamedly so, I was proud of myself.

Somewhere at about two thirds of the way up the hill, the track broke away into a narrow and scarred footpath which, was bordered with electric wire fences designed to keep sheep on their pastures. Ahead of me by just a few yards was Thomo' Thompson. I laughed out loud at myself. *We've been here before.* I liked Thomo'. He was a bloke that just about everyone felt that they could rely. Though we shared the same rank I still looked to him for leadership. In some ways, I envied him. He seemed so at ease with everything.

As the gap between us closed, I called out to the big man and jokingly added, "We must stop meeting like this, people are beginning to talk!" He turned and with an expression which showed a total relaxation with the circumstances, and simply smiled at me. The smile lasted until I drew up level with him, then he silently turned and marched with me further up the path toward the top. I can't remember what words that were spoken, but I do remember that I told him how great I thought all this was and that I was really enjoying myself. Thomo' said little in reply but still I felt encouraged and that urged me on.

That was the sort of bloke that he was. He rarely talked about himself; instead he chose to take an interest in the guys around him. Shortly afterwards, he went off ahead of me. He never got so far that he was out of sight and every now and then he paused to call me. I never though, managed to close the gap. It perhaps sounds cruel, but actually Thomo' was doing me a favour. He knew that I had more to give and he made me work for it.

As the day progressed it got hotter and hotter. For a while as well, I was on my own. I could see men up in front and men behind but no one was close enough to chat. Sometimes I would pass a slowing soldier or two but still I felt alone. I was getting tired, uncomfortable, sore and very hot!

Depression started to unfold over me. The urge to dump all my kit was stifling. This was bad news and I couldn't allow myself to embrace it. I had to shake myself free of it. Banging my head against an invisible wall, I snorted loudly. Arguing out loud with myself, I told the moaning part of my mind to get stuffed! It must have worked because I found a new sense of purpose and strode on with renewed vigour.

The upward climb cut away dramatically into a pleasant country path flanked by dense shrubs and trees. One by one I overtook more exhausted soldiers. Most said nothing, unable even to acknowledge my presence. One chap that I was surprised to catch up to was a good looking blond haired boy of just nineteen years and also from the Royal Engineers, I never knew his real first name. He was just called Smudger Smith.

During Pre-Para he had been amongst the best and he had set a particularly high standard of fitness and strength. Previously I had struggled to match him yet here I was, just about to pass him. Marching alongside, I couldn't help but blurt out some words. I implored him to buck up and stay with me. Smudger though, was obviously not at his best. He was slowly losing ground. Dragging his feet painfully and with his face pale and drawn, he appeared totally exhausted. He lifted his eyes at me before murmuring, "Go Chip, You're doing really well. Go for it." As I opened my pace I glanced back. I had to try again. Cocking my head to one side, I begged him to keep with me. He didn't answer.

Ten minutes later and the closely wooded and darkened path broke out into the sunshine and onto a narrow tarmac road. A uniformed NCO stood alone in the centre of the road, as he did so he waved each of us down the hill. I couldn't see the end but I was able to recognise exactly where I was. This road led to a lovely little country pub that was isolated at the bottom of the hill. This was where the Pre-Para ten miler had ended.

Guessing that this too was the finish for this tab, I accelerated into a run. The sound of hard and fast footsteps from behind convinced me that I had guessed correctly and that at least one other bloke had come up with the same conclusion. He had now decided to try and beat me to the line. With no time to look at whoever it was, I started to sprint. At the bottom of the lane, men shouted their applause, urging one of us on to be the winner. I really don't know who won because it would have been difficult at the finish line to fit a lick of boot polish between us.

As was now quite customary, an SNCO from the staff approached and wrote down our personal details. Helping each other, we two rivals removed our Bergens and webbing. Once free of the burgeoning weight, I dropped to my arse and ripped off my sweat soaked shirt. Somewhere inside my Bergen, packed hard amongst the bags of sand and rocks was a clean shirt.

Pulling it on it felt luxurious. It was just so nice to have something that was dry and smelled clean. With the others who had finished and had sorted their personal admin out, I was allowed to enter the pub. Few of the blokes carried any money so it worked out to be very expensive for those, like me who did.

There is an unwritten rule: when on a course it was expected that you should buy drinks for your Instructional Staff, or at least offer to. Luckily for me, they had already been furnished with pints, so most declined.

The jokes were awful but still the collective humour of the men brought bouts of raucous laughter. Some people called it the last test, this was a command attendance.

The Company Smoker was held upstairs in the NAAFI building and it was for all ranks, Officers, Staff and soldiers alike. The CSM had ordered all of us to be there. Earlier and just before we were due to knock off, he told us to forget all the tests that we had now done. Everyone was to go and get drunk.

For the evening each group was to put on a show of some sort, something like a play, the sillier and ruder, the better.

A lone Cpl. from the Depot staff stood in the centre of a make shift stage. In-between sips from his over-full glass of beer he blurted out jokes happily. The humour was typically lewd and often offensive to just about everyone. I thought that most of his jokes were good but then again it has many times been said that I have a very strange sense of humour.

Over by the bar the Senior Instructors sat sedately, talking only occasionally amongst themselves. Approaching I commented that I reckoned the comedic Cpl. to be rather good but was met with a sharp retort. "No he ain't!" Felling a little puzzled, I questioned the miserable reaction. "He sounds good to you" one said.

"But we've heard it all before". Another member of Staff added.

"Yeah. Every bloody course!"

After the ritual downing of a very hot curry it was time for our hasty and ill-prepared sketches. Just like the earlier jokes most of the plays and sketches were in abysmally poor taste but nobody cared. We all laughed anyway. Our show was no exception. It too was truly terrible.

With my colleagues we had come up with an unimaginative version of the television quiz show, Mastermind. Unfortunately for us, so did two other groups. Ours though, we thought, was far superior. In a cheerful sort of way, all the questions were designed to be insulting to our Instructor, Sgt. Ryder. One silly question was, "What sort of rider was the Horse Artillery very keen to get rid of? The answer was of course, 'Steve Ryder'. To us the questions were hilarious and even just asking the question was enough to bring the whole team to fits of silly schoolgirl giggles.

As the evening wore wearily on and the drinks continued to flow, the men became much less inhibited by the presence of

Officers and Senior NCOs. Worries of who might have passed or might have failed were pushed to one side. Small groups formed and sang their hearts out, all tried to be louder and more disgusting than the next. The atmosphere was bloody great!

With all the tests now over, we breakfasted whilst at the same time holding mini inquests into what had gone wrong. Smudger Smith came and sat at the table. Already there was Kenny Turk, Tom Onions and me. Smudger told me that he thought that he must have peaked physically when we were on the 9 Squadron Pre-Para, subsequently his fitness could only have worsened as the weeks went on. Whereas, he said, I had peaked with perfect timing being at my best during Test Week. The flattery was well intentioned and it certainly did my ego good, but I assured him that the timing was much more of an accident than design, though I was still glad of it.

Looking around so as to ensure that no prying ears could easily over hear we sneakily exchanged verdicts on who should or should not pass P-Company. I didn't feel bad about having a part in this self-righteous act; after all, the blokes at the other tables were surely doing the same to us.

Locally issued kit was returned and the Barrack blocks were cleaned once more.

Halfway through the morning we were marched in our groups over to the Regimental Gym. Inside we were seated in neat rows and just like four weeks earlier, we all wore our Regimental or Corps headdress. The Sgt. Instructors took their places at the back allowing the CSM to take over, briefing the entire course on the order of the day.

The OC threw his beret onto the nearby desk then picked up a clipboard, sighed and sat down. The only noise to be heard inside the hall was the sound of papers being examined.

Amongst the audience was only silence. The men hardly dared to move. In trepidation at what lay ahead, we simply stared nervously into emptiness.

Major Kennett spoke forcibly as he enlightened us with his views. It had been a good course which, he said, had also achieved an equally good pass rate. The OC went on to reassure us, reminding us that there was no such thing as a simple pass or failure. "This is a selection course. Some will be selected and some won't. There will be no disgrace for those who haven't made it this time round."

There was a silent pause and then the blond Major started to read rather abruptly from the list in front of him. Plain, simple and without any elaboration he began to call out the ranks and names. "Gunner Brown!" Shocked into urgent reaction, Gunner Brown leapt to his feet. Ramrod straight and standing formally to attention, he snapped. "Sir!" The OC hardly raised his eyebrows as he casually confirmed the existence of the young Artilleryman. Without any hint of emotion, the Major barked, "Fail!" In a split second the young soldier answered with another but softer, "Sir." He sat down and lowered his head.

A deep sense of shock and anxiety racked my whole being. I knew this lad. He was good, very good. Christ, I thought if he had failed what chance was there for me?

One by one the names were called and men learned of their results from a single word. That word being either, 'Pass' or 'Fail'. Most results appeared much as my colleagues and I had predicted but occasionally, like the case involving Gunner Brown, there were some stunning and shocking decisions announced. Us ordinary blokes without the privy knowledge of the Staff, found some of those decisions very hard to swallow indeed.

Chip Walker

My time came around quickly enough. The feeling of anticipation, similar to stage fright was almost overbearing. I had previously felt confident that I had done alright but now, having seen some blokes fail and who I had thought would have easily passed, I was not so sure.

Sgt. Ryder had sneakily said to me earlier, "You've no problem son. You've done good." Strictly speaking, the instructional Staff shouldn't make singular judgements and certainly they should not inform the course men of their potential results. Unless it was just an exercise designed to cheer up a disheartened soldier. Now I really did wonder.

"Corporal Walker!" The voice shattered the temporary doubts drifting around my head. I pushed myself upward hesitantly into a smart position of attention. With arms tucked in and my chin up, I stood perfectly still. A pause of deathly silence filled the hall. Only the thumping sound of my racing heart interrupted the stillness.

"Sir!" I croaked.

"Pass!"

This simple remark hit me like a baseball bat but the shock fast subsided and was quickly overtaken by a giant wave of excitement rising from deep in my stomach. Trying desperately to suppress an incredible urge to jump up and down screaming halleluiah, I gritted my teeth, composed myself and answered the waiting Major.

Sitting down I glanced slightly to either side and at my already successful companions. With inconspicuous smiles they nodded their approval and congratulations. Hands whipped briskly across our laps for vigorous though discreet handshakes. I was on top of the world.

I was pleased see my matelot friend had passed. With perhaps a little embarrassment from us army folk, the sailor, a commando and a potential transferee from the RAF Regiment picked up Best Recruit awards. Without exception, each one of them fully deserved it.

Back in the accommodation block was a world of gratuitous violence as each of us set about destroying army property. We ripped our old black or blue berets into small pieces. This ceremony met with great cheers, shattering the rooms every time pieces of the unwanted hats were dumped in the bin.

We had earned our maroon berets, the Maroon Machine. Other berets, which were described with an over pronounced, "Hats" were treated with thorough and utter contempt. Even admitting that once you wore such a hat was a matter of deep shame.

P-Company May 1984. Chip Walker is top row, fourth from the right. Tommy Onions is also top row, 7th from the left. Steve Ryder is front row, in blue and first on the left. Front row centre in blue is CSM Ernie Rustelland Major Kennett.

Back in the Married Quarter immediately after passing P-Company, and wearing the near obligatory maroon T-shirt.

DEPOT THE PARACHUTE REGIMENT
AND
AIRBORNE FORCES

PRE-PARACHUTE SELECTION SECTION
REPORT

Number ... 24340155 .... Rank .... CPL .... Name ...... WALKER ....

Unit .... DEPOT ACC .... Regt/Corps ..... ACC .... Course No. .. 3/84 ....

From .. 21 MAY 1984 .... To .. 8 JUNE 1984 ....

PASS/~~FAIL~~

	A	B	C	D	F	
MOTIVATION		X				
DETERMINATION		X				
FITNESS			X			
STAMINA			X			
ATTITUDE		X				
CONFIDENCE			X			
LEADERSHIP		X				
TEAM SPIRIT			X			

KEY TO GRADING

A — Outstanding
B — Above Average
C — Average
D — Below Average
F — Fail

General Comments:

Cpl Walker arrived well prepared for this course. He worked extremely hard during the build up period, however, he experienced difficulties on the confidence training.

During Selection Week he scored high points and was awarded a pass result.

Recommended to serve with Airborne Forces.

Lieutenant Colonel
Commanding Officer

CHAPTER TWELVE

ONE THOUSAND, TWO THOUSAND!

Sunday afternoon was dry and fine. I stood outside by the blue painted front door of my married quarter, kissed Janet and the kids goodbye and waved lovingly as I walked the few yards over to my waiting Austin Maxi. My mind was in turmoil. Of course I was going to miss my family but that wasn't it. Nagging doubts once again filled my head. How well would I cope with the life-long fear of heights? I didn't mind flying but I was now seriously wondering what I would be like with having to jump from a moving aeroplane.

It had not been that long since I had visited the big RAF base of Brize Norton in Oxfordshire but I had never driven there on my own. For all my previous visits I had been a passenger, usually in the back of a truck. My car was a bit of an old jalopy and the pending journey of about eighty miles added concerns.

An hour and a half passed quickly with few hiccups and I found myself exactly where I should have been, at the main gates to the RAF base. An extremely pretty WRAF girl checked my ID card and then pointed me off in the direction of PCAU. The accommodation was on the far side of the camp. To assist us wayward visitors there were little day-glow orange arrows placed strategically alongside of the road, marking the route.

Perhaps the first thing that strikes an army visitor to this massive base was its sheer size; it seemed to stretch for miles. For most soldiers, used only to the cramped living spaces of their barrack blocks and the limited open space of a tarmac parade square, this maze of roads and buildings with all its grass and trees was like another planet. With each yard passing behind me there appeared to be an ever increasing collection of aircraft hangars, administration blocks, accommodation and something which appeared to be of huge importance to the RAF, recreation buildings. There were bars, Messes, clubs, a cinema and even a bowling alley.

The contrast was dramatically stark. Tucked away as if hidden from the view of airmen and their modern red brick accommodation blocks were rows of green wartime prefabricated huts. The initial excitement of being welcomed onto this ultra-comfortable all mod' cons' station suddenly gave way to feelings of being severely dumped upon. I couldn't help but feel that these old decrepit huts would have been demolished years ago if it were not for the fact that the army needed somewhere to lay its head.

Only one of the many huts remained in the service of the RAF. It was the stores and offices of the RAF Police Dog Section.

Sited in the centre of the complex was a hut clearly marked with;

PCAU ADMIN OFFICE.

Snaking away from one of the doors to the PCAU hut was a winding queue of young men. On joining it, I asked if I was in the correct place. Several blokes confirmed that indeed I was.

Having collected my issued bedding and parachuting equipment, I joined another but shorter queue, this time to be given details of where my allocated bed-space would be.

I was fortunate, I think, to be given the top tier of a bunk bed at the end of the last block. I truly felt lucky because in this single hut, there were fifty-six of us but there were only lockers for forty; therefore, some just had to share. This was despite the fact that these lockers appeared hardly large enough to contain the kit for just one man. By my bunk though, there were two lockers.

I busied myself making my bed, storing equipment and generally zipping about in the search for mates who had been quartered in one of the other blocks. I knew most of the lads from P-Company and there were some more that I knew from my days with 7 Para. Most of those were already parachute trained but because of the fiasco which followed the disbanding of 16 Brigade, they were now well out of date for operational parachuting. Such men had to complete a full course as refresher training.

That Sunday afternoon, there was none of the usual running around or over supervision that we as ordinary ranks had come to expect. Once that we had collected our gear and had sorted out our bunk areas we were stood down from duty. It felt quite strange at the time, having this freedom suddenly thrust upon us. What were we to do? Where should we go? Some of the lads wasted no time and headed straight down to the bar, others donned running kit and took in some exercise. I unpacked properly and prepared my uniform for the next day.

As had become very normal whenever I was away from home, I received several visits from other blokes, all of whom repeatedly asked to borrow my iron, the starch, the boot polish or even my boot brushes. It never ceased to amaze me how so many men could exist in this army yet still remain so disorganised. They would forget to bring what most of us considered being essential.

With everything pressed and polished, I decided to examine the contents of the strange looking kit bag that I had earlier signed for. In the PCAU block, the CQMS had warned everyone to take great care of all the items in the bag for they were apparently hugely expensive.

When I tipped the contents out onto the floor, all that I could see was a tangled mess of straps, hooks and buckles. I hadn't the faintest idea whether everything was in good working order or whether it was even there or not?

An unwanted and uncomfortable lump quickly formed in the centre of my chest. It wasn't fear, though maybe anxiety, an anticipation of problems which may lie ahead. I simply didn't know what in Hell I was doing.

It wouldn't be the first time that I had been caught out and had ended up having to pay for something which I actually never had but nevertheless I had somehow signed for. Usually it was because I didn't know what I was signing for or maybe because some short tempered CQMS, frustrated at the large queue, rushed everybody through by demanding a quick signature. It was only after he had received the signature that he would throw the bag of kit to you and order you out of his stores.

I remember once having to pay for a shovel that some store-man had insisted I had signed for. I hadn't seen a bloody shovel but it was on a list of items that were packed up on a truck which I had to take to a different location. Of course I hadn't unpacked the truck to count every item, I simply signed. When the truck was unloaded, a shovel was missing. It cost me two days wages.

Now my eyes were drawn to the jumble of bits and pieces lying about my feet. My mind flashed. Memories seemingly so real filled my thoughts. I was a sixteen-year-old recruit and back in Aldershot. All of us in the new recruit squad had been marched over to the uniform stores. Once inside we were ordered to sign our names on a form, which stated that all the kit had been received and was in good order. Only once we had all completed that task were we allowed to form yet another queue where we could actually collect the already signed for items. Nothing was said as each one of us walked alongside the tall wooden counter. As we passed, the store-men thrust various items at us until when we reached the end of the counter the pile was so big that we could barely manage it.

Like a formation team of forklift trucks, the squad was marched back to the accommodation block to sort out and pack away all the kit. I soon found that missing from my pile was a pair of cap badges. Like a good young soldier I immediately brought this to the attention of my Platoon Cpl. who straight away sent me back to the stores to collect the missing items.

Inside the storeroom I spoke to the SSgt. in charge. He picked up a clipboard and stubbed a nicotine stained forefinger against my name, "You've signed for them. You must have had them". Another but different form was fetched where I again signed but this time I was signing an authority to have the cost of the items retrieved from my wages.

An old hand that I had vaguely known from 7 Para interrupted my memories. "You all right Chip?" The questioner, a stocky blond lad from the northeast, dived straight into my mess of straps, freeing the knotted lengths. Excavating deep inside the tangled pile, he liberated the individual items one by one. Each time that he pulled a piece free he shook it and exhibited the lonely item trophy like, clearly demonstrating his superior knowledge to the growing crowd around me.

Sensing his better understanding and at the same time feeling quite comfortable with it, I hoped that my total ignorance was not making me appear too foolish in front of my watching mates. Every time that the blue eyed Geordie extracted yet another precious bit of kit, the crowd cooed and murmured their admiration. I found their overzealous attention to be a little embarrassing. I half expected them to burst into a round of applause.

Standing rigid, the Geordie looked down at his feet. Laid out in strict military fashion were those few pieces of what had become known as Para-kit, the same items that just a few seconds before had looked so baffling. He pointed a wagging finger at the lifeless kit and counted out loud. "One, Two." Slowly reaching number seven he paused. Everyone stared into Geordie's eyes, almost begging for more.

"There you are." He said confidently.

"You should have seven bits of kit".

Enjoying the attention and with his feet strangely flat on the floor he crouched down into a squat. He took up one item at a time, and with both hands held high he made a mock offering to the Gods. "Helmet!" He called out, clutching the steel green bowl. *Jesus!* I thought, *even I knew that*, but the man appeared to revel in his new found importance. "Strap!" He went on. My self-appointed mentor fingered the thin webbing strap, pausing for a second or two at the small leather pouch designed to fit over the wearers chin. Then unbelievably he demonstrated where the strap should be fitted. I wanted to tell him to stop treating me like an idiot and to get on with it but I knew that he was trying to help and I needed to learn what all this stuff was for anyway.

Having checked that everyone was paying full attention he shouted. "Get some lazzee bands! If you don't, you'll suffer". I didn't like the idea of suffering so; now he definitely had my interest. "You exit the aircraft at a hundred and fifty knots and it's bloody windy! If you don't secure the excess straps with elastic bands they'll whip your eyes out!" I'm sure that the sentence was meant to be taken seriously but instead the knowledgeable Geordie received a fit of silly giggles.

Ignoring the laughter he tried hard to carry on regardless. "Container straps, ground sheet, weapon sleeve." Finally he collected from the floor a strange looking pair of large grey spring mounted clips. "Hooks!" He announced passionately. Watching all those around him nod their approval he continued. "These are worth more than you! If you damage or lose them you'll be up to your necks in shit! I'm telling ya!"

Next on the list of things to do was a visit to the Cookhouse, or as the RAF liked to call it, the main restaurant. It was time to sample the local cuisine. Inside the main restaurant I was immediately taken aback by its modern appearance complimented with plush carpeted flooring, pictures on the walls and even trailing vines, which had been coaxed up attractive looking pine trellises.

My first impression was that it was rather nice, though perhaps a little dark. It was certainly a lot better than most of the cookhouses that I had worked in. Army cookhouses were usually spartan and more often still, in a poor state of repair. Unfortunately my initial observations were shattered when I then noticed how dirty the whole place was. There were food and drink stains everywhere, on the floor and even dripping down the pine cladding. I bet it was nice when it was new though.

The food itself was fine. I think that Service food is comparable wherever you go. The only obvious difference that I could see was that the RAF never ran out of anything whereas in the army, we regularly ran out of something, though scoff was always available. In my own experience, if there were five hundred men to be fed, the cooks were given five hundred portions. If you happened to be the poor sod waiting at the back end of the queue then you got what was left and tough luck with it. Not here though, the guy at the back got the same choice as the guy in front.

The evening passed quickly enough and the new   dawn brought in a wonderful lazy morning. The RAF being much more civilised than the Army, meant that we didn't have to parade until the late time of 08.30. It was a nice, relaxed, almost holiday atmosphere at Brize. However, the PCAU staff didn't seem to enjoy this casual regime. Perhaps they perceived it to be a threat to good order and discipline. We had already been told that we were the Ambassadors of the Airborne Brigade and as such we were to show the Blue jobs how it is actually supposed to be done.

A tall Colour Sgt. with a dark Mexican style moustache marched the few yards from the hut door to the edge of the road and stood momentarily eyeing each one of us. We were standing in loose three ranks and were spread right across the road. The CSgt. hung his head, shook it in abject disbelief then snapped to attention before screaming. "Course! Course 'Shun!"

As if struck by a bolt of lightning, the group shuddered, then stood perfectly still. In positions of attention, the men listened intently to what the big man had to say. "Stand at ease! ... Stand easy!" Turning to a pair of nearby and recently arrived Sgts, he ordered gruffly, "Sort that lot out!" In an instant the Sgts were amongst us. Their arms and fingers stretched right out as they each sliced through the ranks in guillotine fashion. "You over there! You, come here!"

From the chaos quickly came order. There were two courses running simultaneously. One was for recruits to the Parachute Regiment and the other was for everyone else including, Parachute Regiment Officers, Transferees, Marines and us. This was the ALL-ARMS course.

The nominal role was called and some initial ground rules were read to us. The main rule given to us that day was that this is where we were to parade each and every day. We were also informed of what time our meals would be and where the daily routine and orders would be published. There would be, they added, a duty NCO and the course would provide a guard. The responsibilities that went with these duties were slight but it did mean that the duty men had to stay in uniform throughout their tour of duty and that included night time.

A strange whining sound was suddenly noticeable as of a group of ancient Bedford buses came rattling noisily around the corner. I was surprised to see the buses stop right next to where we were standing. The CSgt's speech continued and eventually ended with, "Right! On the buses. Not the front seat, that's mine!"

This was odd indeed. The SNCO had only just told us that we were to go to the Number Two Parachute School which, I knew it was only about half a mile away, so why the buses? I shrugged my shoulders and resigned myself to the fact that either I had missed something or the CSgt. had. On the bus a PCAU Sgt. perched himself in the stair well by the door. "Why the Bus Sar'nt? Where are we going?" I enquired. As if the question was expected, the Sgt. began a well-rehearsed answer. "We're not allowed to march anywhere on the station. It worries and upsets the Blue-jobs." He said, before adding in mock sympathy, "Poor souls."

The exceedingly short journey was quickly over and we got off outside the single storey matt green wartime annex, which adjoined the huge aircraft hangar of the Parachute School. Some time ago this annex had become designated as the offices and lecture room of the School.

Once the Officers had been seated comfortably, the rest of us filed into the hangar. Inside we found ourselves at an area which was covered with exercise mats. The few SNCOs mostly huddled together somewhere at the back and, with the Officers sitting at the front, the rest of us were sandwiched in the middle. Disappointedly I was just pipped at the post when seeing a vacant chair, I darted for it. A lad, much younger than me, I don't remember who, quickly slid himself onto the blue plastic-moulded seat. I don't know about him but I felt like I was a four-year-old again who had just lost a game of musical chairs.

The big CSgt. with the long Mexican moustache entered, arriving to our right through the main doorway of the hangar. He called the men to order and then went about forming us into three ranks. I was silently smirking with childish satisfaction because I now realised that I didn't need the chair, and it made me feel even better to see that the guy who got to the chair before me, was well and truly   ousted.

The moustached man barked some instruction at the SNCOs about having to see him later then screamed loudly, bringing the Course to attention. As soon as he was satisfied that he had achieved the required results, he went on.

"Gentleman!" Then continuing in a softer, more inviting tone, "The Officer Commanding PCAU."

Having received his cue, a middle aged and portly built Major of the Parachute Regiment made his entrance.

I had long since become used to atrociously turned-out middle aged Officers who had lectured smartly dressed lower ranks in the importance of immaculate bearing and this man was no exception. I thought at the time that the trouble with these Officers is that the further up the promotional ladder that they climb, then the fewer people there are to challenge their standards. After all, who would dare suggest to a Major or higher that he needed to get a haircut or to press his trousers?

The forty-five year old OC of PCAU reiterated the Regiment's policy of high standards of discipline and dress, then went on to make a warm welcoming speech designed to ease this large group gently into the new course. As he finished his talk, he turned to his immediate left. Thundering towards him and exhibiting impeccable foot drill, came a barrel chested man. Displayed on his sleeve was the Coat of Arms of a Warrant Officer class one, the RSM. The hangar echoed throughout as the RSM completed his precision halt with two resounding thuds of his boots. Without hesitating, the big man bellowed at the audience of waiting soldiers. "Course! Course 'shun!" Quick as a flash the men responded with a snapped explosion of uniform movement, coming instantly to attention. Raising his hand in a rigid salute, he paused and waited for the Major's reply. "Thankyou RSM. Please carry on." Looking a little uncomfortable as more than a hundred pairs of eyes watched him; the Major turned and walked away.

Now facing us, the RSM stood us at ease and introduced himself as the RSM of the PCAU and reminded us that this unit was only a detached wing of the Depot of The Parachute Regiment and Airborne Forces. He went on to warn us of our behaviour. He too, said that we were Ambassadors and guests of the RAF. Any trouble, he said, with the RAF would be met with an instant RTU. Any discipline offences would be dealt with most severely.

Next came the expected routine. As if we hadn't noticed, he told us that our barrack blocks were very old and of a poor standard, however, he said that there was no alternative for us so we had better just make the best of it that we could. Going on, he advised that every day there would be a barrack room inspection, which, would be carried out by the course NCOs. In addition, on every Thursday, OC PCAU would inspect the blocks. "And beware." He added. "Occasionally the Station

Commanding Officer got the notion that he would like to have a walk around our accommodation and he always expects the highest standards of hygiene and cleanliness in our areas." The RSM stood for a moment, motionless, and then waving his hands about in front he drew an imaginary map, explaining as he did so, the whereabouts and relative positions of the RAF Police dog compounds. "One!" He said. "Is opposite your huts, is surrounded by barbed wire and is home to loads of noisy, smelly hairy dogs with four legs and bad breath." The booming voice of the RSM subsided, allowing the information to firmly sink in. He waited just a few seconds before adding, "The other dog compound." Again he demonstrated by pushing both hands over an invisible map, "Is on the right of your accommodation. It's three stories high and that too is full of noisy, hairy and smelly dogs with bad breath, only these ones have just two legs."

Sudden realisation that he meant the WRAAFs block caused the whole course to erupt into wild laughter. The RSM up to now, a stern looking man was unable to maintain his stereotypical posture and his face cracked, quickly widening to a huge smile. Slowly the giggles fell away and eyes once more turned to the RSM.

With an abrupt change of tone he roared,

"Both are strictly out of bounds!"

Once more his tone altered and he finished off with,

"Now you're going to be handed over to the RAF." Before yelling,

"Course! Course Shun!"

Pivoting to his left he brought his right knee up high to his front before driving his boot to the ground in a tremendous thud that rocked the plywood platform underneath. Already approaching from our right was a young and athletic looking Flight Lieutenant. The Officer Commanding Number Two Parachute School also turned out to be the Senior Instructor.

A few yards from the RSM, the Flight Lieutenant fumbled a very haphazard marching halt and immediately displayed his obvious discomfort with foot drill. Once again the RSM snapped a precision salute then marched away smartly. The RAF Officer took his place on the platform and casually stood us at ease.

It was his turn now to welcome the course to RAF Brize Norton. He reiterated the warnings and their likely consequences that were mentioned earlier. There must not be any trouble between the RAF personnel and the Course, they were not like us, he warned. It was his notion that the men and women of the RAF didn't understand Paras and that meant that they often didn't trust them.

The blond Officer called and beckoned to a waiting Flight Sergeant. He was a short but very smartly turned out man who seemed to fit perfectly into his blue uniform. Recognising that his turn had come all too quickly, the FSgt set about organising us into straight lines. Several other RAF men joined him seconds later. All wore the badge rank of Sgt. They pointed this way and that way and with some expertise they soon had the course in a neat military style file.

The FSgt silenced us chattering men with a shout, then, while holding our attention, he asked if any one present had ever previously attended any parachute course at the station? A scattered handful of arms were nervously raised in admittance. Most of these men had for one reason or another been re-coursed. Some were simply out of date, mostly those from the recently reformed 7 Para RHA. Others had been RTU'd from an earlier course because of injury or sickness. A young PJI

(Parachute Jump Instructor) Sgt quickly gathered up these few men. They were then formed into the first of our new squads.

The FSgt. walked slowly up and down the line of young men. He eyed us, evaluating us. I'm not sure what it was that he was searching for but he seemed to find it because every now and then he would smile and then pull a man from the line. Once that he had extracted eight he called to a PJI SGT who came along and took the group away. The process continued until all the men had been placed into groups.

When my turn came, a very casual looking instructor approached. He appeared to be quite a bit older than the others and certainly a fair bit wider around the waist. Also, unlike the other Instructors, he wore glasses but not just ordinary spectacles. Instead he was wearing those glasses that react to differing levels of light giving the impression that he was in fact wearing sunglasses. His arrival was so relaxed that at first, we didn't know how to react.

The Sgt. pulled the squad into a tight semi-circle and introduced himself as Shaky. The name did absolutely nothing to help with my fast diminishing confidence but strangely, the man himself did. It's difficult to explain, but this man who called himself Shaky, just oozed confidence. A few seconds with this man and I wouldn't have swapped for any other.

Somewhere near the back of the hangar we sat down on a long wooden bench. Shaky began to record our names, Regimental numbers, units and our dates of birth. It turned out that this group was a real mixed bag. We had a Captain from 29 Commando RA, two from the Royal Marines including a bloke from the SBS, a Signaller, and a Sapper from 9 Para Sqn and then beside myself there were two Gunners from 7 Para RHA.

Once Shaky had finished scribbling the scant information onto his rough card clipboard, he moved us around the hangar in   a grand tour. At each area our Instructor explained its name, its purpose and any rules that might have been associated with it. Then, at the back of the hangar our weight was recorded. Shaky explained that in theory, a parachute can safely carry only so much. Therefore, in military terms the maximum safe weight minus the parachutist's own body weight should equate in simple terms to how much equipment, in pounds at least that the parachutist can carry.

The hangar tour came to an end so we sat back down on the benches and started to ask loads of stupid questions. Without saying a word, Shaky just turned away from us and conferred briefly with some of the other PJIs. Then, turning back toward us, he gesticulated wildly, waving his arms all about his head. Not sure what it was that he wanted I looked to my colleagues for an answer who in turn did the same with me.

Shaky, his palms uppermost mimicked a fork lift truck and raised his arms. Following his obvious instruction, we stood up and in unison repeatedly thumped our heels downward allowing the elastics around our boots to fall and thereby pulling our denim trousers straight. Now a little closer to us, Shaky simply said, "Outside."

Feeling a bit bewildered, our Squad ambled over to the giant hangar doors. As we went, we chatted idly, then suddenly our prattle was interrupted by a loud call from a different PJI, "C'mon you lot, or you won't go!" Still none the wiser, we broke into a short trot and joined the remainder of the course outside which was now formed up into three ranks in column of route.

The PJI who had just called at us went up to the column and ejected a Bombardier from 7 Para. It was difficult to make out what was being said but I was just able to hear the PJI asking the Bombardier if knew how to get to the Bowling Alley? Still I was baffled.

Following a brief instruction, the Bombardier brought the column to attention and stepped us off, marching briskly away from the hangar. After about five minutes of regulation foot drill wheeling around huts, trees and various hangars and airfield buildings we arrived outside the Bowling Alley. At last the purpose of the march became clear to me. We were here for a tea break.

For most of us, this routine was hard to get used to. It really did seem the life of luxury. We had started work only about an hour ago and already we were having a break. The bad news though was that for most of us it was a completely unexpected treat and we hadn't brought any money. Even most of those who had had the foresight to carry money were disappointed. There was only one girl on duty to serve the sudden arrival of this mass of soldiers and airman. The queue at the long counter was huge. Some did manage to get served but they needn't have bothered because just as they got their brew we were told to line up outside ready for our return trip.

We all learned a lesson that day. In future, we should carry loose change for a drink. It was also a good idea to buy cold drinks as tea and coffee took too long to serve up and then would be too hot for anyone to drink.

Back at the hangar, we filed into an older nearby building, which had all of its windows blacked out with paint. This was the school's lecture theatre. Most of us found chairs; those that didn't had to stand silently leaning up against walls. With little introduction, the lights were cut and an old and noisy battleship-grey sixteen mm film-projector whirred into life. As it did so it threw out a beam of light filled with glittering dust stars onto a yellowing screen. A black and white countdown led into a scratched and worn colour film of military parachute training. The film itself was shot only about six or seven years previously but already it looked very dated and was threatening to become hilarious.

At one point spontaneous giggles and cheers broke out when portrayed in the film we saw as one of the hapless and very sad looking young recruits a face that most of us easily recognised. It was one of our P-Company instructors. This was an in-joke, a humour that judging by the looks on the faces of our comrades in the RAF, they definitely did not understand.

Back inside the hangar each eight-man squad found its own bit of space and with all the other squads starting at a different piece of equipment we got under way. Our squad formed up at the rear of the hangar close to where the Training Parachutes were stored. Shaky stood at one end and with everyone else in a queue he issued the training 'chutes. One bloke seeing the word Dummy clearly printed in red letters across the width of the parachute asked the first stupid question of the day. "Sar'nt, is this 'cos we're stupid?" It would have been really funny, but he meant it.

It was painfully obvious to everyone else just what these dummy parachutes were for. They were not real parachutes but practice ones. The pack, its straps and extremities were identical with the genuine article but could never be deployed.

With these practice versions we were shown how to check that a parachute is serviceable and also how to fit and wear it correctly. Unlike actors on TV or in films, nobody can simply strap on a parachute, hop out of an aeroplane and expect everything to be fine. If the thing is not fitted properly then the parachute may not deploy and even if it does, the wearer might not stay in the harness long enough for him to land with it.

The fitting instructions at first appeared to be complex. With measurements of three fingers here, elbow to tip of finger there and even palms width used occasionally it was difficult to commit it all to memory. Later, and with constant practice, it started to fall into place and within about half an hour I was relishing my expertise in this new found art form.

Something that became quickly obvious was that these parachutes were not designed for long men like me. The short stocky ones were OK but not me. Whenever I tried to stand up straight, the harness nearly cut me in half! The lower straps seemed to have developed a sadistic mind of their own. No matter what action I took, the bloody things attacked me! Divide and conquer must have been their aim for they repeatedly divided my conkers!

Next was PLD. Shaky mentioned those letters several times but at first nobody had the courage to pipe up and admit that they didn't know what they stood for. When the question came, I was glad because I was one of those who were putting together hundreds of word combinations inside my head in an effort to make sense of the abbreviation. Shaky rolled his eyes to the roof in mock disgust then in a sarcastic tone said, "Parachute Landing Drills! Dickheads".

Shaky insisted that first we had a physical warm-up. I tried hard pleading that we were already quite warm but he insisted. Standing in the centre of a large square of exercise mats he had us run around him in a circle stopping only occasionally to then start a different exercise. "Just shake off the cobwebs", he said.

Once Shaky was satisfied that we were completely out of breath, he lined us up. Then, keeping his feet and knees tightly together, he demonstrated the parachute roll. I couldn't help but think that this all looked incredibly easy. But once I had tried it I found that actually, it really was easy but only if you were fortunate enough to have been blessed with the skills of an Olympic gymnast. I, however, had always been one of those who found success through brute force, bluff and by courting sympathy. I now had a feeling that my troubles were only just starting.

I felt alone and singled out. I am, I considered, to flexibility and co-ordination, what an elephant is to tip-toeing through a rose garden. The basic landing position with both feet and knees tightly squeezed together, arms held out in front and with chin pushed down onto my chest were fine. I only had a problem when I was required to move which, unfortunately for me was most of the time. Shaky said that I was to imagine that my body was sandwiched between two walls and therefore, I could neither bend forward nor back. Once achieved, I was to swing my hips out to the side, bringing my body gracefully to the ground, impacting first with the side of the calf, then the thigh and roll through to the shoulder. Shaky demonstrated it once again and once again it looked easy.

Looking the part of a crumpled heap and getting hurt each time that I crashed to the ground was not exactly what the PJI had wanted from me. To my embarrassment, my efforts were unable to induce any words of advice from Shaky. Instead there was only tearful laughter. I got it in the end but I had to work hard for it. It never did come naturally to me as it most certainly did for many.

A big Royal Marine from Commaccio Company in Scotland was one, who, despite his large frame, had the finesse of a ballet dancer. He was the perfect student. He needed only to be shown a technique once before being able to reproduce it textbook-style every time. Even Shaky thought that the Marine's talents were unnatural. More and more, Shaky positioned the Marine for difficult landings but each attempt brought perfection. The Marine, expressionless and very quiet, simply brushed himself down and went back for more. Shaky turned away from the Marine and faced us with an envious grin moaned, "Makes you sick, doesn't tit?"

A little later and the syndicate were moved onto another set of apparatus which, at least appeared to offer more excitement than jumping off boxes and getting sore. Rows of khaki parachute harnesses dangled at the end of long steel cables that had been suspended from the very high   ceiling.

Initially we were dispatched over to a line of large pigeonhole lockers to fetch our helmets and hooks then half of the squad held step-ladders while the other half climbed into the harnesses. Once we had firmly strapped ourselves in and had fitted a dummy reserve parachute onto the front of the harness, we looked the part and to us novices at least, we felt the part. We were like little boys excited over a big new toy. "Look Mum, I'm a real paratrooper!"

At first we simply practised getting used to climbing in and out of these strange and restrictive sets of straps. It was all easy enough but they say that practice makes perfect and that practice is the time to make mistakes: well some did. At the front of the parachute harness there is a clever four-inch circular device, which locks all the straps of the harness. It works along the same lines as a modern car seat belt. The main difference being that this device locks four different belts at the same time. If the straps are not fitted correctly, then the parachutist will fall out of his fast undoing harness. At one time or another in the practice, we all did exactly   that.

From that dangling position we had to learn and practise all the skills required by a parachutist in flight. Our drills included checking an imaginary canopy by counting out loudly, "One thousand, two thousand, three thousand. Check canopy!" Once shouted, we were required to exaggerate looking up at an imaginary deployed canopy and to check it for any rips, snags or twists. If there were, and sometimes Shaky told us that there were, we would take appropriate action.

It needs to be remembered that when it comes to dropping airborne troops over the right place, the RAF is not infallible. Basic military parachutes at that time did not have any steering rigging yet, as well as avoiding other parachutists in the air, the man on the end of the 'chute must also try and avoid landing in water, in trees or buildings. Each emergency though has its get out or coping technique. For us there were to be many, many hours in those suspended racks, practising hundreds of routine and emergency drills.

The following day started well enough with an expected warm up routine of running around the hangar. Some of the warm-ups were pretty silly like having to get your body at least two feet from the ground. Those who failed to fight their way onto the myriad of wall and off the floor apparatus were punished with more exercises such as press-ups or burpees.

After that there seemed a never-ending session of going over what we had done the day before. Even though I knew that this constant practice was necessary it became very boring. Experts in learning skills reckon that any movement or technique needs to be practised, as much as two or three thousand times before it can become an automotive response. From leaving the aircraft to landing on the ground a military parachutist takes only seconds. He doesn't have much time to think, so his actions must be automatic.

Situated on the floor in the centre of the hangar was a huge plywood mock-up of the fuselage from a Lockheed Hercules. This one in particular had been built to closely resemble the fuselage of the stretched C130 version. The outer skin had been painted in a grey and green camouflage pattern complete with RAF roundels. Inside was a sickly magnolia colour and fitted inside were four rows of bright red netted hammock seats, which were strung out along its length.

Shaky told us to sit down inside the mock-up and then set about orientating us with the apparatus, pointing out the bits to remember. In here, he said we were to learn the safety drills and the preparation required for safe parachuting. We were wearing dummy parachutes, which we then hooked up to the cable above us. It looked extremely comical but Shaky said that this was serious. Still, most of us sniggered loudly when he demonstrated the Parachute Shuffle.

Walking in a line and very close to each other we headed for one of the exit doors. Watching this shuffle had been funny, doing it was even funnier. I had one leg pushed forward with the leg being dragged stiffly behind. This limping shuffle, Shaky explained, was essential if ninety soldiers, all of whom would be carrying heavy equipment, were to move collectively and speedily down the length of an aircraft. At the door of the mock-up I brought both feet together and as taught, I looked straight ahead before pushing hard out of the door, leading with my chest. We were told that it was imperative to make a good and clean exit from the aircraft otherwise all manner of nasty things could happen, like flying down the outside of the aircraft and repeatedly smashing into the fuselage. I had heard of this happening before. It was known in the Brigade as a rivet count.

It was also possible to become hung up, that is caught or trapped under or on a part of the aircraft. However, by far the most common problem associated with a weak or poor exit are twists. Twists occur when the four lift webs or straps which connect the wearers harness to the canopy of the   parachute become entwined which in turn causes the canopy to restrict and only partially inflate.

A whole week passed of what quickly became very routine ground training. All of our time was spent solely on landing drills over by the exercise mats and on flying drills, which were carried out in the suspended harnesses.

One morning during the second week we did actually get to go outside. Shaky and another PJI marched us just a few yards past the hangar doors and then formed us into a wide circle. While we watched, Shaky pulled a parachute canopy minus its harness and cords from a huge green sports bag. The other PJI quickly unfurled the screwed up parachute and then told each of us to take hold of the edge. Like fireman from an old black and white movie holding a catch-blanket, we walked around with the parachute stretched taught. Once we stopped, we were commanded to flick the canopy up into the air, but of course we were not to let go of it. This was, the instructors said, to familiarise ourselves with what an inflated parachute should look like when we look up into it. The whole exercise was repeated several more times. Each time that the 'chute went up into the air one of the PJI's would reel off some   technical stuff, such as the number of panels stitched into the canopy or its weight and width.

For most of the second week we had much more of the same as the first week but there was also some progression onto other bits of kit too. The exciting finale of the week was a promised go on the fans. In common with the other squads our Instructor had promised that if we reached a good standard on the mats, he would allow us to use the fans.

Caged inside large meshed boxes and sited on a high platform, the fans were in fact wide bladed propellers. They were accessible only by a ladder at one end of a suspended gangway.

From these fans hung cables attached to harnesses. They allowed a trainee parachutist to experience a landing in a very safe environment. When a trainee jumped from the high platform the cable pulled on a wheel which then turned the propeller. The propeller with its broad paddles provided air resistance and thereby slowed the descent.

The whole thing looked like it should be great fun. Indeed, on special events there had even been children and old ladies who had had a go. When it was our turn we sat in groups and in queues seated on wooden benches. I looked around at the faces of my eager comrades. It was like watching kids waiting for Santa Claus. All of them sported the widest grins you could ever see. I thought that they were being childish but then I reminded myself that, I too was just like them.

Shaky called us over by giving a thumbs up. With that, three of us sprinted to the steel ladder, which led up to the platform and the fans in the roof space of the hangar. Some way up the ladder I suddenly became a little nervous, fear of heights once more reminded me that it hadn't left. I shook my head in an effort to rid myself of any doubts and continued regardless.

In the open space that passes for a doorway, I secured the harness. Shaky told me to stand back and to face him. When I did so, he then checked that the harness was fitted correctly and safely. Forty feet is a long way to fall if the harness were to come off. As he carried out his checks he quickly reminded me of the exit and landing drills that we had practiced so many times. Perhaps sensing hidden worries, Shaky added, "Little girls have jumped from here."

This fear of heights was certainly with me but it wasn't overpowering and I was not about to give in to it. Inside my head I kept shouting, ordering my conscious mind not to be so stupid. Shaky's voice interrupted sharply, "Go!" As if controlled by someone else, my hands flew across my reserve chute and with my feet squeezed together I propelled my whole body outward, aiming for somewhere up in the roof.

Suddenly I was in mid-air. Having reached up for the lift webs I looked down at the floor. It was all over in an instant. I had touched down well and had rolled into a perfect parachute landing. There was no time to feel pleased with myself. *Up, look at the Flight Sergeant*, I whispered in my head. "Good!" He shouted. I undid the harness and let it slip away and watched as it was pulled back up by the Instructor. Other blokes were already coming down so I had to make a quick exit from the mats and get back to the bench.

Joining the other excited faces it soon became apparent that all of us had enjoyed our few seconds of flight. I wondered then if I might enjoy the real thing as much. That afternoon we all made about five descents each. Every now and then the FSgt. called out one of the men from the line and would offer advice on how to correct a mistake that had just been made, but not me. I seemed to be doing alright.

For me personally the experience had started out as a bit daunting but once that I had completed one of the descents I learned quickly that it was not much more than a fairground ride.

There was now only one part of our ground training left for us to complete. This one had a reputation that seemed to worry just about everyone and was proving to be a menacing prospect. Over on the far side of the base near the main gate was a nasty bit of kit, which was officially known as the Outdoor Exit Trainer. To everybody else though and especially to those who had had the misfortune to have used it, it was the 'Knacker Cracker'.

The Knacker Cracker was a big metal shed, a battle-ship grey sanger. It sat on large steel legs that held the sanger up at around fifty feet from the ground. From the shed and spewing from both sides like giant spiders webs came thick steel cables. Taut and straight, they ran their length of about a hundred yards to a lower wooden frame, which had been decked out with old tyres.

Alongside the Knacker Cracker stood the dreaded crane. The crane was a device for lifting a man up to two hundred feet with an already deployed parachute. He would then be dropped. Standing close to it and seeing it for real, I yawned a huge sigh of relief; for the crane had recently been closed down whilst essential, safety maintenance was carried out. *Perhaps*
there was a God after all.

For much of the time during the days leading up to our eventual deployment to the Knacker Cracker, the barracks were filled with horror stories and great yarns. Old hands delighted in telling the younger and newer lads their tales of terrible injuries and the subsequent gut wrenching fear. It was not, they reminded, called the Knacker Cracker for nothing.

Exiting an old Bedford bus into warm sunshine on the airfield's extensive playing fields, we marched in our squads to form up as a course beneath the shadow of the tower. The mood amongst us was light though perhaps a little anxious. As the bright sun bore down and warmed our skin, the mood slowly became more relaxed.

The Instructors said that the Outdoor Exit Trainer was the most realistic method that there was in simulating the air turbulence that is felt when leaving a big aircraft and one that is travelling at around a hundred and fifty miles an hour. Like everything else in the Army, there is a procedure for jumping from an aeroplane and it was a drill that we were here to learn and practice.

Whilst sat on the grass enjoying the sunshine, the tower looked hardly intimidating at all; instead, it appeared quite plain and even boring. My mind wandered. It's not that fast and not that high, there's surely nothing to worry about? Talking to nobody but myself, I was convinced. Even when those before me leapt from the tower to be greeted by loud laughs and cheers, I failed to get excited, so easy did it all seem.

My turn came soon enough. With my newly acquired Para-smock done up and helmet on, I gently jogged the short distance over to the steps. At the bottom of the steps I met a bloke who had just jumped and took from him a dummy reserve to carry with me. Quietly but in a slight hurry I ascended the stairs to emerge from a hole in the floor at the top.

Inside I blinked several times as I tried to accustom my eyes to the vastly diminished light of the interior. The guts of the trainer appeared to be fitted with some sort of large mechanical device stowed in one corner. Above me there were great pillars of sparkling light bursting through the gaps in the roof. Ahead I could see two doorways or, more accurately, two exits for there were no doors.

Stood by one of the exits and bathed in sunlight was a PJI. I had seen him before but as yet I had never worked with and I didn't know his name. Shaky wasn't here. He was outside somewhere on the ground. The PJI inside the tower beckoned for me to approach. He was standing legs apart but up straight. He sounded confident but more than that, he was in charge. For some reason the sound inside the trainer appeared to be a bit muffled, like when ears pop because of a change in atmospheric pressure.

Standing with the Instructor, we both checked that my helmet was fastened and fitted correctly. Then he pulled a harness from outside, which hung loosely from a cable and pulley. I stepped into the harness and pulled the four straps tightly into my body. Craning his neck to place his mouth nearer my ear the instructor yelled, "Pull 'em tight!" The fit wasn't comfortable but I did feel secure. The straps were extremely tight but that was good. If when I jumped, I was able to move around inside the harness there could be a problem. The instructor likened the fitting of the harness to placing an egg inside a shoebox. If the box were then to be violently shaken, we would expect the egg to be smashed. If instead, he explained, the egg was placed into a good fitting egg box and then shaken, there was a good chance that the egg would remain intact. After those words of comfort, I knew exactly, which box I wanted to be in.

With the harness now on I picked the dummy reserve parachute up from where I'd left it between my feet. It looked and felt just like the real thing. I don't know what was inside it, we were strictly forbidden to tamper with the release handles. I did know though that this one did not contain a parachute. Having secured the reserve to the two upper 'D' clips on my harness I examined myself. Reading those big letters in white paint emblazoned across the front, DUMMY, I began to wonder if it was meant for me or it.

The PJI leaned out from the exit and received a command from down on the ground. He stretched out an arm and gave a firm thumbs up to a small gathering of RAF men below. Straightening his back, he turned to me. There was frantic last safety check then changing his tone, he snapped, "Exit position!" Feeling with my toes through my boots, I made sure that my feet were properly together, and then following a mental checklist, I squeezed both knees tight.

My mind flashed back to just a few days earlier. Shaky had told us that there was once a soldier who was on the Knacker Cracker and who had somehow fallen from the overhead cable, but because this soldier had kept himself in a nice tight position he had survived. Apparently he had landed heavily but otherwise none for the worse. I didn't know then whether that story was true or not but at the time, I believed it. Subsequently, I made sure that my position was really tight.

"Hands across your reserve!" The order shook me from my daydream.

Following a short snappy movement, I found myself instinctively overlapping my arms so that they rested above my reserve and just below my chest. I pushed my hips forward and once more checked my feet. Pointing to the distant horizon the PJI barked, "Out there son. That's where I want you to go, not down. Understood!" Without taking my eyes from the sky I managed a nod of approval. I waited.

It seemed an age but it was probably only seconds. "Go!" The word shot from the Instructor's mouth and hitting like an explosive charge. No more than a tiny fraction of a second later and my bent knees had powered me out into the open. "One thousand!" I could feel myself falling. The hair on the back of my neck prickled. "Two thousand!" There was a crunch. The cable above had reached its maximum length and could descend no further. Unfortunately gravity still laid claim to my body and it continued to drag me downward at a speed that felt like Mach-one. The harness held but the twin thigh straps shot upward reaching high up into my groin and painfully squashing my testicles. As the momentum of the straps continued upward, separating the cheeks of my bum, air was forced from my lungs with a sickening sound.

It was horrible but I quickly gathered my wits about me. I had now discovered what people had said was true. This really was the Knacker Cracker. Less than half a second after my testicles had met my stomach, the cables responded with a vicious bounce and I was wrenched back up to level with the tower again. I could only do as I had been taught; I kept my body tight and tried hard to maintain the right position. "Three thousand!" My voice lost instantly against the twang of steel and the rush of air around me. "Check canopy!" I went through the drills flinging my head back and staring up at an imaginary parachute. I was going down again. I could feel my testicles being pushed awkwardly up against my pelvis. It was painful and I could feel tears of pain as they threatened to fill my eyes. Determination whispered to me, *do your drills* but now I was flying around, lurching in all directions.

Once more I bounced but this time the violence lessened enough to allow me to complete the drills waited for by the audience of Instructors below. Stretching both arms upward I took hold of the two lift webs and forced them apart, which temporarily lifted me inside the harness. I gave an exaggerated glance, craning my neck to the left and then to the right proving that I had remembered to look out for fellow parachutists who may have got too close.

I was spinning, not too fast but nevertheless out of control and hurtling toward the cable end where other soldiers waited. They were there to catch my flying feet and slow me down and hopefully before I slammed into the high poles at the end. I have no memory of who it was that actually did the deed, but whoever it was must have done a good job because I was stopped with at least a yard to spare.

Not everyone was so lucky. Some had struck the wooden apparatus with quite a hard thump but miraculously no one seemed to sustain any injuries apart from some expected bruises to their pride as well as their flesh. The catchers took a heavy risk too. They had caught me without any problem but on occasion there were lads who were still going through their drills, checking for nearby parachutists when they found themselves coming down within catching range. With their feet up in the air and their bodies spinning wildly, they quickly became human flails which, resulted in more than one catcher receiving a swift kick in the head.

Twisting and thumping the lock I dropped free from the harness and watched it disappear as it was hauled back up the line by the PJI working in the tower. The pressure on my groin was immediately alleviated and I began to feel normal again; well in that area anyway.

There was no time to hang about or to even think. With a snappy jog I approached the RAF Officer. He didn't speak much; I guessed that he was generally the quiet sort. Holding a clipboard out in front of him he looked the picture of an officious judge. Shaky was standing behind the Officer. I thought that I must have done something right because he had a great big smile stretching right across his face. Standing smartly to attention with my chest heaving and still trying to regain my breath I managed to blurt out, "Corporal Walker Sir!" The young Officer looked over his nose and without moving his head and remaining expressionless, he spoke. "Good. Good exit, well done". Exhilaration immediately took over and I was chuffed with myself. Now I felt ready.

I awoke the next day to glorious sunshine and a feeling that convinced me that it was great to be alive. This was the last day of the week and, scheduled for nearly the whole of that day, was a flight in one of the RAF's C130 Hercules transport planes. The flight, as explained by the Flight Lieutenant was to be a familiarisation flight where everyone could get the feel of a real Hercules instead of the mock-ups that we had been practising in. Even more it was to give those men who had never ever flown before, the chance of some flight experience, for the next time they climbed aboard they would be expected to jump from it.

Everyone was securely strapped in and properly sat down in their uncomfortably small hammock style seats as the giant aircraft lurched forward and lifted off into the clear sky above Oxfordshire. The first fifteen or twenty minutes of the flight seemed routine with nothing much happening. It was incredibly hot and stuffy inside the aircraft so when the doors were suddenly opened I with everyone else let out a huge sigh of relief and drank in the very welcome cool air. Eventually the aircraft levelled out at an altitude of around eight hundred feet. The Air Load Master, a member of the RAF crew, in charge of the plane's cargo, received via his head set the all clear from captain. Then using the same medium the Loadie (as they were known) gave out instructions to the two PJIs that were by now standing close to the opened doors and positioned on both sides at the rear of the aircraft.

Earlier, while we were still on the ground we had all fully kitted up with parachutes and reserves. For most of us this was the first time that we had ever worn a real parachute and its reserve. It was also our first chance to discover just how hot, sticky and painfully difficult it is to sit in one of these planes with all this equipment on. My back was aching terribly. The parachute pushed awkwardly making it impossible to lean back. At the same time I couldn't sit forward because of the bulky reserve worn across my chest.

The PJIs at the open doors then turned to face up the length of the aircraft. By shouting as loud as they could they gave a well-rehearsed instruction. "Port stick! Stand up! Hook up! Check equipment!" For us who were wearing light order without the addition of too much bulky military hardware, the   instruction was an easy one. It was in fact identical to all the times that we had completed the same training exercises in the hangar.

I didn't have to think for the training took over. The seat was quickly folded and stowed away. Then I reached up and attached the strop, a long piece of webbing fitted with a hook at one end and attached to the parachute; on to a cable, which was strung out along the ceiling of the plane. I twice pulled hard on the strop ensuring that it was fastened correctly then set about checking the remainder of my equipment. Once that was done I checked the bloke in front of me. Behind me there was another man who in turn went about checking me.

Being as confident as I could be that my equipment and the bloke's in front were fitted safely, I placed my right hand on his shoulder and screamed. "OK!"

We stood in a line facing the door and waited. It couldn't have been for very long because it seemed that as soon as we were ready, the line received another command. "Port stick count off!" Starting at the rear and counting downward the last man in the line shouted his numbered position. I shouted my number with an added scream of OK. It didn't take long and very soon the man nearest to the door held his thumb up to the PJI and yelled. "Number one OK. Port stick OK!" The PJI turned instantly to the Loadie and passed the thumbs up signal to him.

Oddly we were then told to sit down. Somewhat gingerly, we released the seats and sat balanced on the edge, being careful not to pull on the strop and trying hard to keep an eye on whatever was about to happen. None of us wanted to miss a thing.

One at a time, when called over by the PJIs, we unhooked our strops then climbed over all the other blokes to get to the starboard door. It was awkward to say the least traversing the sitting men. There was no room to walk down between them so I had to clamber about on and over their legs. At the door, the two PJIs took firm hold of each of my arms, clasping my biceps. One of them then took my strop and hooked it up to the nearby cable.

The air that came gushing in through the open door at more than a hundred and fifty knots stole my breath away, leaving me slightly winded. Pulling me over to the door the PJIs dragged my stiff body to the gap in the aircraft's fuselage. One of them leaned into my ear and quickly reminded me of our complete safety; after all if anything were to go wrong, we were all wearing parachutes. All of a sudden I was on the step and practically outside.

Both arms were pulled tight behind me as the PJIs played tug o'war with the slipstream. The funneled air around the door buffeted my body, leaving me to feel almost helpless. I felt that any second now and I would be dragged away into the open as the plane carved its way through the turbulent sky.

It was a wonderful yet strange feeling. Here I was, a bloke who had always had a fear of heights being held out of the open door way of a moving aircraft and loving every second of it. Up here looking at a Mediterranean type sun over golden fields below, I felt exhilarated. At the same time, the open space was inviting me, almost willing me to break free from my Instructors and jump. The excitement filled my head but then the shutters were drawn abruptly and the two PJIs pulled sharply at my smock, bringing me back into the dark stale air of the aircraft.

Having returned to my seat, I looked around at the happy expressions beaming from those who had already been to the door. Our eyes met as we shared the pure sense of that overwhelming thrill. I had really wanted to jump. It is hard to

Chip Walker
explain why but if one of the PJIs had instructed me to go, I simply would have.

CHAPTER THIRTEEN

A FATE WORSE THAN DEATH

A weekend spent off duty and at home with my wife Janet should have been a relaxing time. She, of course, was great and was, as usual, pleased to have me at home. But I was restless. I suppose that the previous weeks of constant rushing around had turned me into the worse of all fidgets. I couldn't stay still for more than two minutes. It was Saturday afternoon and Janet had suggested that we snuggle up with each other on the settee and watch a film on the TV. I found it very difficult to get myself in the mood to watch anything. I didn't notice myself doing it but I think that I must have been huffing and puffing with boredom because Janet suddenly snapped. "Oh for Christ's sake! Why don't you just go for a run?"

She wasn't stupid. My wife had known exactly what I had wanted, even before I had. Part of me was pleased as now I could relax in my own way. However, another part of me felt seriously guilty about leaving her at home; after all, she had hardly seen me for the best part of seven weeks. In a daft attempt to offload some of the guilt upon her I turned and gave one of my best little boy lost looks. At the same time I pleaded. "Are you sure you don't mind?"

Our eyes met. As always in her attempt to feign anger, her eyes sparkled. "Oh get out! I could do with the peace!" The guilt was still there but now, so was triumph. In less than a minute or two I was ready and was leaving for my run. My body had a need to bleed itself of unspent adrenaline. Twelve miles and an hour and a quarter of pacing the local roads, brought me   back home feeling completely refreshed. A cloud of depression and frustration that had earlier threatened to swamp me, was now blown clear away.

Back at Brize, it was the start of our third week. Monday ticked away slowly with repetitive performances in the hangar of yet more landing and flying drills. The day itself was fairly boring but the following day would be our first real parachute jump. There was some trepidation, but I think that we were all looking forward to it. We had been through a lot to get this far and I know that I wasn't the only one who felt more than ready.

Through bleary eyes and old metal framed window I searched the morning sky for clues of the day's weather. Up to now we had enjoyed sub-tropical conditions with clear blue skies and temperatures regularly reaching into the eighties. Today though, as I looked up I could see that overnight, grey clouds had crept in to spread across the heavens, shutting out the orange glow of the sun. Satisfied that it was at least dry, I swung my legs down, dismounted my bunk and got ready to start another day.

Enroute to the RAF station at Weston-on-the-Green, I noticed how the mood of the men had changed. There was no longer that air of wanton excitement but instead one of sombre silence. A silence interrupted only occasionally with a nervous wisecrack from a soldier trying hard to talk himself out of his mood.

This cloudy day was to be the first in a series of parachute descents, not from the huge lumbering Hercules aircraft in which we had all recently enjoyed a trip but from a balloon. Balloons had been used for parachute practice since the earliest days of parachuting history. Though considered to be an old fashioned tool for a modern army; the RAF had kept hold of a few. The reasons were simple. Because of their ease of use and perhaps more importantly, their low operational costs, they then made good sense.

After rounding a bend in the road, the buses came to a halt opposite a few small buildings. Close by and sitting almost motionless above a shiny blue cage floated a huge grey whale of a wartime type Barrage Balloon. At its base several men in blue overalls could be seen milling around adjusting cables and pulling on levers.

On the bus all we could do was wait for the command to de-bus and form up into three ranks. I could feel knots being tied deep in the pit of my stomach. All I could think about was the idea of having to step off a platform into nothing but thin air. Suddenly all those horror stories that I had heard about the balloon became very vivid in my imagination.

Outside, staff were pacing up and down, occasionally looking upward and then down at their watches. No one on the bus had any idea of what might be going on? We continued to sit there. About twenty minutes had passed before Shaky and another of the PJIs boarded our bus. Halting in the stairwell Shaky and his companion stared for a moment at the murmuring and impatient men in front of them. "Listen you lot! It's off! We're going back to Brize." All of a sudden the depressed murmuring dissipated only to be replaced with whoops of joy and cheers. Within a few moments, those same voices changed once more to sounds of abject disappointment.

Someone from the back of the bus asked why the jump had been cancelled? "The weather!" came the short reply. Quietly and to myself I looked once more out of the window. It surely was cloudy but even a layman like me could see that there was little wind and that it wasn't raining.

"What's wrong with the weather?" I asked.

"Static!" retorted the PJI before adding, "Too much static in the air."

Part of me was disappointed. After all I had been training for weeks for this jump. Also, I knew that this balloon descent was one of the seven essential qualifying jumps. Another part of me however, was mightily relieved.

That night in the Starlight bar of the station's NAAFI building there was a bit of a ruckus. Every now and then there was a disco held there. A disco meant only one thing to most of the blokes and that thing was girls, so just about everybody went. Amongst the flashing lights and strobes the atmosphere was decidedly tense. Despite the happy rhythms booming out from the enormous loud speakers there remained a very volatile feeling, one of 'them and us'. The RAF didn't like us and as far as we were concerned, they were all tossers and wimps anyway.

I sat with some others at a small table somewhere between the bar and the dance floor. Several of us commented on the rather ugly feeling that was apparent all around us. It was clear by the looks on the faces of the lads from the RAF that they were not at all impressed and especially if any of the women were paying attention to any of our blokes. Still, most of us tried to ignore the negativity and instead just relaxed and enjoyed a drink whilst window shopping at the array of young and pretty WRAFs.

On the far side of the room some sort of commotion erupted. Something was going on but nobody at my table had any idea what it was and we didn't particularly care. We continued our conversation but were interrupted when a bloke from our course, panting and excited, pushed through to us at our table. He told us that three blue-jobs had attacked one of ours but the Snowdrops had carted our man off to the guardroom.

Perhaps it was because at the table, we were all NCOs but we were very quickly surrounded by men from the course. Most were outraged and were very verbal in their intentions to storm the guardroom and rescue our stricken comrade.

Others simply wanted to beat the life out of any one who happened to be in the RAF. With a couple of more level headed men around me, we stood and shouted down the group that was fast threatening to become a lynch mob. John Dyer, the RMP Corporal suggested that he alone should visit the guardroom and see if he could sort out this misunderstanding. At the time, it seemed the only logical thing to do and perhaps was the only thing that would calm the crowd. For poor old John though, he may well have bitten off more than he could comfortably chew.

Looking back it shouldn't have been surprising that a near drunk RMP Corporal from the Parachute Course who had demanded a right of access to see his client was told in very plain Anglo-Saxon language by a very less than impressed FSgt. of the RAF Police, to embark on a course of sexual reproduction.

While still at the table in the NAAFI, we were approached by an RAF Sgt. in full uniform. I guessed that he was some sort of Orderly Sergeant. He leaned over the table and shouted above the blaring music. "Are you an NCO?" Keeping eye contact but not bothering to speak, I nodded. He looked around at the potentially hostile crowd of soldiers encircled around us. "Do us a favour mate? Get your lot together and get them out of here before this gets stupid!"

The implication was obvious and we needed no more telling. A couple of us went about quickly gathering up the men and ordering them to return to the block. Not all of them were   too happy about that of course, and there was some defiance but in the end, they all saw sense.

There was just one man missing. No one had seen him for a while but neither did anyone worry, for he was our resident Casanova. He had been with a different girl just about every night so far. True to form, when we got back to the block we couldn't but help notice the missing man's car parked right outside the buildings. The car had the tell-tale signs of steamed up windows and was merrily bouncing up and down.

The sun was once more brightening the sky as I casually wondered if this would be the day that we might actually get our balloon jump. Inside the hangar we learned that the course would continue unabated and on schedule. The balloon jump would be re-scheduled for the end of the course.

At the back of the hangar and in long lines, we drew our parachutes from the stores and fitted them. Four fingers here on this strap and three fingers width on that strap and so on. Still, I thought, I must be a funny shape? I had followed all of the fitting instructions and still the bloody thing didn't fit. Only once in all the times so far that we had done this had it ever fitted so that it was at least reasonably comfortable. Once that it was on, I was able to make some adjustments, though never enough for it to be good.

With the parachute came a very large olive green hold-all. This was for us to fold the parachute into after the jump. For now though, we all folded the hold-all into as small a bag as possible then stuffed it down the chest of our para' smocks.

Excitement began to tingle down my spine, permeating through the rest of my body. Already I could hear the steady drone of powerful engines warming up the waiting Hercules aircraft just outside. The PJIs zipped in and out of the long lines of men busily checking, checking and checking again with a strap pulled here and a strap pulled there until totally satisfied that everyone was ready.

All of a sudden it had started. I hadn't even heard the order but like a sheep, I followed the others. A lengthy line of men all dressed identically and each carrying a khaki X4 parachute on his back, snaked around a winding route which led eventually to a downed ramp at the rear of the aircraft. Hot fumes of aviation fuel spent by the aircraft's four big engines blasted us in the face. Ignoring the furnace-like temperatures, we continued our silent march into the carcass of this flying whale. I don't think that I was scared. I was certainly nervous but I had remained confident and I was still looking forward to it.

I was the second to last man to board our aircraft, which meant that when the time came, I would be the second man out. I knew that it shouldn't have made any difference where in the line that I was placed but at the time, I remember thinking that I would have much rather be somewhere in the middle.

Earlier the Course members had been organised into small groups called sticks. On this occasion we were in sticks of six. Looking around at the cramped conditions inside this full aircraft I started to wonder how many sticks that there were altogether. I reckoned that it would have to fly over the DZ about fifteen times if, as planned, we would drop in bunches of just six.

For an operational jump, the PJIs would try to get as many men out in as short a time as possible but today we were only training. Sticks of six allowed the instructional and safety staff down on the ground to observe each and every parachutist.

The flight had not progressed far when the order came to fit and check equipment. There wasn't any fumbling about, it was now routine enough and God knows we had practised it enough. We sat down again. The parachute doors on either side of the huge aeroplane were opened. From where I was sitting I could clearly see the fields far below. The aircraft levelled out. We were flying at an altitude of about one thousand feet. Trees, hedges and even the odd tractor or car on the road were all easily distinguishable. That was an eerie feeling. I felt unsafe; I could feel fear stick its ugly claws down my throat and start to wrestle with me.

Glancing nervously all around I searched for some sight or sound that might reassure me. There were some excited faces, like kids at the fairground but generally the blokes looked exactly how I had felt. Hardly anyone was talking. Most were thoroughly morose and deep in their most inner and private thoughts.

My mind flashed to all the times that we had been told of the reliability of this X4 parachute. They had remained virtually unchanged since the original design had come into service some decades before. I knew that it was incredibly rare for faults with the parachute and that when accidents do happen, it's usually because the parachutist did something wrong. Still, I was more scared than I have ever been in my entire life.

The motto of the RAF Parachute school is 'Knowledge Dispels Fear'. That may well be true but today, knowledge wasn't even remotely dispelling my fear. I felt empty, undernourished and weak. I could feel my face drain of colour and with my eyes low I must have shown it too. One of the PJIs who had been clambering over the men whilst checking cables stopped momentarily. Making eye contact with me he smiled and held his thumb up and shouted. "Walker! You all right?" Searching deep into his eyes I mouthed. "No!" He laughed. I willed him to say that everything would be all right and that I didn't have to go. He didn't. Instead, he continued to laugh and then moved on. I don't know whether the cause of his new found humour was because he had believed that I was joking or because I really did look funny. But God knows I wanted him to land the plane and let me walk off.

"Stand up! Hook up!" In unison the aircraft's cargo of men stood and reached for their strops. The connection to the cable made a distinctive Ker-click as more than eighty of them were simultaneously snapped together. For a few moments as I went into auto' pilot and carried out the drills and my worries disappeared. The SOP's sequence repeated in my head. I pulled at the strop and made sure that it was   connected properly before checking it all. I did it then I did it all again. In front I checked a Captain from 29 Commando. The Officer stood with his back to me in line toward the door. Almost fumbling I fingered the strap and buckle of his parachute helmet. This was for his benefit rather than mine. It's very noisy inside a C130 and talking is very difficult so an   exaggerated physical check of a soldier's equipment allows him to know that it has been done.

"Starboard Stick, Count off!" The numbers loudly shouted in response from the rear of the aircraft were only faintly heard but then the sounds got gradually louder as they worked their way down to me. The shout was at its loudest when almost instantly afterward there was a tap on my shoulder, a signal to me that the bloke behind me was happy with his kit and also happy with what he could see of mine. "Number Two OK!" I yelled, but at the same time I was thinking that I really was not sure if OK was the right word to describe how I felt.

The red lights illuminated brightly above the each of the two doors. There were abrupt and simultaneous shouts from the PJIs. "Red on!" From up and down the lines voices erupted. The para-shuffle started and we edged closer and closer to the door. The Commando Captain stopped at the open doorway. Both of his arms were held wide as he gripped the steel structure around the door. Just slightly behind and oblique to him, I stared out at the fast moving ground below. Stale air from inside the aircraft disappeared, being replaced instead with intermittent wafts of sweet fresh air and the thick stench of avgas'.

Death was coming. I could feel it. The voice of fear inside my head told me that I was going to leap from this aircraft and die. As I stood there awaiting my fate, I began to even welcome it. Dying was by far a much more preferable course to take than a refusal to jump because that would bring undoubted dishonour. It was better that my life came to an end right there rather than face my comrades after wimping out of the jump. I told myself that death was better than failure. And anyway, I'd come too far to surrender now. I remained absolutely terrified!

"Green On!" More shouts followed. "Go!" The word dug into me. This was it. I shook with fear then the front man was gone and I was in the doorway. "Go!" The PJI repeated his call and patted me on the back. It happened instinctively. I leapt out as hard as I could and flew from the lumbering craft. I was aware of my feet being pulled up in front by the invisible force of slipstream and then there was nothing.

It was a subdued tranquillity, like gently waking from a warm and pleasant dream. My eyes could see but little registered. For some seconds, I was unaware of where I was or what I was doing. Then a voice in the distance called out. It was repeated, this time with some urgency. Consciousness jerked my whole being and suddenly I was fully awake! *Jesus! I'm under a bleeding parachute!* In a flash I was checking myself, trying to convince my mind that I was all right. At the same time, I had this nice feeling of being safe and warm. I was floating and it felt wonderful.

That voice again. This time I had heard it loud and clear. "Starboard stick number two! Complete your checks!" The

The Devil Wears Maroon

loud voice whining from the voice amplifier was now easily understood. On the ground below I could make out a group of three or four RAF men with the Flight Lieutenant holding a blue megaphone to his face. The shout had stirred me into action and immediately I went through my parachute flight checks. There were a couple of other parachutes in the air but none were so close that I needed to worry. I could even still see the giant silhouette of the Hercules. I knew then that I must have blacked out, though it could have only lasted for a few seconds.

The voice again. "Starboard stick number two!" There was a pause. "Parachute landing position!" My training had taken over and the instructions weren't needed. Already I had reached for the lift webs and bent my knees slightly. There appeared to be quite a breeze and it was obvious that I was flying pretty fast and forwards. In an effort to slow down my forward momentum I selected the rear webs and, using every
muscle in my upper body, I pulled the webs down for as far as my strength would allow. Arching my neck, I watched the canopy fold behind me.

Satisfied I looked back toward the ground. Alarmingly the baked brown grass seemed to be rushing up to meet me. The wind direction changed rapidly and suddenly I found myself galloping to the ground to my left. I swung my body frantically round to adopt the position for a landing to the left. There was a thud and I was down. The billowing parachute continued along the ground, pulling me onto my left side as it went. Aided by the remaining lift of air above me, I managed a near perfect para-roll.

The canopy still near fully inflated, bounced along the grass and began to drag. Now on my back, I twisted the locking box on my harness and gave it a good thump. It sprang open instantly, allowing me to pull arm over arm at the webs forcing

308

them to one side and eventually turn onto my belly. Reaching up, I grabbed handfuls of cord and dragged them to the ground until tired of its flight, the canopy collapsed.

In a spin, I shrugged myself free of the harness. I jumped hastily to my feet and raced over to the floundering canopy. Bubbles of air pulsated from inside searching for an escape. Exploring the mass of nylon beneath my feet I located the apex, a small hole at the very top of the canopy. Gripping it firmly in my palm I ran twenty paces away and at the same time drew the parachute into a straight line. With my right arm flailing a wide arc I twisted the outstretched parachute and pulled it in. In seconds the whole thing was packed up and with the locking box showing uppermost, it was stowed away inside the giant green hold-all.

As I jogged the couple of hundred yards over to the waiting trucks I was caught up by two other lads who had also just landed. All three of us were so high with excitement that we were almost floating. We each agreed that this experience had been fantastic and we wanted more.

For now, my part in this phase of our training was over. I sat by the side of the DZ and watched as aeroplanes flew past over and over again, each time spilling a small group of men beneath green or white puffy mushrooms. We watched as one bloke from the Royal Signals pulled instantly at his reserve parachute in the second that he had left the aircraft. Once on the ground he told everyone that his main parachute hadn't deployed properly but from where we were sitting, it had looked perfect. Nobody gave him a hard time about it but everyone reckoned that in truth, he had panicked.

A little while later, whilst still watching the exercise, I and the men around me were amazed to see two civilians, a man and a woman both run onto the DZ. They rushed up to a landed

309

soldier, a young officer from the Parachute Regiment. He was on his knees and trying to finish his ground drills when these two seemingly mad people started to rip at his clothes. One of them pulled his tunic to one side then from a satchel produced wires and then went about plugging the soldier into some sort of portable machine. Discussion on the ground was one of complete consternation. I gathered that whatever was happening, it must have been OK because there were plenty of RAF officers and other personnel standing around and they didn't appear to take any notice of the commotion at all.

Later in the day, I learned that these strange civilians were from some university and were doing a study into the body's reactions to stress. They had apparently earlier measured the young officer's heart rate and temperature back at the hangar. Someone else did it again on the aeroplane and then these two turned up to take the exact same measurements again now that he was down on the ground. I remember thinking at the time that it was a good job that nobody had wanted to measure my stress levels. It's a sure thing that inside the aircraft my heart rate would have blown their equipment apart.

Once that we had returned to the factory (as the hangar became known) we were back to more ground training and even more flight drills in the suspended harnesses.

Bussed in to the parachute school once more on yet another fine morning, I eagerly looked forward to the parachuting that was scheduled for later that afternoon.

As usual though, first came the PT. "To shake out those cobwebs!" Shaky repeated. The morning ritual of running around the hangar interrupted only by the occasional command for press-ups or burpees, had by now become very, very boring. It must have been just as tedious for Shaky too, for he had started to pick men from the group to lead the warm-up session instead of doing it himself.

For much of the remainder of the morning it was repetition of the same ground and flight drills. We practised every conceivable type of landing: landing in water, in trees, landing left or landing right, it just went on and on. Then there were flight emergencies to go through such as collisions and entanglements.

A little while after NAAFI break, there was at last something new on the training programme. Huddled together on a mat around Shaky, we watched as he laid out a bizarre collection of webbing straps and buckles. Almost straining to bring it around to his front Shaky reached round behind him and dragged a heavy jerry-can that had been filled with sand and which, weighed approximately fifty pounds. This was, Shaky explained, our lesson on how to secure and wrap a rifle and a Bergen.

At first, wrapping the square shaped package looked to be complicated but after we had done it several times the packing process fell into place and I soon had it done easily. From now on, all our practice flights in the harnesses would include having a bundled up jerry-can attached with a rope to a strap on our sides.

Once that we were in the harnesses and we had completed the routine of normal flying drills, Shaky would shout an all clear. This would be the signal for us to release the bundle by pulling at a strap, which unhooked the lot and allowed it to drop six to ten feet below and to dangle on a rope while still attached to the harness.

It was a quick lunch that day because we had to hurry up back to the factory. We needed to fit and draw kit ready for our next parachute jump. It took about ten minutes to fit our parachutes and associated gear, then we stood once more at the back of the hangar where we waited. Amongst the lines the PJIs busied themselves checking everybody repeatedly.

Many of the blokes seemed to be a bag of nerves. Old sweats say that the second jump is always much worse than the first. Their reasoning being that initially a trainee or recruit hasn't the faintest idea what it is that he is letting himself in for. The second time round though, he knows exactly what is going to happen and that should scare him shitless.

Personally, my feelings were very much the opposite. That first jump had frightened me more than anything ever has done before, but now I was standing in a line with my shoulders pulled back and I was thinking, so what?

Leaving the aircraft, I concentrated on every tiny second. There was no way that I was going to let myself black out again. The descent was unexceptional and very similar to the first. The only notable difference was that the landing was quite a bit heavier. I had hit the deck like a sack of spuds. However, the RAF told us that any landing where you can get up and walk away is a good one. Well, I walked away so perhaps it wasn't as bad as it had felt.

Before the end of the week there would be just one further jump. That is if the weather permitted it. In between there would be plenty more time for the now dreaded ground training.

Friday morning arrived and again the sun was out raising the temperature and providing us with a glorious day, a day that was perfect for parachuting. The jump had been brought forward slightly, being scheduled for the morning instead of the afternoon.

This jump differed considerably from our previous attempts because this time the men would be dispatched simultaneously from either side of the aircraft and in sticks of six. That allowed a gap of only one second between parachutists as they left.

Soon enough, the red light was on and we were standing alert in the doorway waiting for the light to change with its shouted warning of, "Green on!" A PJI clambered up and down along the inside length of the fuselage. It being obvious that there was no way could most of the men easily hear his words, the PJI paused. Then turning to face as many of the men as possible he exaggerated his mouth movements and with a chest full of air, he bellowed. "It's a bit blowy down there, thirteen to fifteen knots. But you'll be alright if you keep a nice tight position!"

I think that perhaps I should have been scared but I couldn't imagine what fifteen knots of wind were like, it certainly didn't sound very fast.

"Green on!" The shout echoed around the plane as every man repeated the words. I steadied myself then shuffled forward ever nearer to the door. "Go!" The scream was matched with a slap on my back. I propelled my whole body out of the doorway and was immediately taken by the violent turbulence of the slipstream. Jerking my head back to watch my parachute unfurl from its hiding place in the pack behind me, I felt my feet begin to rise lifting me through a somersault. There was a sudden and sharp crack as the canopy opened right out and then thankfully my feet fell, naturally finding their way back down to dangle beneath me.

Before my flight drills could be started, I became quickly aware of another parachutist who with barely a yard between us was very close. As in a mirror, both of us responded straight away with our IAs.

He was a big man and a nice enough bloke. I'd seen him around for a fair bit of the course and had vague memories of him from when I had served with 7 Para RHA. Suddenly there was a blunt collision as the two of us came crashing into each other's space. I flung my limbs out wide in an exaggerated star shape in order to prevent my body from passing right threw his rigging. He did the same. Above us, I watched as both parachutes struck then folded as each forced itself upon the other.

IA's were whizzing threw my mind I thought of all scenarios that we had practised in training. I've always thought it weird that when you're in a crisis, you are able to think through whole procedures and sentences in a flash and in the tiniest part of a second. In my head, I concentrated on the drills for the expected outcome, an entanglement and a collapsed canopy.

I remember a terrible feeling of helplessness as the two parachutes swung us together once more and then brought each parachutists to a sickening crash! For a brief moment it had hurt and it had certainly knocked the wind out of me. Fortunately though, neither of us sustained any noticeable injury and as abruptly as we had collided, we bounced apart. The edges of our twin canopies appeared to be holding on to each other, refusing to let go. Again we mirrored each other's actions as the two of us reached up high to grab at an outside lift web then together with all our strength we yanked those webs down bringing them level with our necks then chests.

At the second fold that now showed in my canopy I could see the periphery strain against the added air now trapped in its hold. In unison our two voices screamed. "Steer away!" Despite all that was happening around me I felt no fear. In fact I was exceptionally cool and calm. It was almost as if I was a third person who was somehow detached from this emergency and was able to stand back and watch.

I tried hard not to take my eyes from the other bloke. Both of us were pulling solidly at our parachutes but seemingly they were stuck like glue. Every now and then they would free themselves separating by as much as a foot or two but then they would crash back together again. Each parachute was now holding much less air than would be ideal. Our descent became erratic and much faster than we had been used to.

Every few seconds I became aware of another parachutist nearby and he would also shout but I could do no more than I had already done. There didn't seem to be any response from the buckled canopy no matter how hard I tried to pull at the webs. Ignoring the shouts and warnings of others, I concentrated on getting away from the parachute still stuck to mine. All the while I could hear myself mouthing through clenched teeth, "Com'on you bastard! Pull away!"

For the other guy and me, time and distance were just about to run out. I looked down, Christ! The ground is bloody close! The most worrying thing for me then was not the speed of the descent but the likelihood of an imminent air-steal. With two parachutes so close to each other as ours were, and both gasping for the air that they needed to stay deployed, an air steal would be difficult to avoid.

There comes a point when at about forty feet from the ground, the air pressure required to fully inflate a parachute rescinds. If that happens then at least one of the parachutes might collapse and the parachutist will fall sharply to the ground. Unsurprisingly, I didn't fancy that.

At last and in the final few seconds of our descent the two canopies separated pushing between us a distance of around fifteen feet. I landed, coming down on my right with an awkward crash. The force of the speedy landing threw me into an involuntary body roll and as my head came round to face the sky I could make out the dark sinister shape of the other parachutist coming down over the top of me. It was with horror that I faced a realisation that he was about to land right on top of me and there was absolutely nothing that I could do about it. There was about a half a second to go before impact and my body was still out of control. Momentum retained its grip on me and I was being dragged through a fierce ground slapping.

Surprisingly there wasn't any pain as the out of control big man, came hurtling down into my bent body. Both pairs of lungs suffering under the immense pressure were quickly purged of any air. It took no more than a second or so and each of us was on our backs, shoulder to shoulder and being pulled at ten miles an hour across the dry open fields of the DZ. The ground had looked flat but now that I was being drawn along it and at speed, I felt every lump and rock.

Cords of rigging from my colleague's parachute wrapped themselves around my face and neck, first tying me up then cutting deep into the loose skin around my throat. Clawing at the strong nylon cords I tried desperately to free myself. The tension was too great and I was unable to shift it. Giving up for a second I decided instead to see if I could release the harness. One arm was partially free but everything else was trussed up like a Christmas turkey. I just managed to get my fingers to the locking box but frustratingly I couldn't exert enough force to turn the cap.

I'm not sure how, but I was fully aware of the other guy and that he was having identical problems. Shouting as loud as I could to my attached friend, I suggested that on the count of three we both turn outward and then once that we were on our bellies we should try to collapse our still inflated canopies. I hadn't yet though, figured out just how exactly it was that we could do that. "One two three!" We turned. Both parachutes still fully inflated continued to bounce and crash into themselves racing further down the DZ. I searched for any rigging that might belong to my own parachute but it was all mixed up and impossible for me to distinguish. Reaching up as far as I could with my free hand, I grabbed a fistful of the uppermost cord and pulled it to me. Thankfully the other lad appeared to be having more luck than I. He was able to utilise both hands and snatched at the rigging from both parachutes. A few seconds later, both canopies collapsed, offering only the occasional flutter in the wind.

We didn't speak but nevertheless managed to come up with identical intentions. We turned over to our backs and started to untangle ourselves. Two men appeared quickly, one an RAF Corporal and the other, a bloke from our Course. The soldier ran straight to our canopies and ensured that they could not re-inflate. The Airman knelt down next to us and scrambled hurriedly at our tangled harnesses. Eventually we finally escaped our cocoon of straps and cord. The RAF guy looking quite concerned picked me up by the collar.

"Are you alright?"

"Yeah, great!"

My answer appeared to shock him and he seemed taken a back. He explained that he had watched the descent and had expected me to be badly injured.

From the outside, it had looked far worse than it really was. Perhaps I should have been scared and fearful over the potential consequences, I just don't know. I do know though that I felt brilliant. The adrenaline buzz had taken me up to be as high as a kite and I loved it.

The weekend came around abruptly but we weren't allowed to go home. RAF Brize Norton was celebrating an Air Day. The Air Day was to be an open day for all the families and relatives of the station's personnel as well as an opportunity for the general public to get an insight into what goes on here at the base. All around, the visitors would be offered different displays and attractions.

Saturday morning was for us another working day. Just like any other day, we paraded outside our accommodation blocks and waited for transport to take us the short journey to the factory. On arrival, we were ordered to various parts of the hangar. My group were to carry out what would appear to be a normal days training but of course it was actually just a show for admiring onlookers.

I counted myself to be lucky because I was in the group that was to undergo flight training in the harnesses. Therefore, whilst all the other groups were busy throwing themselves all over the floor pretending to show how we could land without hurting themselves, we would be dangling happily from a flight harness.

In the harnesses, we went through every conceivable emergency and probably a few that Shaky had simply invented in order to relieve us from some of the monotony.

Later that afternoon my wife Janet arrived bringing with her my kids and a couple of other members of the family. As part of the watching crowd they stood directly in front of me. At that time all I could do was hang there like a puppet. He shared a few words of explanation to the audience then Shaky started to shout out his vision of what emergency was about to occur. "Parachutist left!" We of course would duly respond with the appropriate IA's.

Shaky continued loudly. "You're over water, fifty feet!" We started the drill for landing in deep water.

A water landing is very different from any other sort of landing that we might complete on terra-firma. Subsequently the IA's are just as different. Once a parachutist has realised that he is over water and that a water landing is unavoidable he must climb part way from his harness ready to jettison it and all the associated parachute paraphernalia. For if the parachute were to enter the water with the soldier still attached, it would likely sink and drag its unfortunate cargo with it.

Janet and the others watched intently and no doubt proudly, as I completed the climbing out procedure. Shaky interrupted the process with an added shout. "Thirty feet!" That was a signal for us to lift our arms up to a position of surrender and immediately afterward, slip easily free from the harness dropping a few feet to the floor. Unfortunately for me, my harness caught on the sleeve of my smock jacket and as the rest of the team fell gracefully away, I to my massive embarrassment, stayed exactly where I was. Shaky's face was not one of pleasant surprise; rather it was one of frustrated anger. Meanwhile I of course became the object of much mirth amongst my family and the other members of the audience.

The final week crept up on us and we could hardly believe that this period was actually coming to a close. We had at least a further four jumps to go. A minimum of seven jumps of varying types were what were needed to qualify. There had been talk though that there may be a few more for us.

Morning PT had long since become tedious and this Monday morning proved to be no exception. After our ritual warm-up, the groups were separated and sent to different parts of the hangar to practice again on all the aspects of parachuting. The groups moved around in a circle, each remaining with any one piece of apparatus only for about fifteen minutes.

Lunch came and went and then, we were to parachute with full kit, which included our container and weapon sleeve. With containers held on our shoulders, we marched over to the waiting aircraft. The bloke behind me asked me a question.

"Hey Chip! How comes your parachute was made in America?"

"You what?"

"Yeah he replied, "it says U.S. on the back!"

The joke twigged, in army terminology the letters U.S. are an abbreviation of unserviceable. "Ha Ha, very funny". I quipped sardonically. I really did think that it was funny but I didn't want him to know that. For several minutes, I giggled quietly to myself.

It was the next day that disaster almost fell upon us. It had been another fine sunny day but there was a fair bit of wind about as we flew over one of the training areas of Salisbury Plain. This was to be the biggest parachute jump of the course. By Brigade standards it was nothing, but to us novices it was an exciting time as well as being a little daunting.

According to the programme, this would be an operational jump. Of course it wasn't really. It only meant that it would be treated as such, both in the air and on the ground. There were three aircraft altogether with the entire course split roughly equally between them. In turn, the aircraft took to the skies and rendezvoused before flying in tight formation and at low level, sticking to the contours of the ground below.

The red light was on and we stood at the door. The strain of the weight that I was carrying began to pull at my back and sweat rolled in torrents down my face. I looked around. A few of the men were shouting close to their companion's ear desperately trying to make themselves heard but most were silent. The mood was generally sombre.

Lurching forward and upward the plane started its sharp and sudden climb to its parachuting height of eight hundred feet. The PJIs flitted about here, there and everywhere inside the aircraft checking, and then re-checking again. One of the PJIs worked his way along the lines of men and as he did so, shouted a warning of high winds outside.

The aircraft quickly levelled out. I got myself ready to go. Others around me did exactly the same. Poised to throw myself from the door I tensed my muscles and watched the light waiting for the change of colour from red to green. Before it could change, the warning lights above the door abruptly went out. Climbing quickly over the sub-frame between the two side doors, the Loadie held his arms up above his head and crossed his forearms. He stayed in that position, turning to each of the PJIs until he was sure that they had understood his signal.

The Loadie then joined closely with the PJIs as he continued to listen with one ear into a headset. As he did so, he screamed into the microphone. More unheard words were shouted to the listening PJIs. The PJIs then broke away abruptly from the Loadie and went amongst the men telling us that, because the wind speed was far in excess of what the RAF considered to be safe for a training jump, the jump was off. Following instructions I unhooked the strop and sat myself down.

I was partly elated but also disappointed. After squeezing myself into the hammock seat, I tried to relax for the return journey back to Brize. Seconds later the red light once again became illuminated. To start with everyone just seemed to stare at it as if waiting for it to do some trick. Nothing was said then like monkeys in a zoo the RAF men came hurtling down the lines of men to once more join the Loadie who was by now frantically talking into his headset.

He looked up and to his surprise, the PJIs had pre-empted his call and were almost on top of him. There was a frantic nodding of heads then the PJIs dispersed to position themselves back by the doors and to face their lines of men.

Barely a second apart each of the PJIs shouted. "Stand up! Hook up!" The Loadie moved into to the centre and stood on top of the end set of hammock frames. Looking around the men in his charge, he could undoubtedly see the concern so obviously showing on our faces. I'm not sure whether he in fact turned directly to me or just at the line of men behind me but the Loadie took a deep breath and loudly expelled his lungs shouting, "They've found a window!"

Instantly I guessed that whilst I was not familiar with the term he actually meant that there was a space in time or a place where the wind was not so bad. Perhaps it should have been expected but there was definitely more than one comment from amongst the lads that showed some of them at least had conjured up images of RAF personnel collecting windows from the grass below. Having noticed their baffled faces, I couldn't help but chuckle happily and remind myself that it takes all sorts to make the world go round.

Minutes later, men were spewed from either side of the aircraft. I shuffled nearer to the door and as I did so I could see that something was wrong but I didn't know what exactly. In front of me, each man in turn appeared to hesitate on reaching the door. The PJI though seemed nonplussed, so I wondered if maybe it was just nerves from the men or perhaps I was overreacting to a non-existent situation.

As I readied myself close to the door the bloke immediately in front of me threw his strop to the PJI and shuffled to the doorway, but then started to shake his head violently. Now concerned, the PJI leaned over and looked out of the door. Turning quickly away the PJI shouted something to the Loadie. With all the noise of the aircraft, I couldn't hear what was said but I could hear several anxious voices from behind asking what the Hell was going on?

Chip Walker

The PJIs hands flashed around the static paratrooper in the door and pulled him away. In a continued and fluent sweep of his arms, he guided the man past the door and into the rear of the aircraft. I saw his face. It could have been shame or even disappointment but most of all he looked distressed.

There was a second or two, and then the PJIs voice pierced my baffled thoughts. "Go!" The conveyor belt movement toward the door restarted. Suddenly I was at the exit. With one hand across my reserve and the other holding onto my container, I launched myself into space. Both my knees were squeezed hard together as I felt the furious turbulence of the air as it spiralled in the wake of the giant Hercules. It felt much worse than that on the previous jumps and I felt a little panicky so couldn't help but respond with a profound obscenity. I cleared my head and got back to the drills. "One thousand! Two thousand! Three thousand! Check canopy!" I was already looking up into my deploying parachute. Huge shadows suddenly blotted the sky and I found myself screaming! My voice strained as I watched the tail end of the giant Hercules aircraft sweep over the top of my parachute.

In the speedy tumble of those first few seconds, I was unable to gain any real perspective of time or distance but at the time that aircraft looked bloody close! My mind was instantly filled with pictures of my parachute getting stuck on a part of the aircraft with me being dragged all over the place.

The experience was to prove uncanny because I later learned that the reason that some of the men had earlier hesitated to jump was because a young LCpl. from the RAMC had somehow and unbeknown to the PJIs become hung up underneath the exit. He couldn't be seen until they had already physically committed themselves at the door to leave the aircraft. The poor chap who had been in front of me and had apparently refused to jump had caught a glimpse of the bloke

323

underneath the aircraft and the sight had scared him half to death. Meanwhile, after a terrifying couple of seconds, the trapped medic managed to break free and parachute safely to earth, sustaining nothing worse than a dislocated shoulder.

Still in the air, my eyes darted around me. The air was thick with other parachutists. I worked at the webs of my canopy and fought for a clear space then almost inexplicably it just happened. One second and there was khaki mushrooms all around me and the next; I was suddenly free with nothing else nearer than a few hundred feet.

Underneath my reserve chute my left hand searched for and then fumbled at the yellow canvas strap that secured the container to my torso. I yanked at the strap and immediately the weight fell away. Reaching the end of its tether very quickly the large green bundle bounced on its rope before finally settling.

The wind seemed to erupt swiftly, whipping me around in tight circles. I was spinning and try as I might, I couldn't figure out which direction that the wind wanted to take me. I tried to steady my eyes in an attempt to orientate myself. The ground flashed forward. Acknowledging the ground rush below me I shouted out loud. "I'm coming in backwards". I grabbed at the front lift webs hoping it would slow me down. I checked the ground again. Shit! Now the ground was speeding toward me in front. I was going forward. Before I had even got the chance to select the rear webs I felt the wind change direction once more. Beneath the canopy, I was swinging like a pendulum on a clock.

Hurtling up to meet me and apparently much faster than it should have been, came solid ground. Drawing hard at the front lift webs to at least stabilise my descent I hauled my arms as far down my chest as I could. The container hit the deck with a resounding thud and a scrape and as it did so, I pulled my feet up for a rear landing.

Dust exploded into the air as my arse smashed onto the ground. In that tiny instant I remember noting the pain of the impact but there was no time to think. Downward momentum brought the rest of my body swiftly backward. Sheet lightning zapped across my eye sockets as a loud shock wave slammed my whole body. The back of my head had just hit the ground! Stabs of pain shot down the bones in my neck and in a flash had spread around the sides of my skull. Fingers of agony stabbed at my brow and forced my eyes to tremble in their orbits.

Gathering my senses, I conducted a quick damage check. My brain scouted about for any trace of lingering pain, broken bones or torn tissue. I let out a rough whistling sound and was busy congratulating myself on my survival when unknown faces unexpectedly appeared over me. Two RAF men had seen my landing and thinking that I was most likely dead or at least badly injured, had come running to my aid. Peering up at the men in blue I whispered, "This is becoming a bit of a habit".
One of the men, a Sgt. asked, "You alright son?" The bang on my head and the crash onto my buttocks had certainly hurt, but otherwise I was fine.

For a second I simply sat there motionless. Obviously concerned, the Sgt. repeated his question. "You alright son?" Recognising the admirable interest in my welfare I replied. "It was that bad huh?" Catching each other's nodded approval one of them added, "We thought you'd been killed." I thanked them for their offer of help but reminded them of the saying; "Any landing that you can walk away from, is a good one."

Sitting on the old blue bus on the return trip to Brize I asked one of the PCAU men about the lad who had refused to jump. I was told then that he would be packed and gone before we reached the camp. Sure enough an hour later on our return there was no trace of the man. His bed space had been cleared and I never saw or heard about him again. Now that I had witnessed a refusal and in the circumstances that it had happened I felt immensely sad for the bloke but at the same time I was incredibly glad that it hadn't been me.

During the course, there were several men who on one of the jumps had refused to go. All of them had disappeared from the course having been rapidly returned to their parent units.

The morning brought with it a little rain but after the recent dry spell, it was pretty welcome. We only had to work for a few hours. It was ground training of course but it didn't seem so bad, for tonight we were to complete our qualifying night jump. Operationally the darkness of night would be an attractive tactic. It appeared then to be essential and quite correct that we should complete a night time parachute descent in order to gain our wings.

Once kitted up, the RAF FSgt. gathered us around him to form a three-sided box, a sort of giant horseshoe in order that he could make himself heard. Talking loudly he addressed the men about the size of the parachute sticks and our instructions for when we were on the ground. He went on to remind us of the lack of light. It seemed obvious but he went on to tell us of the main difficulty in night parachuting, that being that we wouldn't be able to see the ground. The knack to learn, he explained was to watch for the horizon and as soon as the horizon appears to be level or above head height, you will know that you are about to impact with the ground. It all sounded quite plausible to me. Because this was our first ever night jump we were allowed the unusual privilege of jumping in clean order, in other words, without the added burden of carrying any sort of attached container.

The green light was on; PJIs on either side swung their hips as they guided their men out of the door at two-second intervals. As I left the aircraft the first thing that I noted was just how warm the night air was and also that much of the hectic turbulence that I had come to expect was missing. It's difficult to describe but the initial exit was very pleasant, even relaxing.

Parachutists moved about the sky but none threatened my air space. Down below I could see the brightly-lit flares of the Alpha. The Alpha was the name given to the shape of illuminated red flares that were positioned on the DZ to guide the incoming troops. As moths to a lamp we would have something to aim at and hopefully the men wouldn't end up scattered all over the training areas.

The descent appeared to be taking longer than I thought it should. I kept my eyes on the horizon but I still seemed to be a long way up. There was virtually no wind and that coupled with the heat, my parachute didn't want to come down. I'd heard of such descents before. In the barrack rooms they were referred to as a "Fairy's Fart".

Widening my eyes and straining my pupils to draw in any available light, I searched for the ground. It was down there somewhere. I could actually see it but I couldn't measure its distance accurately. I could still see the horizon clearly. I was baffled and could not figure out where in hell the ground had gone.

Voices! Loud clear voices penetrated the air. I could hear every word; it sounded like I was in the middle of a bus queue. I looked up. The horizon was still below me. My eyes spun my head to the right; the alpha was still in clear sight too. I must have been lower but how low? How far had I still to go? I guessed that I must have had a good few seconds left of my descent but those voices, so clear, had me worried.

Apprehensively I searched my mind for logical answers. It must be the fine clear air, I told myself smugly though still not convinced. I knew how well sound could travel during the still of the night. Then something visual shook me, a shape stretching up to meet me. A rectangle, then more voices but what was it and how far?

Realisation dawned. This wasn't a shadow. This was the side of a very big truck and I was just about to hit it! The training took over. I pulled my knees high up to my chest and breathed in. Begging for more height, I swore at the approaching truck. Somehow, and with only a hairs breath to spare, the truck passed harmlessly underneath.

Dropping my feet and still clearly observing the distant horizon, I braced myself ready for the imminent impact. With the grace of a world class ballerina my feet gently touched the earth. For a second or two I stood very still. Somewhat bewildered I kept telling myself that this was not how it was supposed to be. I wondered if I had somehow done something wrong. Surely this was meant to hurt and by now I should be rolling around on the ground? As if to reassure me, the parachute folded softly and silently behind me.

As if from nowhere, men suddenly appeared next to me. "Oh Hi Chip. You come down soft too huh?" It seems that thermal heat waves, which arose from the sun warmed DZ had been unusually hot and most of the men who had parachuted that night had come down like a fairy's fart.

Safe on the ground I had the time to think about what had gone wrong during the descent. Initially I was not impressed with that RAF theory of observing the horizon. Plainly, it hadn't worked but I didn't know why. I looked around and answer became very obvious. The bloody DZ was on a hill!

By the time Thursday had come along, the atmosphere at the Parachute School was very relaxed. Most of the course men swaggered around like old pros. We had done seven jumps and there was only the balloon to do before we qualified. To most of us, it seemed a foregone conclusion. Ground training was really boring, after all, there was nothing left to learn, we were all experts, or at least that's how most of us had felt. Looking back it was stupid   really.

The buses took us out to a large open space. The landscape, barren except for a lone fluttering windsock appeared to be dry and lifeless. On one side and running along the length of a high chain fence were the red brick buildings of RAF   married quarters. Nearby and sitting idle with just the odd twinge of movement was a big fat grey walrus of a balloon. Dangling gracefully beneath the giant bulbous shape was   the   dreaded cage, the contraption from which in a few moments men would step into space.

Nearby was an assortment of RAF trucks including a flatbed, which was fitted with a winch, one end of which was firmly attached to the cage.

Looking back, I suppose that it wasn't at all funny, but at the time, when I saw the lightning rods stuck deep into the ground on either side of the truck it made me think of static in the air. Perhaps it was just nerves but to everyone else's consternation, I laughed out loud.

A FSgt. read aloud from a manifest. The manifest detailed who was to jump and when. The half syndicate that I was to go with was scheduled to go quite later on. I sat myself down on the grass and tried to be comfortable, undoing my smock to soak up the warm sun.

It was an odd experience. Here in the sun were around a hundred men, all of whom were dressed identically and   again all of who were arching their necks, straining to watch as tiny men in the distance fell from a powder blue cage.

Our turn came around quickly enough. I joined the queue that had now formed at the back of one of the lorries and where I could draw and fit a parachute.

These parachutes were different to the type that I had been used to. These were the newer mark five. Green and modern looking they had originally been designed to replace the ageing X4's but for some reason it was decided that they were not quite as good as they should have been. In the end someone way up high had relegated the mark five to training purposes only, then they were further demoted and were now only allowed to be used for balloon descents.

Still on the ground but inside the cage Shaky positioned us into each corner then pulled at a huge lengthy strop before hooking it onto the overhead bar. As always, he attended us, checking our equipment. He was an artiste, a shop front designer who was not satisfied unless everything was perfect. Some people would take the mickey out of Shaky and his fastidious nature, even some of his fellow PJIs did, but I found a comfort in his efforts. He made me feel safer.

Satisfied, he turned to the men working the winch and with his hands held to the sides of his mouth yelled, "Up eight hundred! Four men jumping!" The signal was duly accepted and the cable began its journey worming itself along the ground cranking and whirring as it went. At first, it went with a jerk but then slowly, silently, the huge Barrage balloon lifted upward. The ascent, though relatively short on height, seemed to take an age. The atmosphere was eerie. The cage itself coupled to the balloon made absolutely no sound yet every crank of the winch could easily be felt.

This wasn't like an aeroplane. There were no windows, only a belt high panel, which was held together by a thin tubular frame. No engine noise to stifle our conversation, no powerful fumes to choke us: Instead, there was only crystal clear warm air. Under my feet, the cage (or platform as some called it) was unsteady, gently rocking like a boat at sea. Every time that I shuffled my feet, I could feel the platform respond below me. I didn't like that, so I decided quickly that I shouldn't move unless I truly had to.

We hung there like a giant scale pan beneath a grey hand for a few moments in total silence. I peered down to the ground. I could see clearly the other men sitting there as they waited for the spectacle of men falling from the sky. I looked again: it was unnerving. I could see the men so well that I could even make out their returning gaze and could easily hear their words.

Shaky spoke quietly, almost whispering, for up here there were no impediments to the sound. Facing inward from our corners as boxers waiting for the bell, we listened intently to what Shaky had to say. He calmly reminded us of the safety protocols but before he could finish his rehearsed speech, he found himself interrupted sharply by a clanking sound, which, was followed by a sudden jerk on the cable. Shaky leaned over the side and eyed the cable securing the balloon to the ground. To signal that we could begin our descents, a little coloured flag was raised.

To my left stood the Commando Captain. As ever, he appeared quiet and confident. Shaky called him over. The commando moved to the gap ready to exit the cage. He placed one hand across his reserve and with his remaining hand, gripped on the metal frame that passed for a doorway. "Ready?" Shaky asked with little volume. The commando nodded his head and swiftly brought his right hand down to join his left over the reserve. "Go!" Shaky's voice was sharper now. The sound had hardly left Shaky's mouth and the commando was gone.

He checked that all was clear then turned to me. In the corner, I looked once more over the edge and scanned the ground. I was frightened. I felt very unsafe up here. Down below I could see dozens of happy cheery faces. They were laughing and I wondered if they were laughing at me? Could they have known how I was feeling? The skin of my knuckles whitened as my fingers stubbornly refused to let go. Shaky called my name. My feet moved forward a pace but then my arms pulled me back.

Shaky, who was still unaware of my paralysis, casually called me once more. My body jerked. Two sides of my character were fighting a war inside my head, one to go and one to stay. The big PJI believing that I was just mucking around let out a stifled laugh as a wide grin exploded across his cheeks. "Stop buggering about and get over here," he chuckled. Now deadly serious I said, "I'm stuck". With a single pace the RAF PJI gripped my right arm firmly with both hands. Craning his head to place his mouth close to my ear he warned, "Don't be a prat! You've done seven jumps already. This one qualifies you!" As his voice tailed off he stepped closer to wrap an arm around my shoulders and gently but firmly edged me to the gap. I still didn't want to go but Shaky made it difficult for me to resist his argument.

Half a step back from the empty space, which counted as the door, I stood silently staring at the clouds. The voice in my ear continued reassuring me that all was well. Shaky spoke again. "Look, if you find it hard to just step off, well then instead leap into it and make sure that you look up as you go. It's a lot easier that way". Pointing to the spot directly in front of my feet Shaky commanded, "In the door!" I shuffled hesitantly forward onto the edge of nothingness. Both hands involuntarily and automatically raised and seized the frame at either side of the gap. Shaky spoke slowly. "One hand across your reserve,son".

In slow motion, my right hand reluctantly relinquished its grip on the bar and lay itself down on top of my reserve. A thought flashed into my mind. What was the point of this reserve anyway? They had already told us that these parachutes were as good as useless if deployed at below four hundred feet. By my reckoning eight hundred feet of cable was just that. It was impossible for it to be higher. In addition, I could see that because the balloon leaned away from the wind, the cable wasn't vertical. Our true height was more likely seven hundred and fifty feet. My pondering continued. I had watched a parachute deploy from this balloon earlier. It had taken nearly two hundred feet before it began to open. That left less than six hundred feet. If the four hundred feet needed for complete inflation were to be discounted, there would only be around two hundred feet remaining. When falling at sixty feet per second that doesn't leave a lot of time to find out that there is a problem and do something about it. I was scared.

Shaky's calming tones interrupted my worrying thoughts. "When I say ready, I want to see both hands across your reserve. When I say go. Just do it. OK?" I nodded agreement. It wasn't like that very first parachute jump of two weeks previous. This time I didn't believe that I was about to die, I just didn't want to do it. Firm and commanding, Shaky shouted. "Ready!" My left arm swept down swiftly. The problem was that equally as swiftly and at the same time my right arm shot up and gripped the opposite frame. Shaky didn't know whether to laugh or to cry, though he did let me know what it was that he thought of me with just one word. "Prat!"

Shaking his head in disbelief Shaky asked, "Do you want some help?" Of course I need some help, I thought to myself, but I queried in what shape this help would come.

Taking hold of my biceps Shaky pulled me away from the gap. "Right!" He said. His tone had changed and I could tell that he meant it. "Both hands over your reserve!" I complied. "Step into the door!" I did and just as I was anticipating words like ready or even go, there was a sharp slap to my back and I was tumbling forward into nothingness.

Too late to do anything but remember Shaky's advice, I threw my head back to watch my canopy pull free from behind my back. To one side I could just see Shaky's smiling grinning orb suspended over the blue panels.

I was falling and I hate falling. Nerves tingled uncomfortably about my skin. At the same time my testicles forced themselves higher up into my body than they had ever been. It was as if they had a mind of their own and were trying to climb up through me to get back up onto the platform. If they got any higher I would land looking like I had contracted mumps!

As suddenly as it had started, the wind-rush of falling had vanished. I was already close to the ground so I pulled my body in tight. The landing was heavy but I was down and I was safe. Immense sensations of accomplishment and triumph surged through me. The experience and exhilaration was so great that the tiny hairs on the back of my neck were sending tingly electrified feelings down my back and were forcing my shoulders into uncontrollable shudders.

Having scooped up the parachute and its harness then bagged it, I jogged off the DZ. There was a good reason for breaking into the little run. It was important that I clear out as soon as possible because any second now there would be another bloke coming down on top of me.

Chip Walker

On the grass with my mates, it became quickly apparent that they had heard or at least had guessed that there had been some sort of hold up with me. I told them what had happened. Perhaps surprisingly every one of them was wholly supportive and even sympathetic. One slapped me on the shoulders and added reassuringly, "You jumped didn't you?" It was more of a statement than a question. I turned to him now feeling already much better and replied with a simple, "Thanks mate".

The Devil Wears Maroon

Parachute course at Brize. Shaky is front centre with the dark glasses. Chip Walker is top row, second from the right.

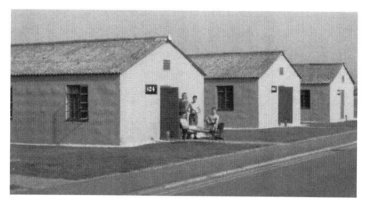

The PCAU accommodation for course personnel.

336

Chip Walker

The balloon, ready for elevation to 800 feet.

Ground training at Brize

Landing from the fan.

Buddy checks for Parachute fitting.

Exiting the Knacker Cracker of Outdoor Exit Trainer.

All dressed up and nowhere to go. Chip Walker at one of the training ramps.

Attached to 2 Para.

CHAPTER FOURTEEN

AN EXCLUSIVE BROTHERHOOD

In our barrack room, each and every one of us got stuck into an identical activity. We sat at our beds sewing parachute wings over the upper arm of our shirts ready for the parade in the morning.

I am sure that there is a right way and a wrong way to attach parachute wings onto a uniform but all I knew was that there was an airborne way. It was just not done to leave all the excess khaki coloured background cloth on the wings, so we shared scissors to remove as much as was possible.

After pressing my shirt with its strikingly new adornment, I held it proudly aloft. This was my World-Cup and I was Bobbie Moore. Carefully, lovingly, I allowed the shirt to hang untouched by other clothing in the locker. For a while, I stood there simply admiring it.

The following morning the RAF found a way to claim its revenge for all the surly, bigoted and abusive behavior that they had had to put up with. Here we were in the hangar and ready for a parade. All of us dressed in our best kit. So that we could look our best for the presentations, we had spent hours polishing boots and pressing uniforms. There had been a quick parade rehearsal where everyone got to find whereabouts they were to stand and where we should march to but then what happened? We found ourselves cleaning the bloody hangar!

Every mat had to be picked up and every inch of the floor had to be swept. The Course was split into smaller groups and was then sent off around various parts of the hangar. At first I found myself at the large wooden boxes which housed the dummy parachutes. Each one was drawn out and checked for training serviceability then replaced in numerical order.

A little later on, Shaky came to our aid. Apparently, he was as pissed off about this farce as we were. He led our group out through the giant doors and told us to walk around the outside of the hangar to pick up any litter and fag ends. I appreciated this because it was a lovely day with the sun shining and I'd rather be outside doing this than inside sweeping and mopping a massive floor. We made the job last as long as possible for we knew that if we went back inside, the bosses would find something else for us to do.

Eventually we did parade. It was held inside the hangar in front of the two mock-up fuselages. I was in the rear rank of a squad that was positioned at the front. The blond Flight Lieutenant stood on the deck of one of the mock-ups just in front. He congratulated all of us on being a good course and went on to wish us the best for our futures. Then we were brought again to attention where upon the RAF man simply walked away.

The contrast in tone was very much in evidence as the RSM bellowed. "Stand at ease! Stand easy". The barrel chested man with a bark that could shake houses slammed his feet into position and took the place of the RAF Officer. It was now the turn of the RSM to congratulate the course. He added that he hoped to see some of us in the future during our service with the Brigade. There were a few mickey taking comments about the Marines and Commandos who had been on the course but before the giggles could get too raucous he snapped with a loud, "Course!" That tiny word was all that was required to instantly bring the entire Course to order.

We stood silently and with our shoulders braced, in anticipation of the next command. He glared threateningly at us, reminding us that ultimately, it was he who was in charge. Then glancing outward and toward the hangar doors he seemed to spy whatever it was that was expected. The RSM shifted his position smartly and brought the Course to attention. The resounding crash of boots slapped the cement floor and echoed around the building. Standing still for around thirty seconds we waited. I could hear someone approaching from my right and then in walked the OC PCAU. The RSM saluted. Something was said then the RSM stood us back at ease again.

The Major went straight into his speech. He also congratulated us but this time not just for completing the parachute training but for getting through the whole selection procedure. He said that we were but a tiny part of the Army, adding that we were though, a select few. Only about three, he said, of every ten men who volunteer for selection actually reach this far. It's been said, he continued, that P-company was amongst the hardest of courses in the Army. It was meant to be, for the Brigade only wants the best. The OC finished his speech and stepped down, and then with the RSM and the RAF Flight Lieutenant he walked amongst the rows of men shaking their hands and awarding them their wings. The RAF Officer followed behind and gave out Irwin badges. Irwin was the company that had been manufacturing our parachutes ever since the Second World War and ever since then had issued each successful soldier with a badge.

Once that the entourage had completed their rounds, the OC returned to his place on the platform. He glanced around seemingly catching each one of us in the eye. His face said it all, he was admiring our efforts, and he was full of pride. Satisfied that he had gained our attention he spoke once again. "With those wings you've become part of a brotherhood. A brotherhood of airborne soldiers, respected, envied and feared throughout the world. It's an exclusive brotherhood. Welcome!"

GLOSSARY

A4	Paper size, approx.' 8"x11".
AAC	Army Air Corps
AI	Assistant Instructor, pronounced Ackeye
ACC	Army Catering Corps
ADJ	Adjutant, usually a Captain.
AKI	Ackeye, assistant instructor.
ALM	Air Load Master
APC	Armoured Personnel carrier
APFA	Annual Personal Fitness Assessment.
APTI	Assistant Physical training Instructor
ATA	Army Training Area
AVGAS	Aviation Gasoline
Basher	Make shift shelter
Battery	A company of Artillery pieces.
Beasting	Arduous physical abuse or training
Bergen	Large back pack
BDR	Bombardier
BFT	Basic Fitness Test
BKS	Barracks
Block job	Personal cleaning task within the barrack room
Blue Jobs	RAF personnel

BN	Battalion
BQ	Battery quarters, Usually used as a short abbreviation for the man in charge of the Battery stores
BQMS	Battery Quarter Master Sergeant
BSM	Battery sergeant Major
Boff	Food
Bulling	Cleaning and polishing
CEFO	Combat Effective Fighting Order
CPL	Corporal
Crap Hat	Non Airborne Soldier
CQMS	Company Quarter Master Sergeant
CQ	Short for CQMS
CO	Commanding Officer
Cookhouse	Main kitchen and dining room for ordinary ranks
CSM	Company Sergeant Major
Denims	Olive green trousers
Depot Para	Regimental Headquarters and Recruit training camp for the Parachute Regiment and Airborne Forces
DMS	Durable Moulded Sole, standard

	issue ankle high army boot
DPM	Disruptive Patterned Material, camouflage clothing
Dressing	A soldiers place in the ranks
Drill	Marching and saluting or a set reaction to a command or situation
DWTI	Drill and Weapons Training Instructor
DZ	Drop Zone
Double	Marching at running speed
File	Rows of two
FN	Belgian automatic rifle
FOD	Foreign Object Damage
Full Screw	Corporal
Gimpy	General Purpose machine Gun
GPMG	General purpose Machine Gun
Hats Stupid	Camouflaged baseball style hat
HQ	Headquarters
IA	Immediate Action
ICFT	Infantry Combat Fitness Test
Ind	Independent
Jack	To give up, surrender
Jacking wagon	Safety vehicle which can also be used to carry those who give in

Knacker Cracker	Outdoor Exit Trainer
Khaki	Sandy coloured
LAAW	Light Anti Armour Weapon
LBDR	Lance Bombardier
LCPL	Lance Corporal
Light Order	Boots, Denims and Shirt
Loadie	Air Load Master
Lt Col	Lieutenant Colonel
Manning	Corps records office
March Out	The inspection and hand-over of a building,
Mess	Living and dining area for senior ranks and Officers
MO	Medical Officer
MOD	Ministry of Defence
MOD 90	Army identification card
MEVE	Military Experimental vehicle Establishment
MI Room	Medical Inspection Room
NAAFI	Navy Army Airforce Institute
Nato Standard	Hot white sweetened tea
NBC	Nuclear Biological and Chemical Warfare

NATO	North Atlantic Treaty Organisation
NCO	Non Commissioned Officer
OC	Officer Commanding
OG	Olive Green Trousers
OR	Ordinary ranks
Para	Paratrooper or Parachute Unit
PAD	Married Soldier
PCAU	Parachute Course Administration Unit
PFA	Parachute Field Ambulance
PJI	Parachute Jump Instructor
PL	Platoon
PLD	Parachute Landing Drills
PT	Physical Training
PTI	Physical Training Instructor
POD	Fuel truck
QM	Quarter Master
QMSI	Quarter Master Sergeant Instructor
RA	Royal Artillery
RAF	Royal Air Force
RAMC	Royal Army Medical Corps
RAOC	Royal Army Ordinance Corps
RE	Royal Engineers
Recce	Reconnoitre

REME	Royal Electrical and Mechanical Engineers
RCT	Royal Corps of Transport
RHQ	Regimental Headquarterset
RHA	Royal Horse Artillery
R&R	Rest and Recuperation
RTU	Return to Unit
RV	Rendezvous
SAC	Senior Aircraft's Man
SAS	Special Air Service
Sangar	A watch/ Look out or Guard post
Scran	Food
Scoff	Food
SHQ	Squadron Headquarters
SF	Sustained Fire
SGT	Sergeant
SI	Sergeant Instructor
SLR	Self Loading Rifle
Snow Drops	RAF Police
SNCO	Senior Non Commissioned Officer
SMI	Sergeant Major Instructor
SMG	Sub-Machine Gun
SO2	Supervising Officer, ACC

SOP	Standard Operating Procedure
SQMS	Staff Quarter Master Sergeant
SQN	Squadron
SSGT	Staff Sergeant
SSM	Squadron Sergeant Major
Stick	A group of Parachutists or a small patrol
Strop	Hanging belt and hook used in parachuting
Tab	Forced march at speed
Tom	Private Soldier
Triple A	Anti-Aircraft Artillery
USSR	Union of Soviet Socialist Republics
Webbing	Collection of belts and straps
WO1	Warrant Officer class one
WO2	Warrant Officer class two
WO	Warrant Officer
WRAC	Women's Royal Army Corps
WRAF	Women's Royal Air Force
7 Para RHA	Seventh Parachute Regiment, Royal Horse Artillery

16 BGDE	16th Independent Parachute Brigade
5 Airborne	5th Airborne Brigade
9 Para SQN RE	9th Parachute Squadron, Royal Engineers
2 Para	2nd Battalion of the Parachute Regiment
2 ic	Second in command
66mm	A light and disposable anti-armour weapon

Corporal Chip Walker was later promoted to Sergeant and posted to Aldershot where he served with 2 Para.

On leaving the regular army Chip Walker served for a while with 10Para (TA) as a machine gunner.

23167238R00200

Printed in Great Britain
by Amazon